Challenging the Myths of US History

The publisher and the University of California Press Foundation gratefully acknowledge the generous support of the Ahmanson Foundation Endowment Fund in Humanities.

Challenging the Myths of US History

SEVEN SHORT ESSAYS ON
THE PAST AND PRESENT

Marc Egnal

UNIVERSITY OF CALIFORNIA PRESS

University of California Press
Oakland, California

© 2025 by Marc Egnal

Cataloging-in-Publication data is on file at the Library of Congress.

ISBN 978-0-520-40245-4 (cloth : alk. paper)
ISBN 978-0-520-40246-1 (pbk. : alk. paper)
ISBN 978-0-520-40247-8 (ebook)

Manufactured in the United States of America

GPSR Authorized Representative: Easy Access System Europe, Mustamäe tee 50, 10621 Tallinn, Estonia, gpsr.requests@easproject.com

34 33 32 31 30 29 28 27 26 25
10 9 8 7 6 5 4 3 2 1

For JUDITH

Contents

Preface

Getting Right with the Past

Since Donald Trump's election in 2016 the battles over American history have grown more intense. Legislatures have ordered schools not to teach aspects of the past that might distress (White) students. Some observers suggest slavery was not all bad. The Florida middle school curriculum declares that "slaves developed skills which, in some instances, could be applied for their personal benefit." Discussions of the Civil War are okay, but references to systemic racism, often referred to as "critical race theory," are taboo. Both sides in this debate recognize the importance of history. How we understand earlier events shapes our view of the present—and the actions we take.[1]

Lost in this noisy dissensus are the broad areas of agreement that most textbooks and courses share. Students in California and Texas, Massachusetts and Florida, learn a narrative marked by high ideals and steady progress toward "a more perfect union." Virtually all texts concur that a desire for "liberty" explains the American Revolution, and that the drive for "freedom"—the determination to end slavery—caused the Civil War. Every textbook condemns slavery (even if some note redeeming features), explores Black resilience in bondage, praises Harriet Tubman, and notes the accomplishments of Black Reconstruction. Civil rights leaders, like Martin Luther King Jr., guide the nation's progress toward racial equality. Most accounts acknowledge foreign policy stumbles, but on balance see America as a positive force in the world.

The seven essays in this book challenge those myths. They question the comforting narrative that shapes Americans' view of the past. This work contends that at the heart of the American story are the demands of affluent citizens for economic growth and territorial expansion. Lofty concerns cannot be ignored. No explanation can be monolithic. But idealism was subordinate, and its secondary role helps explain the nation the US is today.

The relentless drive for expansion, both economic and territorial, underlay the two events—the Revolution and the Civil War—that profoundly shaped the United States. In the Revolution the opposing camps (which would eventually be labeled patriots and Tories) formed by the 1740s. At midcentury colonists divided over fighting the French and their Native allies, just as in the 1760s they quarreled about opposing Britain. The constant for the expansionists, the future patriots, was the promotion of a New World "empire." Significantly, the Revolution also birthed a slaveholding republic. The price Southerners demanded for their allegiance was the protection of bondage. Northerners acquiesced, and the Constitution confirmed that bargain. Racism was a fundamental aspect of the new nation.[2]

The Civil War similarly emerged from calls for expansion, with the lead taken by planters in the southern reaches of the cotton states and by farmers, merchants, and manufacturers around the Great Lakes and in New England. The victorious Northerners' principal concern was the creation of a dynamic industrial state with federal backing—a goal they achieved. The fact that for Northerners emancipation and improving the lives of African Americans were far less important has profound implications for US history. This outlook led to the absence of land reform, the short-lived, troubled era of Reconstruction, the rise of repressive regimes in the South, and pervasive discrimination in the North.

Challenging the Myths of US History explores the nation that the Revolution and Civil War created, a country shaped by expansion, with racism as its noxious corollary. The relentless drive for growth coupled with condescension toward non-Whites was evident in the wars against Native Americans and in the nation's aggressive foreign policy, including the lengthy involvement in Vietnam. Racism has also contributed to the plague of homicides within the Black community, left its imprint on the women's movement, and steered the evolution of American politics, including the broad and sustained support for Donald Trump.

Noble goals are part of the American fabric, but they serve as a counterpoint to expansion and racism, never as the dominant theme. Thomas Jefferson's ringing endorsement of equality, even if uttered by a slaveholder, inspired generations of Americans.[3] With their appeal to lofty principles, abolitionists stirred a national debate in the mid-nineteenth century. As the country industrialized, labor leaders and farmers battled factory owners, while critics of foreign policy denounced imperial ventures. Generations of activists demanded justice for African Americans. The essays note these campaigns and closely examine one: the struggle for women's rights.

This book questions long-held assumptions. It is not a comprehensive survey or a historiographical essay (although the endnotes point to relevant works). The first chapter provides an overview that is both philosophical and broad based. It asks how we can decide which interpretation is better than another. It looks at the changes in the study of history since the 1960s and examines conflicting overviews of the past.

Challenging the Myths of US History draws from a variety of sources, including primary documents and my five books, particularly my studies of the Revolution, the Civil War, and American culture as reflected in novels and art. In addition, a series of remarkable works, most published during the past ten years and referenced in the text and notes, have shaped my outlook. Nor can anyone writing in the early 2020s fail to be affected by recent events. Clashes over race, foreign policy, inequality, and democracy must give any observer pause and force a reexamination of assumptions. Discussions with other historians, family, and friends, whose names are listed in the acknowledgments, have also been important.

These essays are about the past, but they are also about the present. What American is not touched, in some way, by Donald Trump's ascent, rampant violence, foreign wars, and the women's movement? Each of our worlds has been profoundly affected by two foundational events—the American Revolution and the Civil War—as well as by the way history is taught and imagined. In several places I've brought in my own experience. But readers might readily substitute their own involvement with the issues discussed.

I'd be delighted if readers who differ with the book's thesis or any of its contentions carefully consider the material presented and provide their own explanations. This book is about "challenging the myths," a phrase that suggests a dialogue, not a sermon. This modest book will not end disagreements about the past or the present, but I hope it will help elevate the discourse about America's history.

1   *Is There Progress in the Study of US History?*

Is there progress in the study of US history? If you ask a physicist or astronomer a similar question, "Is there progress in science?," the answer will be a rousing *Yes*. At least since the seventeenth century, thanks to what modern observers label the "scientific method," scholars have learned more and more about the physical world. Each generation stands tall upon the shoulders of its predecessors.

When researchers disagree, the scientific method provides a court of law for settling disputes. Everyone leaves that court, eventually, accepting the same conclusion. The method consists of the formulation of a testable hypothesis, then careful observation to determine if the theory is supported or refuted. The propositions set forth lead scientists to reexamine existing evidence or seek new materials that shed light on contentious issues.[1] Between the 1940s and early 1960s, for example, astronomers debated whether the universe began with a Big Bang or existed in a steady state with new matter constantly being created. The discovery in the mid-1960s of faint cosmic microwave radiation uniformly present in all directions settled the matter. That radiation was the remnants of the first explosion, predicted by Big Bang theorists but unexplained by the steady state hypothesis.[2]

History is not a science, but historians often work in ways that are similar to the practices of astronomers, physicists, and anthropologists. Progress is evident when scholars approximate the scientific method and gain a more accurate understanding of the past. That statement clearly points to the need for further analysis. A full response to the question, "Is there progress in the study of US history?" requires an examination of three related areas: methodology, the emergence of new approaches and materials, and the current synthesis of recent findings. The answer to the question that headlines this chapter is positive but cautious: during the past sixty years significant advances have characterized the study of America's past—even if problems remain in analyzing large issues and in formulating the broad overviews that shape textbooks.[3]

I

An understanding of that progress, or at times its absence, demands scrutiny of the methodology that guides historians. A first brush with the practices of American historians is not reassuring. What are casual observers to make of seemingly unresolvable disagreements among researchers? Debates over the causes of the American Revolution and Civil War date back to the events themselves. Scholars with professional training and extraordinary credentials metaphorically lock horns or, more precisely, pound on dueling keyboards to defend their opposing views. The same persistent dissensus holds for other issues: Was the Constitution an economic document? Was the slave South a capitalist society? Highly respected researchers hold sharply contrasting positions.

Still, the picture is less bleak than such quarrels might suggest. Greater agreement—and approaches more akin to that found in science—are evident when the questions are more focused and bodies of evidence more manageable. For example, did the first Africans arriving in Virginia in 1619 enter a fully elaborated slave system? The record is clear that before the 1650s Virginians held some of these women and men as slaves while treating others as indentured servants—individuals who served for a fixed number of years and then were granted land. Only gradually did the colonists tighten laws to create a closed system. Few researchers today dispute this evolution.[4]

Abraham Lincoln's views of slavery and race stand out as another issue about which there is surprising agreement among historians. Scholars, to be sure, differ in their emphases: some highlight Lincoln's racism, others his passionate opposition to slavery. But those underscoring Lincoln's prejudices must acknowledge (and do) his fervent and consistent denunciations of slavery. They recognize the lofty speech he delivered in Chicago in 1858: "[L]et us discard all this quibbling about this man and the other man—this race and that race and the other race being inferior . . . and unite as one people throughout this land, until we shall once more stand up declaring all men are created equal."[5] Nor can these scholars overlook Lincoln's moral and spiritual growth; his emancipation proclamation; his determination to guarantee freedom with the Thirteenth Amendment; and the remarkable "last speech" of April 1865, in which he suggested that suffrage be extended to African Americans, who were "very intelligent and . . . serve[d] our cause as soldiers."[6]

At the same time, anyone regarding Lincoln's racial views in a favorable light must recognize that the Chicago speech, delivered in the most pro-abolition part of Illinois, was an unusual, one-off performance. Far more common were Lincoln's pronouncements affirming White superiority. In his debates with Stephen Douglas he repeatedly echoed local prejudices, stating, for example, "I am not nor ever have been in favor of making voters or jurors of negroes, nor of qualifying them to hold office, nor to intermarry with white people. . . . [A]nd I as much as any other man am in favor of having the superior position assigned to the white race."[7] Lincoln was more cautious than many Republicans in attacking bondage in the District of Columbia and in defending fugitive slaves. When the war broke out, he supported a proposed Thirteenth Amendment guaranteeing slavery where it existed. He also consistently advocated colonization, a proposal that, if fully implemented, would have created a country free of Blacks. Despite strong African American opposition to such plans, Lincoln continued to endorse resettlement—even after issuing the emancipation proclamation.[8]

Virtually all scholarly biographies and essays on Lincoln concur in balancing these divergent views. Some highlight his ardent commitment to the Declaration of Independence and suggest the prejudices he voiced simply reveal a canny politician attuned to public opinion. Others, who underscore his more disparaging statements, argue change came only from the pressures of war. Even with these contrary spins, there is far more overlap than disagreement.[9]

Professionally trained historians agree that, unlike partisans campaigning for a particular cause, they do not have the luxury of ignoring contrary evidence. They are not allowed to cherry-pick certain facts; they must examine all the fruit on the tree—and the pieces that fall to the ground. That too reflects the way science progresses. In the early days of quantum physics, researchers discovered that some experiments showed electromagnetic radiation acted as a wave, while other tests indicated it functioned as a stream of particles. The answer, which physicists came to accept, is that radiation displays both properties. As Albert Einstein pronounced: "We have two contradictory pictures of reality; separately neither of them fully explains the phenomena of light, but together they do."[10]

Such an approach does not always characterize historians' work, but often it does, particularly when questions are clearly defined, the evidence is manageable—and researchers are open-minded. C. Vann Woodward's landmark book, *The Strange Career of Jim Crow*, first published in 1955, epitomizes that constructive dialogue. Woodward's work argues that segregation in the South was not an immutable folkway but emerged with the restrictions that states adopted between 1890 and 1905. Critics praised the work but also pointed out its flaws. Researchers noted that Woodward's conclusions applied more fully to the south Atlantic states than to the newer areas of the Cotton South, where segregation dated from the Civil War. They observed that throughout the South many institutions, like schools and cemeteries, were always subject to apartheid, and that similar practices existed in the North. Far from fighting his critics, Woodward incorporated their suggestions in the three subsequent editions he issued during the next twenty years.[11]

This productive approach, with practices akin to science, works better for more narrowly defined problems, such as the origins of slavery in Virginia, Lincoln's views of race, or the advent of segregation, than for the larger issues discussed elsewhere in this book. The voluminous material involved in answering what caused the American Revolution or the Civil War challenges efforts to apply the strictures of science to the problem. Still, those questions are too important to be set aside, even if those investigations only loosely resemble a scientific inquiry.[12]

II

The strongest case for progress in the study of US history comes from a focus on a second topic: the new findings researchers have presented during the last sixty years. The watershed moment for American historians came in the 1960s, the years when I was in graduate school. While there might be a tendency to view earlier decades through a shimmering haze of glory, the idea of the 1960s as a turning point in understanding the past is now widely accepted. That excitement was evident not only in my Early American seminar (often outside of class, since our professor was from another generation), but also in the exchanges we students had when discussing foreign policy, women's history, the Civil War, and modern America. The civil rights protests, the anti-war movement, the debates over the Great Society programs, and the demands for women's rights were reshaping our world and spurring scholars to look at the past differently.

African American history was one area in which change was striking. Before the mid-1960s most texts regarded Blacks as simple folk, with no "agency" or culture of their own. While authors condemned slavery, they asserted that bondage elevated a primitive people. Observers viewed the high tide of Reconstruction, the years after the Civil War when African Americans briefly exercised political power in the South, as a nightmarish time with ignorant Blacks indulging their worst instincts.[13]

The crescendo of protests in the 1960s, including the demonstrations led by Martin Luther King Jr. and others, encouraged many to rethink those assumptions. Among the loudest voices demanding change were the Detroit Board of Education and the Newark Textbook Council—bodies that spoke for two Black-majority cities.

They called on publishers to provide texts that acknowledged the role of African Americans in building the nation. Such local interventions have not always been forward looking. The Mississippi State Textbook Purchasing Board battled revisions of White supremacist material in its state histories. The Texas State Board of Education, a major force in the textbook market, has insisted upon conservative readings of events. But the demands of Detroit and Newark proved far more positive and coincided with a fundamental shift in the outlook of the historical profession.[14]

Scholars now revised long-held beliefs, scrutinizing materials often overlooked, such as slave narratives, folklore, and spirituals, and examining from a new perspective plantation journals, travel accounts, and planters' letters. Researchers perceived, as never before, that slaves developed a rich culture. Family, religion (both Christian and African), music, language, and various forms of resistance built a sense of community and fostered a deep resilience despite difficult circumstances. These findings became the new norm, reshaping textbooks and lectures.[15]

The rewriting of Black history extended to Reconstruction and the civil rights movement. Texts now depict the courage of the freedpeople in their struggle to secure suffrage, land, education, and fairer taxes. Scholars who once regarded White supremacists as noble crusaders for good government now view them as violent extremists bitterly opposed to an egalitarian society. Textbooks also expanded their coverage of the civil rights movement. Today all students learn about the heroic struggles of Rosa Parks and Martin Luther King Jr., champions who join Harriet Tubman, Frederick Douglass, and Booker T. Washington in the pantheon of prominent African Americans. If we compare the teaching and scholarship on African Americans before and after 1965, progress is unmistakable.[16]

Women's history is another field in which new approaches transformed the traditional story. Like the civil rights protests, the women's movement encouraged scholars to recast the narrative. Some of the discoveries made found their way into textbooks, although the material presented in courses comprises only the tip of a volcanic island whose mountainous base is wide, deep, and fully submerged. Typically, students learn about the struggle for the vote—campaigns that began in 1848 with a meeting at Seneca Falls and culminated in 1920 with the Nineteenth Amendment. Demands, beginning in the 1960s, for fairer treatment usually receive a mention. Survey courses, however, usually overlook the many studies that unsettle the familiar male-dominated narrative. These works examine the women who were active in politics after the adoption of the Constitution, played crucial roles on the home front during the Revolutionary and Civil Wars, provided leadership in settling the West and on the mining frontier, and served as labor organizers. Monographs shed new light on female immigrants, lesbians, and the activism of African American women.[17]

Striking progress has also been recorded in the study of Native Americans—even if survey courses rarely present that material.[18] While assigned works provide more material about Indigenous people than was the case before the 1960s, much of that discourse still comes from an older viewpoint: Indians loom large only when they obstructed European expansion. Most surveys discuss Pontiac's Rebellion of 1763, the forced removal of the Cherokees and other Indigenous people from the southeastern states in the 1830s, and the defeat of the Plains Indians during the last third of the nineteenth century. The "new Indian history" that emerged in the early 1970s has a different focus. It retells the story of Native people from their own perspective, making use of oral history, archaeological remains, the pictographs ("winter counts") Natives recorded, and documents created by non-Indians.[19] Historians, some of them now themselves Indigenous people, have produced remarkable accounts of Comanchería, Iroquoia, and the Lakota Nation, sprawling empires that for lengthy periods held off imperial powers and other Indian nations. Works discuss Native religions, life on the reservations, and the tragedy of American Indian boarding schools.[20]

Textbooks (and scholarly monographs) similarly have recast the Cold War. During the 1950s and much of the 1960s, students learned that the USSR was the villain and America the defender of freedom. The Vietnam debacle challenged that Manichean vision and fostered new research. One school of historians, the revisionists, who faulted the United States and its economic ambitions, gained little traction among textbook writers. But the views of the post-revisionists, who argue both great powers were culpable, became the new norm and shape the surveys students read.[21]

Since the 1970s advances have been noteworthy as well in a variety of fields that earlier generations ignored or judged with crippling biases. (Here too, however, much of the progress remains in monographs.) The study of gays and lesbians, for example, provides a history for individuals often rendered invisible; this research shows that Americans accepted such unions in the nineteenth and much of the twentieth centuries, with rampant homophobia emerging only after World War II.[22] The "new labor history" focuses on the lives of workers rather than simply the large unions. The "new Western history" looks not at sagebrush and gunslingers, but at urban centers, corporations, and conflicts over resources.[23] Environmental history, a field that had coalesced by the 1970s, retells the story of Indigenous peoples, Europeans, and African Americans, emphasizing interactions with the natural world.[24] Disability history, of still more recent origin as a field, discusses how earlier eras treated the deaf and blind, the physically and mentally challenged.[25] Other studies explore how America sounded or smelled in the past.[26] More generally, these studies turn the spotlight on people who worked with their hands—a group too often missing from earlier histories.

Another area that has exploded in recent years has been the digital humanities. Digitizing documents, such as colonial newspapers or Civil War records, makes possible searches for names and terms, allowing for new insights into the past. Enormous databases, such as the records of the ships and individuals involved in the slave trade, allow certainties to replace guesswork. Balancing the enthusiasm that often accompanies these findings are critiques that point to the biases in these data and the dangers that come from a narrow focus on tabulation.[27]

Taken all in all, works completed during the last sixty years represent striking advances in the analysis of America's past—even if the dissemination of these findings is often limited. Each of those scholarly essays must be evaluated individually, and historians do so—in reviews, at conferences, and in further research. Not all measure up to the highest standards, but most do, and collectively they deepen our understanding of the American saga.

III

Finally, any full answer to the question that frames this essay must examine the current synthesis of US history presented in textbooks and lectures. Except for students in graduate programs and historians themselves, few individuals plunge very deep into the specialized literature. Textbooks and lectures are the gateways for most grade school and college students exploring US history—and these sources present with remarkable consistency an overview that might be called the "liberal consensus." It's an approach that reflects the advances of recent decades. But how credible is this summation? Within the terms discussed in this chapter, this is a "larger question," not easily subject to the science-like focus and agreement that characterize narrower topics. Still, there is a need to closely examine this worldview since its wide dissemination says much about how most educated people view America's past.

A review of attacks from the Right and Left highlights the strengths and shortcomings of the liberal consensus, which gradually coalesced in the 1970s. The bitter battles in the 1990s over the National History Standards illustrate the depth of conservative opposition to the new approach. The roots of the clash date from 1990, when President George H. W. Bush urged the creation of national guidelines for various academic areas. With support from Congress, the National Endowment for the Humanities recruited a working group for the US field. Over the course of two years this body consulted with nearly six thousand teachers, business leaders, scholars, parents, and administrators. The guidelines developed affirmed the worldview that had emerged and received wide acceptance since the 1970s. While White men dominated the narrative, the standards also presented the revised view of slavery, Reconstruction, and the civil rights movement; acknowledged the struggle for women's rights; took a balanced approach to America's role in the world; and mentioned Native American activism.

After the working group released its proposed guidelines in 1994, right-wing commentators and politicians unleashed a firestorm of criticism. Most of the attackers had not read the document but thundered within an echo chamber of angry opinions.

Senator Slade Gorton of Washington declared, "With this set of standards, our students will not be expected to know George Washington from the man in the Moon. According to this set of standards, American democracy rests on the same moral footing as the Soviet Union's totalitarian dictatorship." Another commentator remarked, "By the allocation of the text, America today seems to be about 65 percent Indian, with most of the rest of us black, female or oppressive." While professional historians strongly backed the proposals, the Clinton administration, originally supportive, ducked for cover. Early in 1995 the Senate condemned the standards by a 99–1 vote.

That censure did not end the saga. A blue-ribbon panel was formed to reconsider the document. Several foundations supported the new committee's work and approved Albert Quie, a Lutheran minister who had served as Republican governor of Minnesota, as its head. Despite the conservative leanings of its members, the panel accepted the broad contours of the original standards, excluding only the more controversial supplementary material. By the time the panel issued its report in 1996 the controversy had died down. The American Association of School Administrators distributed the new guidelines to the nation's sixteen thousand school districts. The liberal consensus had run the gauntlet and emerged on the other side relatively unscathed and anointed as the national standard.[28]

Although the right-wing attack on the new standards justifiably was repelled, the middle-class values underlying the liberal consensus cannot go unquestioned. To be sure, the new synthesis (properly) highlights the struggles of many groups, including African Americans, women, gays, union organizers, and Hispanics. But does the sum of those episodes support the upbeat narrative arc that characterizes this approach? Typically, each of these campaigns ends with progress and the establishment of a fairer, more egalitarian nation. High-minded ideals, not economic self-interest, underpin seminal events such as the American Revolution and Civil War. But is US history truly "The Story of American Freedom," as one popular textbook is titled? There is a need to explore alternatives before celebrating the current synthesis as a praiseworthy summation of the American past.[29]

What would a history written from the perspective of outsiders and critics of American triumphalism look like? Here are suggestions. In dealing with the seventeenth-century origins of the United States, lectures and texts typically focus on two small English settlements (Jamestown, founded in 1607, and Massachusetts Bay, founded in 1630) and ignore complex, vibrant Native societies, such as the Iroquois, Creek, and Sioux, even though those Indigenous peoples comprised most of the North American population. Imagine the different view students would take away if the balance of coverage were reversed. Indigenous people do not agree that the history of the last several hundred years is "The Story of American Freedom."[30]

The same rebalancing might occur elsewhere in the narrative. Textbooks devote much space to the details of presidential elections, exploring in detail, for example, the clash of the gold and silver standards in 1896 and the battle between New Freedom and New Nationalism in 1912. But they ignore changing attitudes toward homosexuality, rarely mentioning the LGBTQ community until the Stonewall riots of 1969. And while the struggle for women's rights is part of the liberal consensus, the principal actors in US history remain White males, with many of the recent findings about women's role in society relegated to supplementary reading.

Similar oversights mar the depiction of more recent history, painting a rosier picture of American society than might be justified. Few textbooks explore the impact of soaring inequality, which since the 1970s has been the most important development reshaping American society. The increasingly skewed distribution of wealth has exacerbated a broad range of problems, including race relations, violence, and health. Political decisions accelerated this dangerous trend, making America, once the land of opportunity, far less equal than other industrialized nations.

Equally significant are the silences in retelling African American history. Surveys properly celebrate the courage of Rosa Parks and the determination of Martin Luther King Jr. Their campaigns provide an uplifting tale. Few textbooks, however, dare broach the topic of systemic racism, which characterizes the nation despite the genuine advances recorded in the decades after 1948. Typically, the books assigned ignore "redlining," the practice of designating Black neighborhoods as unsuitable for federal loan guarantees. The practice began with the establishment of the Federal Housing Administration in 1934—its manuals instructed banks to shun "inharmonious racial groups."[31] Housing discrimination, which continues to the present day, has played an important role in creating racial disparities: in 2016 the median wealth of Black families was $17,600, while Whites held assets worth $171,000. Some surveys mention the soaring rates of incarceration for African Americans, a trend that has persisted even as crime rates have fallen. Black men are more than five times as likely to be jailed as Whites. Few texts, however, explore the policies that have led to these disparities, including differences in sentencing for possession of powder cocaine (used by Whites) and crack cocaine (more likely to be used in Black communities). A sustained critique of such practices is not part of the liberal consensus, and any text that took such an approach would likely have fewer adoptions. But it would give students a better understanding of the world they live in.[32]

Analysis of the controversy over the 1619 Project suggests further challenges to the liberal consensus. The *New York Times Magazine* launched the 1619 Project in August 2019, four hundred years after the first slaves arrived in Virginia. Along with a special issue of the *Magazine*, the initiative includes podcasts, suggested high school curricula, and most recently a full-length book. In the lead essay in the *Magazine*, journalist Nikole Hannah-Jones explains that the Project "aims to reframe the country's history by placing the consequences of slavery and the contributions of black Americans at the very center of our national narrative." But the Project does more than highlight the importance of slavery, an emphasis most historians accept. More controversially, Hannah-Jones labels slavery the "country's original sin" and states, "Anti-black racism runs in the very DNA of this country, as does the belief, so well articulated by Lincoln, that black people are the obstacle to national unity." Jake Silverstein, editor of the *Magazine*, underscores the point: "We are journalists, trained to look at current events and situations and ask the question: Why is this the way it is? In the case of the persistent racism and inequality that plague this country, the answer to that question led us inexorably into the past—and not just for this project."[33]

These contentions defy the liberal consensus, with its deep-rooted optimism and belief that the various struggles have led to a more perfect union. While the historical profession rallied with one voice to support the standards developed in the 1990s, scholars have divided over the Project in a split that runs partly along racial lines. Very few historians of color have joined the White scholars criticizing the Project; several who were asked to cosign a letter to the *Times* refused.[34]

Dissenters have attacked specific statements in Hannah-Jones's essay, noting that full-blown slavery did not begin with the arrival of the first Africans in 1619 and emphasizing that only a portion of the Revolutionaries feared British threats to their labor system. Critics have pointed out that Lincoln's views of race were complex and evolving, and they question the assertion that "[f]or the most part, black Americans fought back alone." The authors of the Project have conceded some of those points. After reviewing discussions about slavery and independence, Silverstein announced, "The passage has been changed to make clear that this was a primary motivation for *some* of the colonists."[35] As for Lincoln, Silverstein noted that "in an essay that covered several centuries and ranged from the personal to the historical, she [Hannah-Jones] did not set out to explore in full his continually shifting ideas about abolition and the rights of Black Americans."[36]

For both the critics and defenders of the Project the key issue is the presence and pervasiveness of racism. In keeping with the liberal consensus, the dissenters emphasize progress, the cooperation of Whites and Blacks, and the steady improvement in the treatment of minorities. Allen Guelzo remarks, "The 156 years since emancipation are less than a second on human history's long clock, so that such a transformation is more in the nature of a miracle to be celebrated than a failure to be deplored for any seeming slowness."[37] James McPherson, the doyen of American Civil War historians, agrees: "[T]he idea that racism is a permanent condition, well that's just not true. And it doesn't account for the countervailing tendencies in American history as well."[38] James Oakes also challenges the notion that the "Original sin" of racism is "built into the DNA of America." He comments, "These are really dangerous tropes. They're not only ahistorical, they're actually antihistorical." He continues that it's as if "[n]othing changes. There has been no industrialization. There has been no Great Migration. We're all in the same boat we were back then. And that's what original sin is."[39] Gordon Wood adds: "When the Declaration says that all men are created equal, that is no myth. It is the most powerful statement made in our history, and lies behind almost everything we Americans believe in and attempt to do."[40]

This debate has only intensified in the early 2020s. Many states have banned "critical race theory"—by which they mean any effort to suggest that US history is marked by pervasive racism. "It's based on false history when they try to look back and denigrate the Founding Fathers, denigrate the American Revolution," Florida Governor Ron DeSantis remarked recently. "If we have to play whack-a-mole all over this state, stopping this critical race theory, we will do it."[41] Battles over the 1619 Project and similar materials have turned school board meetings into shouting matches. Still, in the midst of this fracas, the "liberal consensus" conveyed in grade school and college textbooks and in innumerable lectures remains deeply rooted. A familiar balance prevails: few teachers base their curriculum on the 1619 Project, and few overlook Rosa Parks and Harriet Tubman. But there has been a perceptible fracturing of the synthesis, with tugs coming from both ends.

Challenging the Myths of US History weighs in on these issues, confronting the liberal consensus. The book is not a comprehensive survey. But in contending that the driving force in America was the demands of upper-class individuals for growth and expansion, it parts company with a narrative that emphasizes lofty ideals and progress. And in noting that the most important corollary of the emphasis on growth was deep-seated racism, it stands closer to the 1619 Project than to its critics.

To return to the question, "Is there progress in the study of American history?," the answer is clearly *Yes*. Remarkable advances characterize a broad variety of fields since the far-reaching changes that began in the 1960s. Still, history is not a science, even if regarding narrow, manageable questions it seems to approximate that methodology. Finally, there is good reason to question the liberal consensus that shapes most textbooks, even if the alternatives force students to launch their boats onto stormy seas.

2 *Why the American Revolution?*

When I arrived at the University of Wisconsin in the fall of 1965 for graduate studies, I already had doubts about the traditional story of the American Revolution. Those concerns, explored in various undergraduate essays, were the reason I chose to work with Merrill Jensen at UW rather than go to Yale and study with Edmund Morgan, a pillar of the academic establishment. Jensen had been a rebel in his early years, publishing works that explored themes left-wing historians would rediscover in the 1960s.[1] But I didn't realize he had grown more conservative. So, with little guidance and faulty assumptions about my adviser, I began my dissertation on the origins of the Revolution in Pennsylvania. By the time I finished in the early 1970s I was teaching at York University in Toronto, a year or two away from evaluation for tenure. Jensen rejected the entire dissertation, all four hundred pages of it. He forbade me to write about the Revolution or any aspect of colonial history after 1763 (the nominal date for the beginning of the rebellion).

Once I got over my shock, I plunged into a new dissertation, drawing on the notes I had accumulated during years in the archives. That thesis, "The Pennsylvania Economy, 1748–1762," got me my PhD and, along with several articles, helped me secure tenure. But my concerns about the Revolution did not go away. In the ensuing years I broadened my research, leading in 1988 to my first book, *A Mighty Empire: The Origins of the American Revolution*.

But what is that "familiar story," and what were those doubts? At its heart, the widely accepted explanation for the Revolution is straightforward and patriotic: the colonists revolted because they believed in noble ideals. Patrick Henry illustrated this outlook when he (reportedly) declared in 1775: "Give me liberty or give me death!"[2] This approach has triumphed in academe and popular culture. It offers authors writing about the Founders a convenient armature, around which tales of lofty or despicable behavior can be wrapped.

Expanding on that patriotic premise, researchers mapped out the colonists' ideas. That scholarly undertaking began in the 1950s when historians, often called the neo-Whigs or consensus school, pointed out the flaws in the writings of their predecessors, the Progressives. The Progressives (such as Charles Beard and Carl Becker) argued that economic interests pitted the mother country against its colonies. They also emphasized internal conflict; in Becker's well-known phrase, the Revolution was not only about "home rule" but also about "who should rule at home."[3] Neither of those contentions, the neo-Whigs explain, stands up to close scrutiny. They point out that the British empire was a harmonious realm, at least until 1763, when the mother country began imposing taxes. And even then, the duties levied imposed little hardship. The conflict would be over principle, not burdensome imposts. These historians also emphasize that social conflict was incidental in a society where most White settlers had the prospect of owning land.[4]

According to the neo-Whigs, the colonists (or at least the ones these scholars examine) were students of history and knew that power corrupts and that leaders left unchecked endanger society. The best protection came from a balanced government that combined the three ideal forms: monarchy, aristocracy, and democracy. For a while Britain achieved that equilibrium with its king, House of Lords, and House of Commons. The colonies too seemed to be on the right track with their governors, upper houses, and lower houses.

But in the 1760s (in this recounting by the consensus school) that tidy world fell apart, with corrupt ministers in Britain seizing the reins of power and royal governors in America expanding their prerogatives. Patriots viewed these encroachments in the light of history and recognized that any threat to liberty demanded stout resistance. Neo-Whig historians offer explanations of what happened next with two flavors: the vanilla and the raspberry swirl versions of the colonists' reactions. For Edmund Morgan and Helen Morgan the colonists responded to these dangers in a reasoned, principled manner. The outcome of the Stamp Act crisis of 1765, the Morgans explain, was the Americans' enunciation of "well-defined constitutional principles" that rejected Parliament's right to levy any taxes, internal or external.[5] No free people—slaves were ignored in this formulation—could tolerate such threats. Bernard Bailyn and Gordon Wood, however, suggest that protests came not from any rational response, but from heightened emotions and a concern about shadowy conspiracies. Bailyn writes: "Inflamed sensibilities—exaggerated distrust and fear—surrounded the hard core of the Anglo-American conflict and gave it distinctive shape."[6] By most measures, the consensus school, often with the two versions blended together, has triumphed. Textbooks today elaborate "republican ideology," the constellation of beliefs explored by the neo-Whigs, and conclude that ideas caused the revolt.

But what about those doubts—the concerns I had when I studied the Revolution at Swarthmore? Those questions only intensified as I continued my research at Wisconsin and in the years that followed. One problem lies with the loyalists. The neo-Whigs explain patriotism, but not support for the Crown. Many loyalists came from elite families long resident in America, others from communities of less wealthy farmers. John Adams suggests they comprised "nearly one-third" of the population, although modern estimates set the proportion at 20 percent.[7] If a belief in liberty quickened the hearts of many colonists, why were others unmoved?

Two other problems challenge the traditional interpretation. The patriots didn't rebel simply to defend liberty—with independence they unleashed a great surge of expansionist and entrepreneurial energy.[8] They founded banks, opened trade with a host of countries that had long been off limits (because of the British Navigation Acts), and dramatically enlarged the boundaries of the new nation. The consensus school ignores that fervor. Finally, the neo-Whig historians focus on a small group of upper-class writers, and even then they tease out only one strand in the tracts those individuals wrote. These difficulties argue for a new interpretation of the Revolution, one that better explains the events of these years.

I

Before exploring an alternative explanation, there is a need to examine another crucial body of material: the social transformations that helped shape the Revolution. The involvement of (and these categories overlap) less wealthy citizens, African Americans, women, and Natives holds great importance for interpretations of the rebellion. These outsiders did not lead the struggle against Britain; independence emerged from a colonial not a class revolution. But the fight could not have been waged without them, and their actions left an indelible stamp upon the revolutionary years as well as the writing of the Constitution.

Studies of those individuals—history "from the bottom up"—exploded in the late 1960s and early 1970s. It made for an exciting time to be in graduate school and to debate revisioning the past. Early American history stood in the forefront of the new scholarship.[9] These findings soon made their way into lecture courses and textbooks, where they were inserted into chapters alongside the neo-Whig interpretation. The two narratives coexist uneasily together; they are like guests with sharply differing political views sitting side by side at a Thanksgiving dinner. Amity is possible, but only when great restraint is displayed. The neo-Whigs minimize class conflict, even if such clashes are difficult to completely ignore. Social historians, for their part, offer only a perfunctory nod to republican ideology, choosing to focus on activities they consider more important for understanding the era.[10]

A variety of monographs make clear the importance of the common folk in the revolutionary movement: affluent patriots could not oppose Britain without their support. During the clash over the Stamp Act (which taxed newspapers, playing cards, magazines, and many legal documents), upper-class revolutionaries in each of the large towns actively recruited artisans, shopkeepers, and others to nullify the hated impost. Broadening the opposition to British measures had a dynamic of its own: the people who worked with their hands became increasingly militant—and self-aware. They benefited from and enthusiastically supported the boycotts of British goods, recognizing that these pacts spurred demand for colonial products. They also realized that such demonstrations amplified their voices within a polity that had long excluded them—and everywhere demanded more say in local politics. Wealthy patriots were of two minds about their unruly allies. They needed these individuals to keep British officials and recalcitrant merchants in line. But having sowed the winds of protest, the affluent feared the whirlwinds of dissension they now reaped.[11]

Even before the revolutionary movement broadened to the countryside in 1774, upper-class patriots confronted rural discontent. In 1764 Philadelphians, led by Benjamin Franklin, rejected the demands of the Paxton Boys, who marched from their backcountry homes to the capital. In 1766 affluent patriots in New York called upon the Regulars to put down an uprising of tenants, who had taken up arms to demand freehold tenure. A British officer observed that the Sons of Liberty "are of opinion no one is entitled to Riot but themselves."[12] In the Carolinas merchants and landowners living near the coast showed no sympathy for the western settlers who organized as "Regulators."[13]

News of the Boston Port Act, which closed the harbor, arrived in the colonies in May 1774, opening a new chapter that would draw more and more of the common folk into the revolutionary movement. Parliament had adopted that repressive measure in response to the Tea Party; the preceding December, Bostonians of all ranks had boarded the tea ships and dumped that dutied product into the icy waters. Throughout the colonies the wealthy patriots now sought the support of small farmers as well as townsfolk. The revolutionaries had no choice, with British soldiers and frigates present in Boston, New York, Virginia, and Charleston, and measures such as nonimportation and nonexportation under discussion. The First Continental Congress, which convened in Philadelphia in September 1774, accelerated the involvement of the common folk. The body met in Carpenters' Hall, acknowledging the crucial role artisans played, adopted a nonimportation agreement to begin in December, and directed every locale to create a committee of observation and inspection to enforce the pact. Bringing small farmers into the revolutionary movement and expanding the role of the "lower orders" in the towns heightened social conflict. One flash point was the formation of militia units, since freeholders in every colony insisted on choosing their own officers.[14]

The clash of social classes had a decidedly mixed impact on the march to independence and on the wealthy revolutionaries, who continued to lead their provinces and direct the continental congresses. Most artisans backed independence, as did some affluent patriots who concluded that bold actions were the best way to ride this tumultuous wave. But other prominent leaders drew the opposite lesson, viewing internal conflict as an argument for a more measured approach; they hoped to establish stable institutions before breaking with the mother country. Still, escalating military clashes helped the more outspoken revolutionaries make their case, and on July 2, 1776, Congress voted for independence, adopting the famous declaration two days later.[15]

Internal conflicts only intensified with the establishment of new state governments and the widening war with Britain. Disgruntled farmers in the Carolinas and New York became loyalists and fought the patriots. Clashes emerged as states crafted new constitutions, with the less wealthy demanding fairer apportionment, debtor relief, broader suffrage, and more responsive institutions. A desire to counter the turmoil in the states was one reason the fifty-five delegates, almost all drawn from the upper class, came together in Philadelphia in May 1787 to draft a new frame of

government. The existing agreement, the Articles of Confederation, had created a weak central government. The representatives
in the Philadelphia convention were frank about their intentions.
Virginian Edmund Randolph opened the sessions, declaring, "Our
chief danger arises from the democratic parts of our [state] constitutions.... None of the constitutions have provided sufficient
checks against democracy."[16] The Founders erected a cumber-
some frame to restrict dissent without denying the common folk
some voice in their governing. In every state the citizenry clashed
over ratifying the Constitution, with the line of division, broadly
viewed, pitting merchants, planters, and other well-off landowners against the poorer farmers.[17]

The less wealthy citizenry was not the only group that helped
shape and was shaped by the revolutionary movement. On the eve
of independence African Americans comprised 20 percent of the
population, about 500,000 of the 2.5 million colonists. Ninety percent lived in the Southern colonies, and only a few thousand were
free. The proclamation Virginia's Governor Dunmore issued in
November 1775, offering loyal slaves freedom, intensified opposition to Britain. Richard Henry Lee exclaimed that "Lord Dun-
mores unparalleled conduct in Virginia has, a few Scotch excepted,
united every Man in that large Colony."[18] More broadly, the revolutionary era altered the status of Blacks. During these years
the river of abolitionist sentiment swelled in the North, drawing
strength from various tributaries. Enlightenment ideas influenced
educated colonists, as did Quaker teachings. Slaves in Massachusetts petitioned for freedom, and several towns supported them.
Remarkable individuals, like the poet Phillis Wheatley, who was
born in Africa and educated by the Boston family that purchased
her, eloquently condemned bondage. After independence the

Northern states ended slavery, although some did so gradually. The Southern states, however, rejected those arguments, secured protections for the institution in the Constitution, and oversaw an era of rapid growth in bonded labor.[19]

The Revolution also affected the roles of White women, particularly those from the "middling" and upper classes. Women launched nonconsumption agreements to support the boycotts and produced record quantities of homespun. They managed farms when their husbands marched off to war, ably overseeing the complex transactions large estates required. Historians differ in assessing the impact of these new responsibilities on gender roles. Despite Abigail Adams's plea to her husband John ("in the new Code of laws, . . . I desire you would Remember the ladies"), legislators did not ease oppressive rules. Courts continued to enforce coverture, the doctrine that a married woman's legal existence was subsumed by her husband. But in other ways progress was evident. Education advanced; by 1800 women in many New England towns had likely achieved near universal literacy. They became an important audience for (and in some cases, the authors of) sentimental novels. Scholars also suggest discussions of women's rights became increasingly common in the decades after independence.[20]

For Native peoples, the revolutionary era proved disastrous. Long before independence, land-hungry colonists had pushed westward from the Carolinas, Virginia, and New York's Hudson Valley, sowing the seeds of conflict.[21] In 1774 Dunmore's War, waged with the full support of Virginia's patriots, drove the Shawnees from Kentucky. Fighting intensified after independence as the British encouraged their Native allies to strike. In 1776 South Carolinians, along with troops from other colonies, repelled Cherokee attacks, burned their crops and food supplies, and forced the Natives to abandon their villages. General John Sullivan employed the same scorched earth tactics against the Iroquois in western New York, shattering the Iroquois Confederacy and subjecting Indians to the harsh winter of 1779. The 1783 Peace Treaty with Britain gave the Americans the land to the Mississippi with no mention of Native sovereignty.[22]

The American Revolution was an earth-shaking experience, unsettling the social landscape. The new scholarship that erupted in the late 1960s makes those ramifications clear. The rebellion could not have occurred without the support of the less wealthy Whites, and in turn it transformed their lives as well as the worlds of African Americans, middle-class women, and Natives. Still, these individuals did not lead the revolt; their activities do not explain the Revolution.

II

Why then was there an American Revolution? Any rethinking of the causes must accept the findings of the social historians. That's a start, but not enough. A new interpretation also must address the issues the neo-Whigs fail to explain: the deep fissure that separated the colonists into patriots and loyalists, and the extraordinary energy the victorious patriots displayed in pursuing their expansionist and entrepreneurial goals. This essay argues that in each colony the revolutionary movement was led by upper-class individuals whose commitment to American growth was evident long before 1763.

A full understanding begins with recasting the long-standing framework that defines studies of the rebellion. The roots of the patriot movement lie not in the years after 1763 but in the mid-century wars involving Britain, France, and Native Americans. Starting the narrative in 1763 is like walking midway into an action movie. You get to see a lot of explosions and chases, but you're not quite sure why everyone is so angry.[23]

The colonial elite divided during the midcentury clashes—King George's War (1744–1748) and the French and Indian War (1754–1763)—creating factions that would shape politics in the decades to follow. One group in every colony was passionate about defeating the French and their Native allies. They were determined to fund the wars, provision the troops, and promote enlistments. These leaders (we can call them "expansionists") include George Washington in Virginia, Benjamin Franklin in Pennsylvania, Thomas Hancock (John's father) in Massachusetts, the Livingston family in New York, and Henry Laurens in South Carolina.

The expansionists supported the British war effort—after all, the Regulars were fighting the French and Indians. But that alliance was a marriage of convenience. Their first loyalty was always to American interests. None of these leaders offered the mother country unconditional support. "O let not Britain seek to oppress us," Franklin told a London correspondent in 1753, "but like an affectionate parent endeavor to secure freedom to her children."[24] The Charleston firm of Austin & Laurens in 1755 extolled the value of American soldiers: "Our Ministry would do well to prosecute a War in America with Americans."[25] Writing to a local journal, William Livingston proposed an essay, "The equal rights of British subjects in the plantations, to the privileges enjoyed by their fellow subjects in Great Britain, asserted and vindicated."[26] These partisans also sought to unite the colonies, an important step in shifting the locus of power to the New World. In 1754 at an intercolonial conference in Albany, Franklin proposed a Plan of Union, and many others, like Austin & Laurens (who urged "the several Provinces to unite their strength"), agreed.[27]

Other individuals in every colony were reluctant to support the war effort and resisted spending for the troops or quartering British soldiers. Among these "nonexpansionists" were Thomas Hutchinson and Peter Oliver in Massachusetts, the DeLanceys in New York, the Quaker Party in Pennsylvania, Peyton Randolph and Edmund Pendleton in Virginia, and William Wragg in South Carolina. Students familiar with the revolutionary movement will recognize these midcentury divisions. Most expansionists became patriots; most nonexpansionists turned into loyalists.

What explains the lines of division that split the colonial elite at midcentury? Three factors—geography, religion, and economic activities—shaped the factions. Individuals whose estates lay close to the frontier or along the routes leading into disputed territory usually joined the expansionists. In Virginia, landowners like the Washingtons, Lees, Carters, and Masons, who backed the war effort, lived along the Potomac River and the Blue Ridge Mountains. The Potomac, with its headwaters deep in the Appalachian Mountains, directed the planters' gaze toward western Pennsylvania, an area the French also coveted. "The [Indian] Trade can be better supply'd from the Heads of Potomack than any other way," Lawrence Washington, George's half-brother, explained in 1749, and continued: "[T]he further we extend our Frontier the safer we render the Interior Dominions," because "the French having possession of the Ohio might easily invade Virginia."[28] These estate owners came together in a land company and defiantly erected a stockade at the forks of the Ohio (later the site of Pittsburgh). In what proved to be the opening exchanges of the French and Indian

War, the French captured that outpost in April 1754 and in July defeated a company of soldiers led by George Washington. Virginians whose estates lay along the more protected river valleys bridled at supporting these efforts and paying the onerous taxes needed to battle the French.

Geography shaped divisions in other colonies. In New York the Livingstons, with their vast fiefdoms on the upper Hudson River, realized, as a 1735 petition pronounced, that "their estates would not be near the value they bear at present" if New France and its Native allies were left unchecked.[29] By contrast, the DeLanceys, who headed the opposing faction, held tracts nearer to New York City. In 1746 Philip Livingston lamented that "the [Assembly] members of the Lower Counties Seem against doing any thing Effectually for the Fronteers, which is really a most melancholy Case."[30] In South Carolina rice planters with estates in the upland parishes supported the campaigns, as did the majority of Charleston merchants, like Henry Laurens and Christopher Gadsden, many of whom also owned tracts in exposed areas. The opposition came from the landowners, like William Wragg, who lived on the coastal islands and had little interest in defending the western reaches.

Religion also affected party lines. In Pennsylvania the Quakers, who resided in the eastern counties, affirmed their peace testimony and opposed military outlays. German sectarians, including Moravians and Mennonites, supported that pacifism. The expansionists counted on the Presbyterians, many of whom lived in the western counties, while others, like Charles Thompson, were Philadelphia merchants. Most Anglicans favored this group, which initially was called the Proprietary Party and later, the Presbyterian Party. Benjamin Franklin, who by his own account "had been religiously educated as Presbyterian" but became a Deist, guided the faction with his words and deeds.[31] In Boston much of the sorting reflected church membership. Expansionists filled the pews in Jonathan Mayhew's West Church and Charles Chauncy's First Church, whose pastors set forth an optimistic view of the future. Nonexpansionists inclined toward Anglicanism and the strain of Congregationalism that emphasized authority and tradition, as reflected in the messages expounded in the Second Church and the New North Church.[32]

Finally, merchants who invested in frontier estates, pursued military contracts, or were involved in smuggling usually sided with the expansionists. Those more focused on trade with the mother country joined the nonexpansionists.[33]

A sustained faith in America's ascent guided expansionists during these years—and after 1763. Bostonian Jonathan Mayhew broadcast these beliefs in the sermons he delivered at the West Church. After the capture of Quebec in 1759, Mayhew declared the colonies would become "*a mighty empire* (I do not mean an independent one), in numbers little inferior perhaps to the greatest in Europe, and in felicity to none."[34] (Mayhew used "empire" in the eighteenth-century sense of an extensive country.) John Adams, a rising member of this outward-looking faction, concurred. He told a friend in 1755 that he foresaw the "transfer of the seat of empire into America," adding, "If we can remove the turbulent Gallicks, our People according to the exactest Computations, will in another Century become more numerous than England itself."[35] In his newspaper, *The Pennsylvania Gazette*, and other tracts, Franklin shared a similar, bountiful vision of America's prospects. In *Poor Richard's Alamanack* for 1750 he contrasted "old settled countries, as England" with the New World: "I believe People increase faster by Generation in these Colonies, where all can have full Employ and there is Room and Business for Millions yet unborn."[36]

By contrast, the nonexpansionists were more cautious about the future and repeatedly grumbled about the war. In Massachusetts Thomas Hutchinson called the 1745 campaign against a French fortress at Louisbourg "rash" and complained that talking about the value of the fortress was "like selling the skin of a bear before catching him."[37] (Expansionist Thomas Hancock declared the contract for the soldiers attacking Louisbourg was "what I am fonder of than anything in the world.")[38] In the 1750s Hutchinson, along with Chief Justice Stephen Sewall, opposed British demands to quarter troops, and sighed for "a peace if but tolerable."[39] In New York the emissary of the Crown "found Mr. Delancey and his party rather cold and backward" and turned to the Livingstons for assistance.[40] The DeLanceys, along with the Quaker Party in Pennsylvania, denounced Franklin's call for a colonial Plan of Union. In South Carolina William Wragg, whom the governor labeled an "insolent and litigious spirit," condemned defense spending.[41]

III

After 1763, with their vision of America's rise serving as their compass, the expansionists led the response to the British enactments. The policies the mother country adopted between 1763 and 1773 did not in themselves cause the revolt. The Proclamation of 1763 (which prohibited settlement beyond the Appalachian Mountains) and the Declaratory Act of 1766 (which stated Parliament had complete power over the colonies) were not enforced. Only the Stamp Act, a measure quickly repealed, disrupted the colonists' lives. The Townshend duties of 1767 targeted a few incidental items, such as glass, paint, paper, and tea. The Tea Act of 1773 would have made that drink cheaper. The Sugar Act of 1764, as amended in 1766, raised most of the revenue Britain got from the colonies during these years but rarely was an object of complaint. But thanks to the expansionists' determination to make America a "mighty empire," these measures provided the tinder for a conflagration.[42]

Defiance came naturally to those convinced of America's ineluctable rise. "This country, it must be allowed," Pennsylvanian Charles Thomson observed in 1765, "is as well calculated for Trade, Manufactures, & Commerce as any in the world. Our Hills abound with iron and other rich minerals, our plains produce the richest verdure.... [But] no sooner did the colonies begin to improve these advantages than they were restricted by acts of P[arliament]."[43] The next year Virginian George Mason asked a group of London merchants, "Do you, does any sensible Man, think that three or four Millions of People, not naturally defective in Genius, or in Courage, who have tasted the Sweets of Liberty in a Country that doubles its Inhabitants every twenty Years, in a Country abounding with such Variety of Soil and Climate ... will long submit to Oppression?"[44] New Yorker William Livingston echoed these sentiments, declaring in 1768, "Liberty, religion, and sciences are on the wing to these shores: The finger of God points out a mighty empire to your sons."[45] Thomas Hutchinson, who would become a loyalist, emphasized the impact of this ideology, rather than any specific measure, in fomenting opposition to Parliament: "The prevalence of a spirit of opposition to government in the plantations is the natural consequence of the great growth of the colonies so remote from the parent state, and not the effect of oppression in the King or his servants."[46]

Expansionists questioned the restrictions imposed by Britain's Acts of Trade. South Carolinian Christopher Gadsden remarked in 1766, "What a boundless & alluring prospect of advantages must even the most distant idea of an open Trade to all Europe, nay to all the World, be to the Americans."[47] In his 1774 tract, *A Summary View of the Rights of British America*, Thomas Jefferson denounced the navigation acts as an "unjust encroachment" on "the exercise of a free trade with all parts of the world possessed by the American colonists, as a natural right."[48]

The deep, prolonged depression that followed the French and Indian War further heightened the expansionists' determination to resist Britain. The torrent of credit and manufactures flooding into the colonies after 1745 proved a mixed blessing. It raised the standard of living, but as the British economy slowed after 1763, soaring debt (colonists owed over four million pounds), along with the unsold goods piling up on merchants' shelves, became an onerous burden. Everywhere the boycotts of British goods that emerged in 1765 and again in 1768–1770 had twin purposes: to chastise the mother country and to ease the pressures that traders and planters felt. Joining together for nonimportation in 1769, Virginians announced: "Having taken into our most serious Consideration the present State of Trade of this Colony and of *American* Commerce in general, [we] observe with Anxiety that the Debt due to *Great-Britain* for Goods imported from thence is very great, and that the Means of paying this Debt in the present Situation of Affairs are likely to become more and more precarious." Bostonians, New Yorkers, and Philadelphians explained their boycotts in similar terms.[49] While the colonists did not go to war to escape debt, the hard times shaped the protests and encouraged expansionists to imagine a new commercial order. During the decade after 1765 boycotts were the principal cudgel colonists wielded against Britain. Expansionists, along with artisans, shopkeepers, and other townsfolk, were the strongest supporters of these pacts.

In every colony nonexpansionists criticized these protests. Individuals like Thomas Hutchinson and Peter Oliver in Massachusetts, the DeLanceys in New York, the Quaker Party in Pennsylvania, the Pendletons and Randolphs in Virginia, and William Wragg in South Carolina denounced the boycotts and opposed the resolutions championed by patriotic lawmakers. These individuals, who once had been hesitant to fund Britain's wars, now were the Crown's loudest defenders. The continuity in their actions and outlook lay in their cautious vision of growth: confronted with demands for independence, they had little faith that the colonies could flourish on their own. Thomas Hutchinson observed that if the colonies ever separated from Britain, "A few individuals may attain to greater degrees of dignity and power, but the inhabitants in general will never enjoy so great a share of natural liberty as they would have done if they had remained a dependent colony."[50]

A fine-grained reading of the conflicts in each colony adds nuance to this narrative but does not overturn it. For example, in New York the Great Rebellion of 1766 led the Livingstons temporarily to mute their criticism of Parliament: they called upon the Regulars to suppress the tenant farmers. But by the end of the decade the Livingstons again stood in the forefront of the resistance—and would remain patriots, while their opponents, the DeLanceys, became loyalists. In Virginia, many nonexpansionists chose to remain in the new nation. The relative lack of tensions within the White population before 1774 encouraged such cooperation, distinguishing Virginia from most other colonies.[51]

IV

The goal of the expansionists was never simply independence. That was just one step in the journey to create a prosperous, powerful, dynamic nation-state in the New World. The convictions of these outward-looking individuals were reflected in the wars against the Natives, the chartering of the Bank of North America, the peace treaty that pushed the western border of the new nation to the Mississippi, and the opening of trade with China. The desire to set the American "empire" on a sound foundation was a crucial motive (along with the need to check the "excess of democracy") that brought delegates together to write the Constitution. During a pause in the convention's work, Franklin, the spiritual father of the gathering, called everyone together in prayer, asking, "If a sparrow cannot fall to the ground without His notice, is it probable that an empire can rise without His aid?"[52]

This expansionary ethos would reverberate through the centuries of American history. It was evident in the expedition to chastise the Barbary Pirates, the wars against Native Americans, the Mexican War of 1846–1848, and the many foreign ventures of the industrialized nation.

Still, the American Revolution cannot be reduced to this one central theme. The revolt was like the bursting of a high dam, unleashing a torrent that pushed aside rocks and boulders in its path. The rebellion animated the movement for the abolition of slavery, breathing new life into ideas that had been quietly exchanged among Quakers and others. The refashioning of the political world encouraged some Americans to explore the daring ideas of the Scottish Enlightenment, expressed in the work of Francis Hutcheson, David Hume, and Adam Smith. Those philosophers emphasized the "moral sense" as well as the value of social happiness and human equality. Persuaded by such ideas, Jefferson declared "all men are created equal." He rejected Locke's trinity of "life, liberty, and property," positing instead "unalienable" rights to "life, liberty, and the pursuit of happiness."[53] Those words, even if written by a slaveholder, had a lasting impact on how Americans saw themselves. "Republicanism" also plays a role in this era. While not the cause of the revolt, it helps explain the checks and balances embodied in the new state and national constitutions.

Hence, if expansionism stands at the center of any understanding of the Revolution, the full legacy of the rebellion is far ranging and at times contradictory. Revolutionaries condemned slavery but also laid the basis for its spread and, with the Constitution, provided a strong legal foundation for a slaveholding republic. They affirmed the rights of all citizens but created governments to restrict those rights. They declared, as Thomas Paine did in *Common Sense*, "[t]he cause of America is, in a great measure, the cause of all mankind," but founded a nation determined to aggressively promote its own interests, often at the expense of other countries' well-being.[54]

3   *What Caused the Civil War?*

My first in-your-face encounter with strikingly different views of the Civil War came in July 2009, when paleoconservative John Lofton interviewed me for his radio program, *The American View.* I was promoting my recently published book, *A Clash of Extremes: The Economic Origins of the Civil War,* and did not heed my publicist's warning about Lofton's outlook. Had I checked I would have learned that Lofton was a provocateur who had appeared on shows like *Crossfire* and *Politically Incorrect* and had famously debated with Frank Zappa about rock lyrics. (When Lofton launched into one of his screeds, Zappa responded, "Tell you what—kiss my ass!") Lofton opened our session by asking me what I thought of the "murderous tyrant 'Dishonest Abe.'" He followed up by demanding to know which side I would have supported in the War of Northern Aggression: the invaders or those who heroically defended their homes. Painfully simplifying my book, I told him I backed the side that wanted to end slavery. The interview did not go well.[1]

Few academics share Lofton's view or even regularly encounter it. Overwhelmingly, historians assert that a dispute over slavery lies at the heart of the sectional conflict. The war came about, they suggest, because Northerners felt slavery was wrong and were determined to end it, while Southerners believed it was a proper system and resolved to preserve it.[2] If this explanation were presented as a sermon, Abraham Lincoln's words would supply chapter and verse. Writing in 1860 to Alexander Stephens of Georgia, Lincoln stated simply: "You think slavery is *right* and ought to be extended; while we think it is *wrong* and ought to be restricted. That I suppose is the rub. It certainly is the only substantial difference between us."[3]

Lofton, however, hardly stands alone. Several best-selling authors, often on the fringes of the academic community and occasionally with neo-Confederate links, also deny the role of slavery. They argue the South seceded to defend states' rights and to resist Northern demands for a centralized government.[4] Many Americans applaud that viewpoint and reject the idea that bondage led to the breakup. In a 2011 poll, 48 percent of those surveyed pointed to states' rights as the cause of the war, while only 38 percent identified slavery.[5] Still, neither the vote of university professors nor the views of the general population can decide which interpretation best explains the conflict. This essay suggests there is good reason to be skeptical of both approaches and presents an alternative. It argues that the demand of affluent citizens for economic and territorial growth is the key to understanding the causes of the Civil War.

I

A close examination of the reigning scholarly interpretation—the argument that deeply held beliefs about slavery brought on the clash—stands as the first step in understanding the origins of the war. James Oakes's *The Scorpion's Sting: Antislavery and* the *Coming of the Civil War* (2014) and Charles Dew's *Apostles of Disunion: Southern Secession Commissioners and the Causes of the Civil War* (2001) present this thesis clearly and forcefully.[6] Oakes argues that Lincoln and the Republicans were unwavering opponents of slavery and regarded the sectional battle as a "conflict over the right versus the wrong of 'property in man.'" The Republican strategy to secure freedom, Oakes emphasizes, was *not* military emancipation. That terrible swift sword would strike the South, but only under the unusual circumstances of a prolonged war. Rather, the Republicans' plan was to "surround the South with a 'cordon of freedom.'" The slave states, deprived of any opportunity to expand, would find slavery increasingly unprofitable and be forced to free their slaves, much like the (mythical) "scorpion girt by fire" stings itself to death.[7]

The Republicans' unyielding stance on expansion, Oates asserts, made secession inevitable. It undercut the compromises proposed and all but guaranteed the South would leave the Union. Oates explains: "Secessionists were not fantasizing this doomsday scenario; they were simply repeating what Republicans themselves promised to do. It is hardly surprising, then, that secessionists were completely unmoved by ritualized Republican promises not to interfere with slavery in the states where it already existed."[8]

With a focus on the South, Dew, in *Apostles of Disunion*, reinforces Oakes's argument. Dew begins engagingly with autobiography. He grew up in Florida, "a son of the South," accepting that the section "had seceded for one reason and one reason only: states' rights." Only later, reading the actual words of the secessionists, was he "stunned" to see that slavery lay at the heart of the matter. Dew points out how assiduously Confederate leaders labored after the war to obfuscate their earlier emphasis on slavery.[9]

Dew examines the speeches of the fifty-two men who served as secessionist commissioners. The first five states to leave the Union appointed these individuals as emissaries to visit the rest of the South and persuade those states to join the Confederacy. Much as Oakes suggests, none of the secessionists were reassured by Republican blandishments about respecting slavery where it existed. Rather, the speakers, who fanned out across the South, rehearsed a litany of horrors that would assuredly follow the Republican ascendancy. Mississippian Fulton Anderson, for example, told Virginians that the Republicans were set on "the ultimate extinction of slavery, and the degradation of the Southern people." Southern Whites would be forced "to bend our necks to the yokes which a false fanaticism had prepared for them."[10]

Oakes and Dew present a strong argument that deep, principled concerns about slavery caused the war. But how convincing is that case? To begin with, it must be made clear that rejecting the emphasis on convictions about bondage does not mean accepting the states' rights argument. "Slavery" versus "states' rights" is a false dichotomy. They are not the only choices. The states' rights interpretation, as the work of Dew and other historians makes clear, is the product of post–Civil War propaganda and comes tinged with racism. It seeks to obscure the commitment to White supremacy that drove the secessionists. There are strong reasons for dismissing that explanation.

But there are also good grounds to question an interpretation that highlights convictions about slavery as the cause of the conflict. Scrutiny begins with Dew's explanation of Southern behavior. Outside of the Deep South the secession commissioners proved remarkably unsuccessful. Virginians listened respectfully to their visitors' lurid prophesies and chose to remain in the Union—even though their state had more slaves than any other. The same was true of all the states of the Upper South and the Border: none felt that Lincoln's election in itself warranted secession. Only when fighting broke out in April 1861 did the four Upper South states—Virginia (except for a group of western counties), North Carolina, Tennessee, and Arkansas—cast their lot with the Confederacy. The Border states—Kentucky, Delaware, Maryland, and Missouri—remained with the Union, although Kentucky had a larger slave population than either Florida or Texas.

Even in the seven states of the Lower South, the secession conventions reveal deep divisions among the citizenry. In Georgia, Alabama, Mississippi, and Louisiana at least 40 percent of those voting for delegates, and in some cases half, opposed immediate secession. Nor was the split in the cotton states between slaveholders and small farmers. Both groups divided along regional lines. The key question becomes not "Did the South secede to protect slavery?" but rather "Why was a particular group in the Deep South attuned to secessionist ideology, while planters and nonslaveholding farmers elsewhere in the South rejected that outlook?" That second question points toward the need to explore economic and regional concerns to understand the Civil War.

Oakes's conclusions also seem questionable. *The Scorpion's Sting* concentrates on the years just before the Civil War and only briefly touches on earlier decades. It does not explain why the North and South were able to compromise repeatedly between 1820 and 1850. The debates over Missouri in 1819–1821 reveal fervent convictions strikingly similar to those expressed in 1860–1861. Northern congressmen and their constituents vehemently opposed admitting Missouri as a slave state. James Tallmadge of New York introduced a bill to ban slavery from the new state and supported the measure with the strongest language. "If civil war, which gentlemen so much threaten, must come, I can only say, let it come!" he thundered. "If blood is necessary to extinguish any fire which I have assisted to kindle, I can assure gentlemen, while I regret the necessity, I shall not forebear to contribute my mite."[11] A chorus of voices supported him. "The existence of slavery," Pennsylvanian William Darlington pronounced, "seems to be universally considered a great moral and political evil."[12] Southerners responded in kind, threatening secession if the North blocked the expansion of slavery. The result of these angry exchanges was not armed conflict, but compromise, with the admission of Missouri as a slave state, Maine as a free state, and a line of demarcation (the 36°30′ parallel) north of which slavery was banned.[13]

Any persuasive interpretation of the Civil War must explain why, despite the vitriol spewed by both sides, the two sections repeatedly found common ground before the 1850s. They came together in the Missouri Compromise, the Nullification controversy of 1832–1833, the clash over abolitionist petitions in the 1830s, and the battle over admitting California in 1850. One school of twentieth-century historians suggests wise statesmen kept the nation together before a "blundering generation" allowed it to fall apart. Historians today uniformly and justly reject that explanation. But at least that earlier school saw the need to explore the shift from compromise to conflict.

Oakes also fails to explain why the Republicans triumphed in 1860. Without that success in the electoral college, Republican plans for a cordon of free states would have remained a historical footnote, much like the Know Nothing Party's proposals on immigration. The Republican victory was hardly a foregone conclusion. The Free Soil Party, in many respects the predecessor of the

Republicans, had not done well. In 1848 it received 14.5 percent of the Northern vote, while in 1852 that proportion fell to 6.7 percent. Some historians argue that during the 1850s antislavery sentiment welled up like a mighty wave, and in cresting carried Lincoln and Republicans into office.[14] But that hypothesis does not stand up to close analysis of those who rallied to the Republican standard and why.

Finally, historians like Oakes who see the Republicans as principled crusaders provide a celebratory and reductive depiction of Lincoln's party. They ignore the Republicans' determination to transform the economy and the broad array of measures the Republicans supported before the war and implemented once they gained power. These initiatives included higher tariffs, a Pacific railroad, and internal improvements. This wide-ranging, coherent program attracted voters who had little interest in campaigns against slavery. Indeed, free soil was for most Northerners more an economic program—preserving the West for small farmers—than a means of hastening emancipation. Emphasis on the Republicans as antislavery idealists before 1861 creates an unsettling discontinuity. In the years after the war, most observers agree, the seemingly noble-minded Republicans became the party of big business, piloted by corrupt spoilsmen. Of course, parties do evolve, but the overall continuity in personnel and leadership is striking. Because the Republicans dominated national politics during most years between 1860 and the Great Depression, understanding the origins of that party is important for any analysis of US history. Oakes and like-minded historians ask us to look at the early days of the GOP through rose-tinted glasses. Any convincing explanation of the Civil War must move beyond the interpretation that strongly held convictions about slavery brought on the clash.

II

Why then the Civil War? This essay argues (in keeping with the larger themes of the book) that the demand for economic and territorial growth set forth after 1850 by a group of cotton planters, and by farmers, merchants, and manufacturers around the Great Lakes and in New England, is the key to explaining the conflict. Economic change underpinned the emergence of these groups and their increasingly fervent demands.

Retelling the story of the coming of the Civil War begins with the era of compromise, from the 1820s to 1850.[15] The economy of the young republic provided the foundation for decades of deal making and resilient national parties. In the West, the Mississippi River created a powerful north-south axis, tying together the Northwest and Southwest. The advent of steamboats, whose numbers increased dramatically in the 1820s, spurred the commerce of an inland empire, which stretched from New Orleans to Pittsburgh. Politicians North and South celebrated this booming region. In 1850 Stephen Douglas told his fellow senators, "There is a power in this nation greater than either the North or the South. . . . That power is the country known as the great West—the Valley of the Mississippi, one and indivisible from the gulf to the great lakes."[16]

A second set of economic ties—the links between the manufacturers and merchants of the North and the cotton planters of the South—drew the sections together. Northern mill owners purchased about a fifth of the bales produced, while New York merchants financed the cotton trade. Political cooperation tracked this business relationship, angering those who wanted the North to take a stronger stand. Charles Sumner, the reform-minded senator from Massachusetts, roundly denounced the "unhallowed union ... between the lords of the lash and the lords of the loom."[17]

The prosperity of the Deep South also fostered sectional cooperation. Before the 1850s planters enjoyed fertile soils and favorable profits. They were pleased the federal government opened new areas to slavery, with the purchase of Louisiana (1803) and the annexation of Florida (1821) and Texas (1845). Before they became sectionalists, Southerners were nationalists who ardently supported the War of 1812, a national bank, and internal improvements. During the heated exchanges over the admission of Missouri, South Carolinian John C. Calhoun told an Alabama friend, "Our true system is to look to the country; and to support such measures and such men, without regard to sections, as are best calculated to advance the general interest."[18]

The Border States, with their strong ties to the North, comprised still another force for national unity. These marchlands increasingly were drawn into the Northern commercial orbit. The section elevated peace weavers, with Kentuckian Henry Clay helping to broker three deals: the Missouri Compromise, the resolution of the Nullification controversy, and the Compromise of 1850.

Finally, two national parties, the Whigs and Democrats, who differed on many issues but shared a commitment to preserving the Union, provided a powerful glue that bound the sections together. Wealth, not geography, separated the parties. The Whigs drew their support from manufacturers, merchants, planters, and other well-off landowners. The Democrats enjoyed the backing of the poorer farmers and the working folk of the cities. These lines of division characterized most locales, even with several exceptions to the pattern, primarily in the South.[19] The two parties feuded over economic issues, with the Whigs rallying around

Henry Clay's "American System" and its call for internal improvements, a strong banking system, and tariffs to promote manufacturing. Whigs favored schools and asylums and the sale of public lands at high prices to pay for their programs. The Democrats dissented on all these counts, leading to pitched battles in statehouses and in Congress. While divided on the role of government, both parties relied on constituencies that spanned sectional lines: they recognized that only broad coalitions could control Congress and triumph in the electoral college. Party leaders joined in supporting sectional compromises. In 1850 Whig Henry Clay and Democrat Stephen Douglas together crafted a multipart deal and shepherded it through Congress.[20]

The Compromise of 1850, however, proved to be the last hurrah for the era of cooperation, as a far-reaching reorientation of the US economy transformed politics, amplifying the voices of extremists. Change in both the North and South ushered in an era of confrontation, culminating in the Civil War.

III

The realignment of the economy and society of the North shattered the party system of Whigs and Democrats and fostered the rise of the Republicans. Around midcentury the trade of the Northwest, a vast region stretching from western Pennsylvania to Iowa, pivoted from a north-south axis to an east-west one. The first step in that change was the completion in 1825 of the Erie Canal, a 339-mile ditch that allowed Great Lakes ports to ship goods to New York City. Opening this water route encouraged the settlement of western New York and the northern counties of Ohio, Indiana, and Illinois, as well as three new states: Michigan (1837), Iowa (1846), and

Wisconsin (1848). Families with New England origins populated this area, their views sharply contrasting with the pro-Southern leanings of the migrants from Virginia and Kentucky who earlier had moved to the southern districts of Ohio, Indiana, and Illinois. The shifting concentration of population within states and the expansion of Great Lakes commerce reshaped the North. In 1835 shipments from the Midwest to eastern destinations amounted to only 5 percent of the total those states sent to New Orleans. By 1840 the proportion had reached almost 40 percent, and after midcentury most goods in the North flowed east-west. Railroads accounted for an increasing portion of this swelling trade, carrying 20 percent of interregional shipments on the eve of the Civil War.[21]

The needs of the Great Lakes economy were unrelenting, a welter of demands with important repercussions. Since the lakes had no natural harbors, endless work—building piers and dredging—was needed to keep ports open. "The truth about the Chicago harbor," Senator Robert Toombs of Georgia observed in 1858, "seems to be that if you run your pier out into the lake three hundred yards this year, you must run it out five hundred next year, and seven hundred the next year, and so on until you run it across the lake."[22] Lake shippers also sought funds to clear two choke points—the Falls of St. Marys River (near Sault Ste. Marie) and the St. Clair Flats (near Detroit).

Shared interests united the politicians living around the lakes, with Democrats defying party leaders and joining with Whigs to back internal improvements. Charles Stuart, Democratic congressman from Michigan, remarked, "I tell you here to-day that the man who shall start in the State of Michigan with the declaration that he is opposed to all harbor improvements cannot get one hundred votes, however great, however popular he otherwise might be."[23] Congressmen from the lake districts pushed for higher tariffs to fund needed outlays and elaborated a self-serving doctrine of *nationalism* to justify their demands. "Long John" Wentworth, a Chicago Democrat, expressed a common sentiment in 1854, "The commerce of my constituents is that of the whole nation."[24] New Englanders agreed: manufacturers recognized that measures that helped their customers benefited them. Connecticut Senator Truman Smith applauded a Michigan lawmaker's call to open the St. Clair Flats, remarking: "The people of the Northwest must stand up resolutely for their rights.... [C]an we not believe that the prosperity of each party is the prosperity of the whole?"[25]

Along with the east-west flow of goods, a second development—the growth of the abolition movement—affected the outlook of Northerners. Demands to end slavery date back to the colonial era, reaching one crescendo after independence, when Northern states ended bondage. In January 1831 William Lloyd Garrison's call for immediate emancipation reinvigorated the movement, and a growing number of Northerners joined antislavery societies. African American abolitionists, including Frederick Douglass, Sojourner Truth, Henry Bibb, and Henry Highland Garnet, helped lead these protests. Still, what must be emphasized is how few individuals supported this campaign. Angry mobs pelted speakers with rotten eggs and vicious epithets in the 1830s and 1840s. The high-water mark for the abolitionist Liberty Party came in 1844 when it received sixty-six thousand votes, or about 3 percent of the Northern total. Contemporary estimates suggest adherents comprised no more than 5 percent of the Northern population, although support was higher in parts of New England.[26]

Perhaps another 10 percent of the North backed "radical" politicians like Charles Sumner, Salmon Chase, and Benjamin Wade.

These individuals accepted slavery in the South but argued the federal government should attack slavery where it had the power to do so, as in federal shipyards and the District of Columbia. Most Radicals and abolitionists also favored strengthening the rights of African Americans in the North, where discrimination and racist practices were endemic. The success of such campaigns was limited. Only the states of northern New England, where about 8 percent of the Northern Black population lived, enfranchised all African American men. Modern observers justly praise the abolitionists and Radicals. But these individuals comprised a small fraction of the Northern population and would be a minority within the Republican Party.

The realignment of Northern society helped birth the Republican Party. The Kansas-Nebraska Act of 1854 shattered the party system that had flourished since the early 1830s. This measure, which repealed the prohibitions of the Missouri Compromise and opened Kansas to slavery, angered Northerners of all persuasions and led many to cast off their old moorings. Support for the Democrats plummeted, while the Whig Party, torn apart by the yawning sectional divide, disappeared. The Republican Party, which emerged out of this chaotic situation, rested on a very different foundation than earlier factions. In 1856, in the Republicans' first election, they swept New England and won the electoral votes of New York, Ohio, Michigan, Wisconsin, and Iowa. Most counties voting Republican were in New England or around the Great Lakes.

The 1856 platform included planks boosting both economic and antislavery goals, but practicality was more important than idealism. What evidence supports that assertion? The sole resolve unmistakably directed against slavery was nonextension. Despite the advocacy of a few individuals, the party shunned initiatives such as ending bondage in DC, banning the interstate slave trade, excluding servants from federal shipyards, nullifying the fugitive slave act, and of course, abolition. The demand that the West be kept open for free farmers reflected both principled and economic motives—but not in equal proportions. An observer in the *New-York Tribune* explained the Republicans' outlook: "There are Republicans who are Abolitionists; there are others who anxiously desire and labor for the good of the slave; but there are many more whose main impulse is a desire to secure the new Territories for Free White Labor, with little or no regard for the interests of negroes, free or slave."[27] The 1856 platform also called for river and harbor improvements and a Pacific railroad by a "central and practicable route."[28]

Republican commitment to economic development broadened over the next four years. Party leaders recognized that opposition to slavery expansion was a weak springboard for an organization that needed the support of almost all Northern states, and particularly Pennsylvania, to win the presidency. Nonextension did not distinguish Republicans from Northern Democrats. Overwhelmingly, Democrats in the North had voted in the 1840s for the Wilmot Proviso, which sought to ban slavery from territories gained from Mexico. When President Buchanan tried to introduce slavery in Kansas by high-handed means, Stephen Douglas, leader of the Northern Democrats, broke with the administration. Further underscoring the need for a broader platform was the failure of David Wilmot's campaign in 1857 to become the Republican governor of Pennsylvania. In a state that demanded tariff protection for its iron and coal industry, Wilmot (whose proviso had made clear his position on nonextension) was branded a "Free-Trade and abolition Agitator ... who is ignorant of the business and politics of the State."[29] Horace Greeley, editor of the *New-York Tribune*, summarized the challenge Republicans faced. He explained that an "Anti-Slavery man *per se* cannot be elected; but a Tariff, River-and-harbor, Pacific Railroad, Free-Homestead man, *may* succeed *although* he is Anti-Slavery."[30]

Republicans triumphed in 1860 thanks to a campaign that emphasized economic issues rather than opposition to slavery. Party leaders made clear their determination to raise the tariff and assist the lake districts, a region Ohio congressman John Sherman declared would "in a short time control the destinies of this nation."[31] Republicans also backed land grant colleges, although President James Buchanan vetoed the bill they pushed through Congress. The 1860 platform expanded the party's commitment to economic development but did little to broaden the attack on slavery. As in 1856, the chief measure directed against slavery was nonextension. (Uncontroversially, the platform also condemned efforts to reopen the African slave trade.) Republicans now added demands for a homestead act and higher tariffs to their earlier calls for internal improvements and a Pacific railroad. The *New York Times* reported from the Chicago convention, "The tariff clause gives universal satisfaction, and was received with a storm of enthusiasm seldom witnessed in any popular gathering."[32] This expansive platform allowed the Republicans to gain almost all the North's electoral votes.

IV

Economic and social change also reconfigured Southern politics, drawing parts of the region closer to the free states while setting other districts on the path to secession. These developments shaped responses to the "first secession crisis" of 1849–1850 as well as to the battles over secession. Gradually the Border States had become less dependent on slave agriculture and more tightly bound to the North. In each of these four commonwealths the proportion of the population enslaved fell between 1830 and 1860, with Maryland and Delaware recording an absolute decline. Politicians from the Great Border, far more than their counterparts further South, backed compromise measures. They spurned Calhoun's "Southern Address," a document drafted in 1849 that foreshadowed the arguments secessionists would later make. (The appeal informed the nation that "aggression has followed aggression, and encroachment encroachment, until they have reached a point when a regard for your peace and safety will not permit us to remain longer silent.") Only one of the thirty congressmen from the Border signed this statement.[33]

The Upper South was tugged in different directions. Towns such as Richmond, Norfolk, and Memphis were drawn into the Northern orbit; the politicians, like John Bell of Tennessee, who were connected to the region's commercial activities voiced moderation. The small farmers of the Upper South, many of whom lived in the Appalachian highlands and the Ozarks, also leaned toward the Union. Concerns of class guided their outlook. Even more than their counterparts elsewhere in the South, these yeomen resented the extraordinary power the large slaveowners exercised in an era of mounting democratic ferment. Planters, influential beyond their numbers, were sympathetic to the grievances voiced in the Deep South.

But the key to understanding the sectional clash was the changes occurring in the Deep South. The prospect that geography—the "natural limits" of staple production—and decisions in Washington might end the expansion of the cotton kingdom unsettled many landowners. Like those species of shark that must keep swimming to survive, some cotton planters believed they required new land to prosper. New soils would counter the ravages of soil exhaustion, provide an outlet for the growing slave population, and make possible new slave states that would preserve the balance in the Senate. Restrictions on the expansion of slavery, evident at midcentury as never before, threatened that future.

Still, what must be emphasized is that even the Deep South was divided, and concerns about the storm clouds on the horizon evoked very different reactions. The northern districts of the Gulf States from South Carolina to Mississippi rejected dire prophesies. This area was populated by individuals who came from the Upper South and could trace their family ties back to Northern Ireland and Europe. The small farmers in these counties grew grain and supported local commercial centers. Along with the cotton planters in these districts, they were more likely to trade with the Upper South than with the port cities in their own states. They did not see the limits to expansion as a harbinger of doom. Rather, these individuals regarded diversification of the economy as a path to prosperity. A Milledgeville, Georgia, newspaper remarked that "our copious and unfailing water power, the abundant supply of raw materials, and the cheap labor which we command, invite us to apply a portion of our labor and capital to manufactures."[34] Benjamin Franklin Perry, who lived in the Greenville district of South Carolina, near the North Carolina border, told his countrymen: "Let the Southern people take lessons from the Yankees, in industry, wisdom and economy."[35]

The southern districts of the Gulf States had a very different outlook. Settlers in these counties had migrated from South Carolina, while their ancestors came from southern England. They grew fewer food crops and directed their exports to nearby ports. These landowners dismissed diversification as impractical. Jefferson Davis remarked, "Ours was an agricultural people, and in that consisted their strength."[36] These individuals, both planters and their small farmer allies, regarded Northern actions as an existential threat.

These fault lines underlay the clashes in the Deep South at midcentury and in 1860–1861. In 1849–1850 bitter conflicts over Calhoun's "Southern Address" rived the cotton states. One observer reported: "Almost all the Counties of South Alabama have responded most emphatically 'to the Southern Address' without distinction of party. North Alabama is much less interested and will be slow in her action."[37] Similar divisions split Georgians. "For the sake of harmony," one politician explained, "the subject of the Southern Address was not touched. It would have torn us to atoms."[38] The pitched battle in Mississippi led to the defeat of the secessionist governor John A. Quitman. Most townsfolk in the Deep South, Germans in Texas, and Louisiana sugar planters, who depended on tariff protection, shared the moderate outlook of the landowners in the northern districts.

The clashes of 1860–1861 replayed earlier conflicts, if with more dire consequences. What earlier had been feared had now come to pass: a Northern party, adamantly opposed to slavery expansion, had seized the reins of power. More than ever before, planters and farmers in the southern districts of the cotton states feared what the future held. *The Charleston Mercury* put it simply: "The issue before the country is the extinction of slavery."[39] These landowners shunned talk of diversification and applauded the Confederate constitution, which banned tariffs "laid to promote or foster any branch of industry."[40]

Still, in 1860–1861, as at midcentury, the landowners in the northern districts of the Deep South took a more moderate stance and again suggested that the future of the South lay in diversification rather than battling over new territory.[41] Except for South Carolina, sizable minorities opposed immediate secession in each of the state conventions. Settlers in the Tennessee Valley of northern Alabama decried rash steps, with one politician remarking, "If the people of South Alabama should succeed in putting the State out of the Union, he favored putting the Valley out of the State."[42] Once the decision to leave the Union was announced, most dissidents "went with their state." But in Georgia 89 delegates (out of about 296) refused to sign the secessionist ordinance. About fifteen thousand White farmers in the Deep South, mostly from the Cajun regions of Louisiana, northern Alabama, and northwestern Texas, joined the Union army.[43] The vitriolic rhetoric put forth in the southern districts certainly echoes the diatribes Charles Dew analyzes in *Apostles of Disunion*. But what is important to remember is that they were the sentiments of only one regional group within the Deep South, and their outlook was shaped by patterns of trade and settlement as well as the broad changes transforming the Southern economy.

For the Border and Upper South states, the Republican victory in November 1860 did not justify separation. Despite their substantial slave populations, these states rejected pleas from the Lower South. The eruption of fighting in April 1861 altered the equation for the Upper South. A Tennessee politician explained, "It is no longer the negro question but a question of resistance to tyranny."[44] Many small farmers, however, defied their state ordinances. West Virginia broke from Virginia, while the mountainous regions of western North Carolina and eastern Tennessee contributed almost fifty thousand White volunteers to the Union armies.[45]

Just as economic development had realigned the North, helping to foster a party, the Republicans, who refused to compromise, so long-standing changes in the South encouraged a group of planters and small farmers (those in the southern districts of the cotton states) to spearhead the campaign for secession.

V

The policies Republicans adopted during the Civil War and Reconstruction highlight the different roles that economics and principled concerns played in the counsels of the new party. When the war began, the Republicans had no plans to free the slaves. During the first months of fighting, they reaffirmed their reluctance to disrupt the South's "peculiar institution." But ultimately Republicans did end slavery, thanks to military necessity, the flight of tens of thousands of African Americans to Union lines, and idealism. During these same months, Republicans barreled ahead with a comprehensive program of economic measures. John Sherman explained the goal: "The policy of this country ought to be to make everything national as far as possible: to nationalize our country, so that we shall love our country."[46] The Republicans taxed local banknotes out of existence and replaced them with a national currency. They created a system of national banks, instituted an income tax, raised tariffs, financed internal improvements, adopted a homestead act, created land grant colleges, and chartered a Pacific railroad.[47]

After the war Republican plans for the freedpeople were limited to guaranteeing their civil rights and protecting them from violence. Despite the urgings of a few radical politicians, they restored estates to former Confederates, did not provide farms to African Americans, and stood by while landowners forced the former slaves into a repressive labor system, sharecropping. Republicans did not plan on enfranchising Southern Blacks; after all they had not done so in most of the North. Nonetheless, they took that bold step out of necessity: to counter the former Confederates who were determined to send unreformed Southerners to Congress and very possibly endanger the measures Republicans had adopted.

Although Republicans only reluctantly and briefly empowered Blacks across the South, the results from those few years were noteworthy, and are justly celebrated today. Blacks demanded land, civil rights, schools, a prominent role in government, and more broadly, the respect they had long been denied. Whites responded with anger and guns, launching a bloody conflict discussed more fully in the chapter on homicides.

Democratic state governments soon replaced the short-lived Reconstruction regimes. At the 1876 Republican convention Frederick Douglass summed up the plight of African Americans: "What does it all amount to, if the black man, after having been made free by the letter of your law, is unable to exercise that freedom, and having been freed from the slaveholder's lash, he is to be subject to the slaveholder's shot-gun?"[48]

While Republicans abandoned Black allies, they strengthened their ties with the business community. Congress expanded the national banking system and repealed the income tax, the one progressive impost. Troops that had once been stationed in the South to protect African Americans were redeployed to the West to fight Natives and to the cities to suppress worker protests. Although denying freedpeople farms, Congress awarded the Central and Union Pacific railroads millions of acres to build a line to California. The end of Reconstruction, with Blacks free but subordinated to racist Whites and big business stronger than ever, was not an aberration. It reflected the deep-rooted values of the Republican Party. More broadly, it was the product of a Civil War whose origins in the victorious North lay not in principled convictions about slavery but in the self-interested demands of farmers, merchants, and manufacturers for economic and territorial expansion.

4 *Homicidal Nation*

Why Do Americans Kill Each Other So Often?

Compared to the citizens of other wealthy countries, Americans kill each other far more often—a disparity that has been evident since the late nineteenth century. The United Nations Office on Drugs and Crime presents a comprehensive international survey, providing data that exclude wars. As table 1 indicates, the gap between the United States and other rich nations is striking. If the comparison provides any comfort for Americans, many poorer countries are still more murderous. In 2018 the homicide rate per 100,000 population in Mexico was 29.45; Jamaica, 45.71; and El Salvador, 53.80.

Scholars offer a welter of hypotheses to explain why Americans are so inclined to bump each other off. Some researchers highlight the "civilizing thesis," an approach that draws upon the work of German sociologist Norbert Elias. According to this explanation, the long-term decline in European violence reflects the rise of settled societies, an evolution that lagged in America.[1] Others point to the influence of the lawless West, the prevalence of guns, questions of race, demography, immigration, and poverty, or to a "culture of honor."[2] Randolph Roth argues for a correlation between murder rates and "trust in government."[3] Richard M. Brown sets forth a

TABLE 1. Homicide Rate in Selected Wealthy Countries, 2018

Country	Homicide Rate	Country	Homicide Rate
Japan	0.26	Germany	0.95
Netherlands	0.57	France	1.06
Switzerland	0.59	England & Wales	1.08
Italy	0.60	Canada	1.78
Australia	0.88	United States	4.89

Source: United Nations Office on Drugs and Crime, Victims of Intentional Homicide, https://dataunodc.un.org/content/data/homicide/homicide-rate. Measured in deaths per 100,000 population per year.

sweeping indictment of the United States: "Our history has produced and reinforced a strain of violence, which has strongly tinctured our national experience.... [R]epeated episodes of violence, going far back in our colonial past, have imprinted upon our citizenry a propensity to violence."[4]

Any effort to sort through these explanations must pay close attention to locales and trends. Homicide rates in the United States have varied greatly from place to place and over time; indeed, in the 1820s and 1830s, the settled parts of the United States were as peaceful as western Europe. This essay examines that evidence and argues that while the abundance of guns serves as an accelerant, the fuel tossed on the fire, the high levels of violence reflect the drive for expansion and systemic racism. The argument of this chapter thus dovetails with the broader themes of the book.

I

Although the connection between the tidal wave of guns that floods the United States and killing may seem obvious, assessing that link demands a careful review of the evidence. Ever since the first European settlements, America has been a gun culture. In the colonial era perhaps 60 percent of all White households owned a firearm. These weapons, typically smooth bore muskets, accounted for about 40 percent of homicides, a higher proportion than in Europe, where swords and daggers remained more common. Farmers used these long guns for hunting and brought them to musters of the local militia, troops that played a crucial role in the Revolutionary War. With the Second Amendment, the Constitution acknowledges the importance of keeping the citizenry prepared for such service. It reads: "A well regulated Militia, being necessary to the security of a free State, the right of the people to keep and bear Arms, shall not be infringed."[5] Southerners, as Carol Anderson points out in *The Second*, had an additional reason to create a "well regulated Militia": the suppression of rebellious slaves.[6]

The reliance on guns rose during the nineteenth century, although before the Civil War these weapons, for Whites, were involved in only half the homicides, and for African Americans, about a third. During the Civil War and the decades that followed, mass production made firearms more affordable and easier to use. In 1873 the army adopted the Colt Peacemaker, a revolver that fired six shots, cost $13, and soon became the weapon of choice throughout the West. Both Blacks and Whites now used firearms in most murders.[7]

The number of guns in private hands increased dramatically in the twentieth century and has soared in the twenty-first. By 2017 the civilian population of the United States had acquired a Mt. Denali-sized stash of firearms, legal and illegal, estimated at 393 million weapons. That amounts to 121 guns for every one hundred persons in the population. No other country comes close. Among nations with populations over a million, the next four, measured by guns per one hundred people, were Yemen (fifty-three), Serbia (thirty-nine), Canada (thirty-five), and Uruguay (thirty-five).[8] With only 4 percent of the world's population, the United States has over 40 percent of the guns in private hands. The United States also leads in the proportion of households—44 percent—that report owning a weapon. Noteworthy as well is the proliferation of handguns: 21.9 percent of American households have one. Switzerland comes next with 10.3 percent, but in most countries the percentage stands well below 5, for example, France (3.7), Canada (2.9), and the UK (0.4). The *average* number of firearms—seven—in each gun-owning household is also remarkable. Americans don't own guns—they accumulate arsenals.[9]

This deluge of guns makes possible, but does not determine, the high levels of killing that mark American society. Racism, mental illness, and interpersonal conflict exist in other countries, but with fewer guns at hand, individual murders and mass killing become less likely. Easy access to firearms made possible a violent decade like the 1920s, when Prohibition fostered an illegal liquor trade and violent gangs. Guns also fueled the violence between 1985 and 1993, when the crack cocaine epidemic wreaked havoc on American cities. During those years the use of handguns by Black youth rose 300 percent, and firearms accounted for over 70 percent of all murders. In the 2010s the proportion of all murders committed with guns again climbed to new heights.[10]

Like King Canute confronting the sea, the United States has had limited success in holding back the surging tide of guns. The National Firearms Act of 1934 prohibited transporting certain weapons across state lines, and in 1939 the Supreme Court, in

United States v. Miller, affirmed that law. When the owner of one of the banned firearms, a sawed-off shotgun, challenged the statute, the Court concluded that "[i]n the absence of any evidence tending to show the possession or use of a [sawed-off] shotgun . . . has some reasonable relationship to the preservation or efficiency of a well regulated militia," the law must stand. The Gun Control Act (1968) banned felons from purchasing or possessing firearms; the Brady Handgun Violence Prevention Act (1994) mandated background checks for purchasers, while the Federal Assault Weapons Ban (1994) prohibited the manufacture and sale of military-style long guns and high-capacity magazines.[11]

Such efforts did little to restrict the ownership of firearms, while the gun rights lobby grew ever more vocal. The transformation of the National Rifle Association at its 1977 convention (the "Revolt at Cincinnati") was indicative. Previously, the NRA had been largely an organization of hunters and sportsmen and backed measures like the Gun Control Act. But after a dramatic change in leadership, the NRA took point in the battle against restrictions. Gun rights, along with abortion and same-sex marriage, became "hot button" issues in the culture wars. In the twenty-first century, advocates demonstrated ever more vociferously for both "open carry" and "concealed carry"—and all but a handful of states acceded. Congress allowed the prohibition on assault weapons to expire in 2004. A measure adopted in 2022 tightened background checks but was silent on assault-style weapons and the "gunshow loophole," which allowed private sales without federal scrutiny. Laws about registering firearms and background checks remain on the books. But Americans register less than 1 percent of their guns, and more than 20 percent of firearms are bought without even a cursory examination of the purchaser's suitability.

Significantly, a pro-gun majority dominates the Supreme Court. The justices ended DC's ban on handguns in *District of Columbia v. Heller* (2008) and nullified Chicago's effort to limit weapons in *McDonald v. Chicago* (2010). In *New York State Rifle & Pistol Association v. Bruen* (2022) the court struck down state laws restricting "concealed carry."[12]

On the state level, laws have proven more effective. Measures banning military-style weapons, removing firearms from dangerous individuals ("red flag laws"), and enforcing registration make a difference. They have reduced the murder rates in California, New York, Minnesota, Connecticut, and New Jersey.[13]

Still, for the country as a whole, both the regulation and deregulation of guns appear to have little measurable effect on the homicide rate. The Australian and British experiences suggest that bold, restrictive measures *can* make a difference. After a series of murderous rampages, in 1996 Australia adopted the National Firearms Agreement, banning handguns and military style weapons. A buyback program took 700,000 firearms out of circulation. Since the law went into effect there have been no mass killings. After a horrific school shooting, Britain took similar steps in 1997, again with positive results.[14] But in the United States the Assault Weapons Ban of 1994 was far less rigorous: it grandfathered 25 million large capacity magazines in private hands as well as 1.5 million assault weapons. Owners were allowed to sell or transfer these arms. There was no reduction in mass murders during the ten years it was in force. Similarly, despite the fears of some gun control advocates, the adoption of concealed and open carry did not noticeably change the homicide rate.[15]

While guns make possible higher levels of killing, the simple presence of firearms does not cause homicides. For example, residents of the Dakotas, Idaho, Montana, and Wyoming own many guns but have levels of violence well below the national average. Any analysis of American homicides must acknowledge the role of firearms, but also note that they do not explain where killings take place, who pulls the trigger, or who the victims are. To fully understand the patterns of American homicides, there is a need to look more closely at the impact of expansionism and race.[16]

II

Any analysis of high rates of homicide in America must focus on two lengthy, overlapping periods. The first part of the story examines the frontier, from the earliest settlements to the "Wild West" of the nineteenth century, while the second part of the saga, an era stretching from the 1880s to the present, looks at the extraordinary levels of violence involving African Americans.

From the time of the earliest English settlements at Jamestown (1607) and Plymouth (1620), the combination of racism and expansionism proved a dangerous mixture. English settlers with rare exceptions viewed Native people as inferior and applauded their removal.[17] The determination to drive Indigenous people from their lands, combined with Native resistance, sent homicide rates for the colonists—measured as victims—skyrocketing to over one hundred per one hundred thousand adults in New England, New Netherlands, and Virginia. The pace of these murders dropped precipitously after victories in the Pequot War (1636–1638) in New England and the Anglo-Powhatan Wars (1610–1646) in Virginia. Researchers have not tallied the deaths of Indigenous people in these conflicts, but assuredly the toll was high.[18]

By the eighteenth century, homicide rates, at least in the long-settled eastern counties, had fallen sharply. Attacks by Natives virtually disappeared in Massachusetts and eastern Virginia. In New England, where the pace of killing had once topped 120 adults per 100,000, this measure plummeted to 1.35 during the first seventy years of the eighteenth century. The homogenous towns of Massachusetts and Connecticut eschewed violent conflicts. The decline was almost as steep in Virginia, where the levels of murders fell from 248 in the early seventeenth century to 8.4 between 1710 and 1775.[19] To be sure, violence toward Natives had not ceased. During the Revolutionary War clashes occurred along the length of the colonial frontier, invariably with disastrous results for Indigenous people. But the areas along the coast were now more peaceful.[20]

Violence continued as European settlers moved steadily west. From the Revolutionary War to the slaughter at Wounded Knee, South Dakota, in 1890, a recurrent pattern shaped dealings with Indigenous people. European settlement expanded; clashes, sometimes involving groups of homesteaders or militia units and often the federal army, pushed the Natives off their traditional farming and hunting grounds; treaties were solemnly concluded and then broken, as the White population increased. Murder rates were high along that moving border, although the deaths inflicted by the US Army are not classified as homicides. One estimate suggests these wars killed fifty thousand Indigenous people, with many more dying from illness and malnutrition. Historians vigorously debate whether US policies should be labeled genocide.[21]

Violence continued even when Native people settled in supposedly protected enclaves. In California, for example, White Americans, or Anglos, assaulted tribal villages, including a Pomo community in 1849 and a Tolowa settlement in 1853. Clare Mc-Kanna, who studies the legal system in nineteenth-century California, shows that settlers murdered with impunity: of the thirty-five Whites charged with killing Indians in six counties, only one was convicted. Violence and disease reduced the Native population throughout the West. In California their numbers fell from 300,000 in the eighteenth century to 150,000 in 1848 to 30,000 after American rule was established.[22]

Natives were not the only group Anglos harried in the West. White settlers were determined to curtail the economic and political power of the Hispanics, and used laws, court proceedings, and violence to gain their ends. During the 1870s the Texas Rangers attacked Tejanos, the Mexicans who had resided in Texas for many years. The Rangers targeted the communities in the Rio Grande valley, killing the innocent along with outlaws. Whites hounded Hispanics in California: the legislature forced Mexicans to pay a Foreign Miners' Tax, even though they had lived in those districts their entire lives. Vigilantes descended on Spanish-speaking settlements; one Anglo community resolved that it was "the duty of every American citizen . . . to exterminate the Mexican race from the county." Homicides soared, especially in those locales where Anglo settlement surged. Between 1850 and 1865, murders in San Luis Obispo County averaged 228 per 100,000 population, while in Monterey County the rate climbed to over 600 in 1855–1857. These campaigns and the continuing influx of newcomers from the East diminished the role of Hispanics. Californios, whose roots in the state went back many years, formed 82 percent of Los Angeles's population in 1860, but by 1880 only 19 percent. In 1900 Hispanics comprised 2 percent of California residents, a smaller percentage than Indians and Chinese.[23]

Anglo Californians also persecuted the Chinese, driving them from the more productive goldfields and eventually from their marginal holdings. Rampages against Asians were common. In 1852 White miners torched Chinese camps in Tuolumne and El Dorado counties, while in 1871 a massacre in Los Angeles's Chinatown killed about twenty immigrants. Attacks on Asians occurred as well in Colorado, Wyoming, and Washington State. Workers called for a ban on immigration, and Congress readily complied, first with the Page Act of 1875, which blocked Asian women from entering the United States (alleging they would become prostitutes), and then with the Chinese Exclusion Act of 1882, which virtually ended all immigration from the Far East. Doors would not be fully open to Asians until 1965.[24]

Still, if the fell mix of expansionism and racism explained much of the killing along the moving frontier, a second source of regional violence must be noted. That was the drive for the "incorporation" (borrowing that term from Alan Trachtenberg's work) of the West. Railroads, mining interests, and cattle barons sought to control land and water rights, using courts and compliant officials when they could and violence when needed. Opposed to that elite were small farmers, ranchers, and cowboys, who resented the land grabs, the barbed wire fences blocking trails, and the pressure of legal battles.[25] This conflict too fits with the argument of this book and reflects the demands of a group of affluent Americans for growth.

One facet of these "incorporation wars"—the clash of gunfighters in western towns—left its stamp upon the American psyche. The era of these cowboys was short lived, stretching from the 1860s to the 1880s, and involved relatively few people. Still, high homicide *rates* characterized Kansas towns, such as Dodge City, Ellsworth, and Abilene, where cowboys ended their drives and herded cattle onto rail cars. Cattle brokers and others resolved to pacify these communities and hired lawmen to do so. Richard Maxwell Brown distinguishes between *incorporation gunfighters*, like Wild Bill Hickok, Wyatt Earp, and Pat Garrett, who were typically Northerners and Republicans and sided with the local businessmen, and *resister gunfighters*, like Jesse James and Billy the Kid, who more often were Southern and Democrats, and who defied pleas for law and order. In the conflict that culminated with the 1881 gunfight at the OK Corral in Tombstone, Arizona, the Earp brothers, Wyatt, Virgil, and Morgan, worked closely with the town's business interests. When the dust settled, the real victors were mining firms and other capitalists, who tightened their grip on the local economy.[26]

Expansionism, racism, and the drive for "incorporation" made the nineteenth-century American West a violent region, but the links between those murders and modern homicide rates remain indirect. Many of the states where in the nineteenth century bullet-riddled bodies were carted out to potter's field now rank among the most peaceful. For example, between 1865 and 1868 homicide rates per 100,000 soared in Montana (212), Wyoming (167), and Colorado (137). But in the years 2017 to 2019 these states stood well below the national average of 5.2, with levels of 3.5, 2.3, and 3.9, respectively. California and Texas, murderous locales in the mid-nineteenth century, stand just above the present-day median. Similarly, Kansas and the Dakotas, where gunfighters unleashed deadly fusillades (Wild Bill Hickok was killed in Deadwood, Dakota Territory, in 1876), record few fatalities in recent times. Killing had a purpose in the nineteenth-century West, and once those larger goals—the restriction of non-Whites and the "incorporation" of the economy—were achieved, homicides decreased.[27]

Still, the echoes of nineteenth-century frontier violence resonate down the mean streets of modern US society. Americans redefined *justifiable homicide*, abandoning the principle of a "duty to retreat" embedded in English common law. That hallowed tradition argued only the state could legally kill (with executions and wars) and labeled "all homicides as public wrongs." When confronted, the victim had a responsibility to walk away, because "the right to defend may be mistaken as the right to kill." Americans viewed such behavior as cowardly and rewrote the law. Fittingly, a western state, Texas, announced the change in its 1856 penal code, which declared "[n]o duty to retreat." Other states soon followed, while the Supreme Court in 1921 affirmed the doctrine in *Brown v. United States.* Justice Oliver Wendell Holmes explained that "it is well settled" that "a man is not born to run away." A recent study notes how this practice fosters violence, since in many instances "both killers and victims could easily have de-escalated the seriousness of the situation by retreat." "No duty to retreat" did not make peaceful individuals violent, but it contributed to a climate of opinion in which Americans, more than citizens of other wealthy nations, accept the necessity for killing when threatened.[28]

III

The second part of this saga, which focuses on African Americans, provides the key to understanding levels of homicide today. An examination of the origins of this problem and the toll this killing wreaks upon the Black community presents a scathing indictment of racism in the US.

Statistics offer a good starting point for this analysis. In 2019, a typical recent year, African Americans, who comprise 13 percent of the population, committed 51 percent of all homicides. They were disproportionately victims as well as killers. Most of those murders—82 percent of them—were Black-on-Black homicides. African American crime drives up the homicide rate, making the United States an outlier among wealthy nations. In 2005, for example, the US toll of 5.7 homicides per 100,000 reflected a rate of 2.7 for non-Hispanic Whites, 8.1 for Hispanics (who then formed about 14 percent of the population), and 23.0 for Blacks.[29]

This carnage cuts a broad, devastating swath through the Black community. Every month, on average, more than six hundred African Americans are murdered, a number about 30 percent higher than the toll for non-Hispanic Whites, despite the disparity in the size of the two populations. Elliott Currie's *A Peculiar Indifference: The Neglected Toll of Violence on Black America* details the physical and psychological damage wreaked on neighborhoods. He notes that young Black men, aged fifteen to twenty-nine, are sixteen times more likely to be killed than young White men. Homicide is the leading cause of death for those individuals, while for non-Hispanic White men it ranks eighteenth. Although levels of violence diminish with age, a sixty-year-old African American is still three times as likely to be murdered as the White individual at the highest risk—a thirty-year-old man.[30]

Against that background, the question becomes why Blacks are more likely to kill, and be killed, than Whites. Researchers today uniformly reject racial characteristics and look to the environment for answers.[31] Studies indicate that economic hardship explains about half the difference between White and Black homicide rates. Violence rises for all groups as poverty deepens. Social scientists analyze the impact of deprivation by comparing Black, Hispanic, and White neighborhoods, selecting districts where variables—such as wealth, unemployment, and family structure—are similar. If race was not a factor, homicide rates should be about the same in these neighborhoods. That presumption proves true for the comparison of Whites and Hispanics. Hispanics who live as well as Whites have similar levels of violence. But since more Hispanics live in poor neighborhoods (their poverty rate in 2019 was 17.2 percent, compared to 9.0 for Whites), their overall homicide rate is higher.[32]

Living conditions are still worse for African Americans, and that immiseration—largely the product of systemic racism—contributes to the frequency of murders. Over 21 percent of Blacks live below the poverty line. Discrimination in the funding of schools, in health care, and in hiring has limited opportunities for generations of African Americans. Deep-seated biases help explain why fewer Blacks own homes: 40 percent against 73 percent for Whites. During the decades after the Civil War, many of the Blacks who gained property lost their holdings because of violence and intimidation. That discrimination continued in the twentieth century. The Federal Housing Administration, founded in 1934, refused to insure mortgages in Black neighborhoods, a practice known as "redlining," and withheld support in subsequent decades. After World War II developers, with tacit government approval, built lily-White suburbs around the big cities.[33] The GI Bill, adopted in 1944, helped White servicemen become homeowners, while few Black soldiers, because of local ordinances and practices, benefited. Differences in homeownership, in turn, foster the disparities in family wealth: in 2019 the median Black household was worth $24,100, compared to $188,200 for White households.[34] Taken all together, these concerns have created across the United States an archipelago of impoverished, violent Black cities within cities.

IV

Still, poverty only partly explains why African Americans kill each other: any full analysis must focus on the evolving pattern of Black-White relations. Before 1880 homicide rates for African Americans, both as assailants and victims, were low, and usually well below the levels recorded by Whites. In New England, for example, between 1677 and 1797 fewer than 1 out of 100,000 Blacks killed or were killed in a given year. Slavery, which governed the lives of most African Americans, was a brutal institution, with historians debating only the extent of that cruelty. And while bondage unquestionably shortened lives, it was not marked by high rates of homicide.[35] The one exception to this pattern during the colonial era was the surge in White-on-Black killing in Virginia between 1690 and 1729, when planters shifted their labor force from indentured servants to slaves. The attacks were a harbinger of the waves of repression that would come after the Civil War, when Whites sought to reestablish hierarchical relationships. These homicides subsided after 1730 (planters had achieved their goals) and remained low for the balance of the eighteenth century.[36]

In the antebellum South, home to 90 percent of African Americans, Whites consistently had higher homicide rates. Florida, a particularly violent state, illustrates the disparity. While the homicide rate for Black adults stood between 10 and 14 per 100,000 persons per year, the level for Whites ranged between 36 and 86 per 100,000.[37]

The relatively few instances in the United States in which slaves singly or in groups killed their masters cannot be read as a sign of contentment or loyalty, as some slave owners and later mythmakers allege. Given a chance, Blacks with remarkable alacrity fled bondage and took up arms against their oppressors. That was evident in the Stono Rebellion (1739), the response to Lord Dunmore's proclamation (1775), the uprising in St. John the Baptist parish (1811), Nat Turner's rebellion (1831), and the waves of "self-emancipation" as Union forces advanced in the Civil War. Before 1861 the infrequent and short-lived nature of such outbursts reflected the extraordinary strength of the forces of repression.[38]

The era of Reconstruction transformed African American society and left it more violent. For Blacks, the postwar years began as a time of hope and empowerment. Republicans ended slavery in 1865, guaranteed civil rights in 1866, and enfranchised Southern Black men with the Reconstruction Acts of 1867 and 1868. Across the South, African Americans voiced their demands in conventions and churches, in Republican Party meetings, and in the Union League. Freedpeople called for land, education, more equitable laws, and a role in local and state politics. "The negro of today," a reporter for the New Orleans *Tribune* observed in September 1866, "is not the same as he was six years ago. . . . He has been told of his rights, which have long been robbed." Blacks served on town councils and in state legislatures; a few went to Congress. African Americans now stood up to landowners and refused to take their hats off to Whites who passed by.[39]

These changes horrified Whites, and with a frenzy of violence they sought to restore the racist hierarchy. "Southern whites," a Freedmen's Bureau agent remarked, "are quite indignant if they are not treated with the same deference that they were accustomed to" before the War. In Texas the Bureau recorded the "reasons" for the one thousand murders of Blacks by Whites between 1865 and 1868. One African American "did not remove his hat" and another "wouldn't give up his whiskey flask"; in another instance a White man simply "wanted to thin out the niggers a lit-tle." In 1867 a Nashville paper reported, "regulators . . . are riding about whipping, maiming and killing all negroes who do not obey the orders of their former masters, just as if slavery existed." The violence came in waves, beginning with individual actions, then focused by groups such as the Ku Klux Klan, and finally driven by well-organized White militias. In most instances, the Freedmen's Bureau, the Republican governors, and the Union soldiers over-seeing Reconstruction offered only token resistance, and in 1877 even that check disappeared when all federal troops were removed from the South.[40]

Determined to reassert control, Whites murdered Blacks in staggering numbers. Gilles Vandal's study of rural Louisi-ana shows that between 1865 and 1876 White mobs, often led by planters, killed 1,371 African Americans. Just one attack, the "Col-fax massacre" of 1873, slaughtered over 100 African Americans. As table 2 indicates, during Reconstruction White-on-Black mur-ders in Louisiana far exceeded the toll of White-on-White kill-ing, Black-on-Black violence, or Black-on-White homicides. The carnage intensified with the struggles to overthrow the Republi-can regimes. In Mississippi, during the winter of 1874–1875 mobs of angry Whites shot Blacks who came to Vicksburg to vote, then ranged through the countryside, killing perhaps 300 more. In South Carolina the 1876 election was marked by pitched battles between rival militias and by a White reign of terror that swept through the Piedmont counties. One planter informed a freedman that Democrats would take over the state "if we have to wade in blood knee deep."[41]

The slaughter of Blacks during Reconstruction was only one example of White mobs suppressing outspoken African Americans.

TABLE 2. Homicides in Rural Louisiana

	Percent of All Homicides	
	1865–1876	1877–1884
Whites by Whites	14.2	18.3
Blacks by Whites	46.5	13.2
Whites by Blacks	3.2	4.7
Blacks by Blacks	10.7	22.1
Unknown	25.4	41.7
Total homicides	**2,943**	**1,056**

Source: Gilles Vandal, "Black Violence in Post-Civil War Louisiana," *Journal of Interdisciplinary History*, 25.1 (1994): 53.

In the 1890s and early 1900s violent campaigns ended Black suffrage, the last remnant of Reconstruction. In Wilmington, North Carolina, for example, in 1898 a crowd of 2,000 White men killed between 60 and 300 African Americans. Lynching surged as well, peaking in the 1890s. Violence continued in the new century. During the "Red Summer" of 1919 unruly Whites in cities and towns attacked Blacks, including soldiers who had returned from Europe and strikers demanding their rights. Vigilantes killed 38 in Chicago and 15 in Washington, DC. In Elaine, Arkansas, rioters crushed a tenants' union, shooting between 100 and 240 Blacks. In Tulsa, Oklahoma, during the summer of 1921, Whites razed the town's "Black Wall Street," killing between 75 and 300 people and displacing 10,000.[42]

The disproportionate incarceration of Blacks and discriminatory policing compounded that repression. Soon after the Civil War, many Southern states introduced a convict leasing system, facilitated by the "loophole" in the Thirteenth Amendment. The measure ended slavery, "except as a punishment for crime whereof the party shall have been duly convicted." Historian Douglas Black-mon calls the practice of penal work a form of slavery, "a system in which armies of free men, guilty of no crimes and entitled by law to freedom, were compelled to labor without compensation." The practice, which proved lucrative for state governments, continued into the early decades of the twentieth century. More broadly, in both the North and South, Blacks were jailed at far higher rates than Whites—or Hispanics. Discriminatory approaches to prose-cution further reinforced the caste system. In practices that date back to the antebellum period, White-on-Black murder was treated with impunity, Black-on-Black killing was regarded with indiffer-ence, and Black-on-White homicide was vigorously prosecuted.[43]

This violence and repression brought about striking changes: beginning in the 1880s the rate of Black-on-Black homicides soared. Local studies document the new pattern. For example, in Chicago between 1900 and 1910, African Americans comprised 1.9 percent of residents, but 14.3 percent of murderers and 13.8 percent of vic-tims.[44] Analysis of Southern cities in 1922 paints a similar picture. In New Orleans the Black homicide rate was 57.5 per 100,000 pop-ulation, and the level for Whites, 9.8. In Memphis the two figures were 145.3 and 24.5; in Atlanta, 105.4 and 16.5; and in Birmingham, 108 and 26.7.[45]

In *The Condemnation of Blackness: Race, Crime, and the Making of Modern Urban America* (2010), Khalil Gibran Muhammad high-lights the impact of racism on crime rates. Focusing on the early twentieth century, he points out that "police bias and discrimina-tion were baked into the arrest statistics." Lawlessness within the Black community, he notes, reflects a variety of concerns including the lack of recreational activities for Black youth and the relocation of red-light districts to Black neighborhoods.[46]

Discrimination in law enforcement—another aspect of repression—continues to the present. In 2017 Blacks were locked up at nearly six times the rate of Whites and twice that of Hispanics.[47] In 2020 the US Commission on Civil Rights examined the impact of the "Stand Your Ground" laws adopted since 2005, analyzing when courts accepted that line of defense. The conclusion? A verdict of innocence was "[t]en times more likely if the shooter is white and the victim is black, than if the shooter is black and the victim is white."[48]

Hemmed in by oppressive policing, judged by a biased court system, and battered by repeated paroxysms of White violence, the anger that rages in the Black community often seems to have few outlets. Urban insurrection stands as one possibility. In *America on Fire: The Untold History of Police Violence and Black Rebellion Since the 1960s* (2021), Elizabeth Hinton examines the nearly two thousand separate uprisings in American cities since the 1960s and argues these actions should not be called "riots." Rather, "violent rebellion offered a means for people of color to express collective solidarity in the face of exploitation, political exclusion, and criminalization."

Homicides must be understood within the same context of repression.[49] The persistence of intraracial violence makes a strong statement about the lack of real change. Certainly African Americans have recorded significant gains since World War II. Throughout the United States Blacks now can vote, sit where they like on public transit, and know that public schools will not reject them on racial grounds. Black entertainers and movie stars are part of the mainstream. African Americans hold top positions in the armed services. The election of Barack Obama stands as an important milestone.

Still, more noteworthy is what has *not* changed. As one Black pastor, the Reverend Charles Koen, observes, "voting rights could not be eaten or made into clothing and shelter."[50] Progress has made a few cracks in the caste system, but it still stands intact. Blacks continue to live in the poorest communities and face levels of employment, education, and health that are far lower than those Whites experience. The COVID pandemic exacerbated those disparities. Residential and school segregation persist, not de jure but de facto. It is no coincidence that homicide rates today are highest in the most segregated cities, such as Detroit, Chicago, St. Louis, and Baltimore. Black-on-Black murders may not be political in the way that Hinton describes urban rebellions, but they make a powerful statement about American society and should temper any optimistic reading of racial progress.[51]

Reflecting back on American history since the first settlements, the answer to the question of why Americans murder each other so frequently seems clear. While the abundance of guns facilitates this killing, the ruthless drive for expansion and systemic racism, directed at Natives, Hispanics, Asians, and African Americans, lie at the heart of this violent legacy.

5 *Why Did the United States Fight in Vietnam?*

For those of us in a certain cohort—the young men and women who went to college and graduate school in the 1960s—Vietnam was our war. It shaped our view of the United States just as World War II had done for our parents. For the most part we did not serve, clinging to student deferments that allowed us, (largely) White, middle-class kids, to stay out of the draft, while poorer and often brown and Black young men were sent to Southeast Asia. We protested, knowing in our marrow this was an unjust war. I took part in teach-ins at Swarthmore, marched and got tear-gassed at Wisconsin, and joined demonstrations in London during the year I spent there as a Fulbright fellow. At the time, our analysis of the conflict was more slogan than scholarly, more Country Joe and the Fish than Marx or Marcuse.

During the years of fighting and since then, politicians, historians, political scientists, and others have sought to explain why America became so deeply involved in Vietnam. The reason most commonly put forth at the time was *anti-Communism*: the US went to war to block the spread of a malevolent ideology bent on world domination. A second interpretation, related to anti-communism although with a very different emphasis, is *modernization*: a desire to help other nations become prosperous, liberal democracies. A third argument is *expansionism*: the war reflected the desire of upper-class individuals to spread the influence of American capitalism across the globe. Any full understanding must acknowledge all three approaches (as well as a fourth concern, racism, which affects so many US activities). Still, this essay argues—fully in keeping with the larger themes of the book—that expansionism best explains the Vietnam War and, more broadly, the Cold War and American foreign policy.

I

At first glance, scholarly opinion and the pronouncements of various leaders make a convincing case that the resolve to check the fire-breathing red dragon was the reason for America's involvement in Southeast Asia. George Herring, the doyen of Vietnam War authors, asserts: "The United States intervened to block the apparent march of a Soviet-directed Communism across Asia, escalated its commitment to halt a presumably expansionist Communist China, and eventually made Vietnam a test case of its determination to uphold world order."[1] Even with that "apparent" and "presumably," Herring's point is clear: the United States went to war to block the red menace. Other researchers agree. Mark Philip Bradley remarks, "Without question the Cold War provided the larger frame that shaped American involvement in Vietnam."[2] Vietnamese scholar Luu Doan Huynh concurs: "The Cold War was instrumental in causing the United States to launch a massive intervention in Vietnam."[3] These historians are not arguing (as did the war-era presidents) that such reasoning made for a just war. But they accept that the resolve to protect Vietnam from Communist expansion underpinned US involvement.

The declarations of five presidents (and their advisers) also point to the importance of stopping Communism. Harry Truman's secretary of state, Dean Acheson, explained that the United States supported the French in Southeast Asia because America was "convinced that neither national independence nor democratic evolution exists in any area dominated by Soviet imperialism." Building on that premise, the United States in 1945 approved France's efforts to reimpose its will on a nation, Vietnam, that had just declared its independence—and that was led by an avowed Communist, Ho Chi Minh. During the ensuing years, American assistance to the French ratcheted steadily upward, and by 1952 the United States was covering 40 percent of the war costs.[4]

Dwight Eisenhower reaffirmed that resolve, offering familiar reasons for US support. "Asia, after all, has already lost some 450 million of its people to the Communist dictatorship," he told a press conference in 1954, "and we simply can't afford any greater losses." He expounded the "domino" theory, arguing that defeat in Vietnam might lead to "the loss of Indochina, of Burma, of Thailand, of the Peninsula, and Indonesia." Indeed, a setback could "threaten Australia and New Zealand."[5] Ike's administration matched deeds with words. By 1954 the United States was paying almost 80 percent of France's war costs. Nor did the French defeat in the spring of 1954 weaken American resolve. The United States refused to sign the Geneva Accords, which divided Vietnam at the seventeenth parallel and provided for a vote on reunification within two years—a ballot all agreed that Ho Chi Minh would win. Although America initially announced it would not "disturb" the Accords, that promise was short-lived. The United States made certain no vote took place and approved Bao Dai's appointment of Ngo Dinh Diem as prime minister of South Vietnam.

John Kennedy continued Eisenhower's commitment to Vietnam and like his predecessors made blocking the spread of malevolent Communism his mission. In September 1963 broadcaster David Brinkley asked him, "Mr. President, have you had any reason to doubt this so-called 'Domino Theory'?" Kennedy replied: "No, I believe it. I believe it. I think that the struggle is close enough. China is so large, looms so high just beyond the frontiers, that if South Viet Nam went, it would not only give them an improved geographic position for a guerilla assault on Malaya, but would also give the impression that the wave of the future in Southeast Asia was China and the communists."[6] Although Eisenhower had ignored the Geneva Accords' directive on elections, he had abided by the limits on advisers, keeping the number of Americans to 685. Kennedy gradually expanded the US contingent to 16,000.[7]

Lyndon Johnson picked up where Kennedy left off, echoing a familiar credo: Vietnam stood as that line in the sand, or jungle, where the free world must halt Communist aggression. In an April 1965 speech that I remember well, he explained: "The first reality is that North Viet-Nam has attacked the independent nation of South Viet-Nam. Its object is total conquest." The stakes were enormous: "Around the globe, from Berlin to Thailand, are people whose well-being rests, in part, on the belief that they can count on us if they are attacked."[8] That speech delivered at Johns Hopkins occasioned a teach-in at Swarthmore, where the political science professor leading the discussion praised Johnson's call for a speedy settlement of the dispute—once North Vietnam recognized an independent, American-dominated South Vietnam. I stood up, disagreed, and said the real message of the speech was a wider war, which Johnson threatened if American terms were rejected. When the professor scoffed at my comments, I, with the self-confident petulance of an undergraduate, stomped out of the room.

Johnson did, in fact, widen the war, with two hundred thousand military personnel stationed in Vietnam by December 1965 and more than five hundred thousand by 1968. The reality on the ground, however, did not comport with the picture Johnson depicted in his speeches. Not only the North Vietnamese, whom LBJ condemned as aggressors, but also many South Vietnamese wanted the Americans out. The Tet Offensive during the first months of 1968 made clear how widespread opposition was. That coordinated onslaught, combined with mounting US casualties and an ever more vocal peace movement at home, made Johnson realize that further escalation was pointless.

Richard Nixon, who assumed the presidency at this critical juncture, similarly denounced the evil Communist nations bent on world domination. He explained to the American people in 1969: "Fifteen years ago [i.e., in 1954] North Vietnam, with the logistical support of Communist China and the Soviet Union, launched a campaign to impose a Communist government on South Vietnam by instigating and supporting a revolution."[9] But with public opinion turning against the war, Nixon, the quintessential Cold Warrior, was thrust into an odd and uncomfortable situation: he was charged with extricating the United States from Vietnam. Nixon did draw down US forces, leading to an agreement in early 1973 and the final departure of American troops in March. But he did so reluctantly, intensifying the bombing in both the north and south and overseeing incursions into Cambodia and Laos. More than a third of the 58,800 Americans killed in Vietnam died while Nixon was winding down the conflict.[10]

In short, many historians as well as a series of presidents concur: the United States got involved in Vietnam to stop Communist aggression. The evidence for ideology driving the conflict seems overwhelming. But is it?

II

Militant anti-Communism must be part of any analysis of US involvement in Vietnam. But as a full or fundamental explanation of America's role in Southeast Asia (or elsewhere in the world), this approach is deeply flawed.

During the long sweep of American foreign policy, ideologies changed while actions exhibited a strong continuity—undercutting the explanatory power of any single worldview, such as anti-Communism. America's expansion beyond its continental borders began in 1898 with President William McKinley, the Spanish American War, and paeans to a beneficent Christianity. In this brief conflict, America wrested Cuba, Puerto Rico, and the Philippines from Spain. Calling for war against Spain, McKinley emphasized America's high-minded Christian goals: "The spirit of all our acts hitherto has been an earnest, unselfish desire for peace and prosperity in Cuba. . . . If this measure attains a successful result, then our aspirations as a Christian, peace-loving people will be realized." Those lofty ideals did not extend to the Cuban rebels, who had long battled their Spanish overlords and had helped the Americans achieve their victory. The United States barred them from the new government, limited suffrage to property owners (hence excluding most rebels), and backed a pro-American political party. While Cuba was granted independence, the Platt Amendment (1901) reserved for America the right to intervene for "the maintenance of a government adequate for the protection of life, property, and individual liberty."[11]

Militant Christianity also justified the American decision to capture and retain the Philippines. Here too the United States pushed aside the rebel forces. "Did we need their consent to perform a great act for humanity?" McKinley asked rhetorically. He continued: "We were doing our duty by them as God gave us the light to see our duty, with the consent of our own consciences and with the approvals of civilization." The goal? "[A] people redeemed from savage indolence and habits, devoted to the arts of peace, in touch with the commerce and trade of all nations enjoying the blessings of freedom." The Philippines would remain an American colony until 1946.[12]

Intertwined with those Christian goals was a noxious strain of racism. In the US the 1890s were marked by attacks on African Americans, including a surge in lynching and the imposition of segregation—a campaign that culminated in the first years of the twentieth century. Theories of racial hierarchy proliferated, an outlook graphically demonstrated in the St. Louis World's Fair of 1904. The exhibition offered onlookers a series of Filipino "villages," with a total of a thousand Indigenous people. These groupings illustrated different levels of civilization, beginning with the "wild tribes," the Moros, Negritos, Bagobos, and Igorots.[13] Even as justifications for imperial ventures shifted in the ensuing decades, prejudice continued to shape the outlook of many Americans and particularly affected interactions with Asian people. These biases, loosely gathered under the heading "yellow peril," were revealed in crude caricatures and harsh epithets.[14]

Between 1900 and 1945 successive presidents offered a variety of reasons to explain American interventions. Such incursions, which usually targeted the smaller nations of Central America and the Caribbean, remained a constant during these years. Marines landed and stayed in Cuba (1906–1909), the Dominican Republic (1916–1924), Haiti (1915–1934), and Nicaragua (1912–1925, 1926–1944). With the occupation of Panama (1903–1914), the United States birthed a new nation and secured the right to build an isthmian canal. American troops entered Mexico twice (1914, 1916). The United States also supported long-serving dictators, including Fulgencio Batista in Cuba (1930–1961), Rafael Trujillo in the Dominican Republic (1933–1959), and the Somozas in Nicaragua (1937–1979).[15]

The "reasons" for these ventures shifted from one administration to the next. Theodore Roosevelt preached a muscular imperialism. In what came to be called the "Roosevelt corollary" to the Monroe Doctrine, he declared: "Any country whose people conduct themselves well can count on our hearty friendship.... Chronic wrongdoing, or an impotence which results in a general loosening of the ties of civilized society ... may force the United States, however reluctantly, in flagrant cases of such wrongdoing or impotence, to the exercise of an international police power."[16] Woodrow Wilson, no less an interventionist than TR, at least in Latin America, declaimed loftier aims. In putting forth his plans for Europe after World War I, he declared the United States wished only that the world "be made safe for every peace-loving nation which, like our own, wishes to live its own life, determine its own institutions, be assured of justice and fair dealing by the other peoples of the world as against force and selfish aggression."[17] With his "good neighbor" policy, Franklin Roosevelt also presented high ideals: the

United States will be "the neighbor who resolutely respects himself and, because he does so, respects the rights of others."[18] FDR did improve ties within the Western Hemisphere, responding in part to the looming threat from Nazi Germany. But Roosevelt continued to support dictators and perpetuate old inequities, for example, retaining the US naval base at Guantanamo, Cuba.

During the Cold War, from the late 1940s through the fall of the Soviet Union in 1991, anti-Communism replaced those shifting justifications. Emerging from the war as the strongest nation in the world, America strode boldly onto the global stage. The United States fought wars in Vietnam (1950–1973) and Korea (1950–1953); helped unseat governments in Iran (1953) and Chile (1973); landed troops in Lebanon (1958, 1982–1984), the Dominican Republic (1965), Grenada (1983), and Panama (1989–1990); supported paramilitary forces that overthrew the government of Guatemala (1954) and attacked Cuba (1961); and was deeply, if covertly, involved in Greece, Guyana, Indonesia, Zaire, Brazil, Libya, East Timor, and other countries. A focus on the red menace allowed Americans to trumpet idealistic goals while dismissing issues such as poverty, dictatorial rule, and the desire of countries to control their own resources.

Spokespersons broadcast the new US stance. In 1950 the State Department's expert on the Soviet Union, George Kennan, met with US ambassadors in Rio and told them, "[W]e should not hesitate before police repression by the local government. . . . It is better to have a strong regime in power than a liberal government if it is indulgent and relaxed and penetrated by Communists."[19] Anti-Communism became the constant refrain. It stood front and center in 1954 when the CIA overthrew Jacobo Arbenz, the duly elected president of Guatemala. Secretary of State John

Foster Dulles rejected Arbenz's criticism of the United Fruit Company, the country's largest landowner. "Communist infiltration," Dulles declared, is the "problem, not United Fruit."[20] Eisenhower explained US intervention in the Middle East by pointing to Russia's involvement: "Considering her announced purpose of Communizing the world, it is easy to understand her hope of dominating the Middle East."[21] Similar arguments were put forth in 1965 when the United States invaded the Dominican Republic, blocking Juan Bosch's ascent to the presidency. Although journalists and senators pointed out that Bosch was a reformer not a red, Lyndon Johnson proclaimed, "[T]he American nations ... will not permit the establishment of another Communist government in the Western Hemisphere."[22]

While anti-Communism was one of the many shifting justifications for American interventions, it also became embedded in the fabric of American society in ways that other ideologies never had. The federal government promoted this outlook with elaborate policy documents and campaigns against dissenters. In an influential paper, NSC 68, written in 1950, the National Security Council declared that the Soviet Union is "animated by a new fanatic faith, antithetical to our own, and seeks to impose its absolute authority over the rest of the world." NSC 68 became the basis for government pronouncements during the ensuing decades.[23]

Anyone who has grown up since the collapse of the Soviet Union can hardly comprehend how pervasive Cold War ideology was, particularly in the late 1940s and 1950s. I was born in 1943 and attended public schools in Philadelphia. Regular air raid drills reminded us of the danger of Russian bombs. The four-page newsletter *The Weekly Reader*, which was distributed to my elementary school class (and to thousands of other classes across the United

States) featured accounts of Soviet repression along with stories about the change of seasons. Movies, books, and newspaper columns sounded similar themes. The House Un-American Activities Committee (HUAC), created in 1938 and made a standing body in 1945, systematically harried leftists, spearheading a purge of Hollywood in 1947 and investigating scientists like Robert Oppenheimer in 1949. Joe McCarthy began his meteoric rise and fall in 1950 with an attack on "Communists" in the State Department.[24] In 1952–1953 HUAC turned its attention to public schoolteachers. My dad, Abe Egnal, who had helped organize the Philadelphia Teacher's Union in the 1930s, was summoned to Washington to testify. He quoted Jefferson in response to demands that he name names. The school board fired him along with thirty-one other teachers, and my parents went into the housewares business.[25]

Between 1945 and 1991, when the Soviet Union collapsed, the influence of anti-Communism on decision-makers was unmistakable. The "manufactured consent" (a term first introduced by Walter Lippman) that accompanied this world view proved useful as the United States emerged as a superpower after World War II. It justified the many interventions—including the deep entanglement in Vietnam—that marked American foreign policy during these years. It facilitated actions that, given its long history, the United States would have pursued under any circumstances. It allowed a nation that had emerged from World War II as the undisputed leader of the "free world" to pursue its interests around the globe.[26]

After 1991 American ideology evolved once again. Instead of fighting Communism, US forces mustered to defend freedom. There was much to defend. Even before the dissolution of the Soviet Union, the United States sent nearly 700,000 troops to Kuwait in the First Gulf War (1990–1991). American forces battled in Somalia (1993), landed in Haiti (1994), bombed Bosnia (1995) and Serbia (1999), and in 2011 cooperated with other nations to oust Libyan dictator Muammar Gaddafi. With the invasion of Afghanistan in 2001, the United States commenced what would become the nation's longest war (2001–2021). The Iraq War (2003–2010) overthrew Saddam Hussein but failed to find weapons of mass destruction. With drone and missile strikes, special forces teams, and CIA operations, the United States was involved in dozens of other countries in Asia, the Middle East, Africa, and South America.

These actions were undertaken in the name of freedom. Speaking in a newly reunited Berlin in 1994, Bill Clinton told Germans: "You have proved that no wall can forever contain the mighty power of freedom."[27] He struck the same notes in 1995, discussing the Dayton agreement, which ended the Bosnian conflict: "Because previous generations of Americans stood up for freedom and because we continue to do so, the American people are more secure and more prosperous."[28] In the aftermath of the September 11, 2001, attacks, George W. Bush told Americans, "Tonight we are a country awakened to danger and called to defend freedom. . . . The advance of human freedom—the great achievement of our time, and the great hope of every time—now depends on us."[29] Barack Obama and (at times) Donald Trump cast American foreign policy in the same terms. Explaining in 2009 his decision to send more troops to Afghanistan, Obama told West Point cadets, "[W]e are still heirs to a noble struggle for freedom. And now we must summon all our might and moral suasion to meet the challenges of a new age."[30] Even Trump, who usually set forth his views in less expansive terms than his predecessors, told the

UN General Assembly in 2019, "I have the immense privilege of addressing you today as the elected leader of a nation that prizes liberty, independence, and self-government above all."[31]

III

Like the emphasis on anti-Communism, modernization—a second explanation for America's involvement in Vietnam—has grave shortcomings. Those who highlight this interpretation contend that underpinning US actions was the desire to help other countries enjoy the success it had experienced. "The modernization theorists," Nils Gilman observes, "sincerely believed that the United States represented the most enlightened form of civilization yet known, and felt as if they were doing the world a favor by aiding 'them' to become more like 'us.'"[32]

Influential figures broadcast this ideology in the decades after World War II, with David Lilienthal and W. W. Rostow among the most prominent spokespersons. During the 1930s Lilienthal headed the Tennessee Valley Authority, the successful New Deal agency that harnessed Southern rivers and provided hydroelectric power. After the war he founded a consulting business, the Development and Resources Corporation, which built infrastructure, such as dams and roads, at home and abroad. With the encouragement of the US government, the company undertook mega-projects in countries such as Ghana, Iran, and Vietnam. David Ekbladh notes that the "TVA provided a modernization model of American origins to hold up against those of communist competitors." Lilienthal enthused about developing the Mekong Delta, writing to LBJ about the many benefits of the undertaking "based on the experience in helping to liberate the creative energies of people in America and overseas."[33] Rostow, author of *The Stages of Economic Growth: A Non-Communist Manifesto* (1960), was still more influential. He served as Kennedy's speechwriter and Johnson's national security adviser. Rostow's book presents "the uniformities in the sequence of modernization" and provides "an alternative to Karl Marx's theory of modern history." America, Rostow felt, had a duty to set Vietnam on the path to prosperity—a high road similar to the one the US had followed.[34]

The modernizers influenced American policy. Kennedy's Alliance for Progress, which was designed to buoy the economies of Latin America, bears their imprint, as does the Peace Corps. Lilienthal, a strong supporter of that initiative, helped train the corps' volunteers, who then assisted countries around the world.[35] In his Johns Hopkins Speech, LBJ called for the creation of a billion-dollar development fund, once the North recognized an independent South Vietnam. "The task is nothing less than to enrich the hopes and existence of more than a hundred million people," he stated, observing, "The vast Mekong River can provide food and water and power on a scale to dwarf even our own TVA."[36] Michael Latham notes that the US presented the Strategic Hamlet Program as "the centerpiece of its nation-building efforts." This initiative forced peasants into secure settlements where they would be taught the advantages of a modern nation-state.[37]

Still, modernization is a flawed explanation for American actions in Vietnam or elsewhere in the world. Many of America's interventions had no plans for improving the local economy, while in other cases the US *opposed* development (as in Iran, Guatemala, the Dominican Republic, and Vietnam), if the new head of government was not fully open to American investment and control. At times, for example with the Strategic Hamlet Program, the label of modernization appears far-fetched. Latham states bluntly, "[I]n practice the programme was a disaster from the start."[38]

IV

While anti-Communism and modernization played a role in shaping foreign policy, a far better explanation for US involvement in Southeast Asia, and across the globe, was the desire of upper-class individuals to expand the reach of American capitalism. Many historians agree. Gabriel Kolko, my colleague at York University, argues that US motives went far beyond efforts to block the red menace and embodied an "intense commitment to create an integrated, essentially capitalist world framework."[39] Marilyn Young, whose *The Vietnam Wars, 1945-1990* remains a key study of the conflict, contends: "In the largest sense, the United States was in Vietnam as a crucial part of the enterprise of reorganizing the post-World War II world according to the principles of liberal capitalism."[40] Odd Arne Westad, a leading historian of the Cold War, concurs, stating that "American leaders *consciously* took on the role of leader of global capitalism, and were willing to bear at least short-term burdens in order to ensure that the system worked."[41]

Three reasons suggest that the self-interested agenda of American financiers and industrialists shaped US intervention in Vietnam and elsewhere. First, the shifting arguments for American intervention point to the need for an explanation that transcends any one ideology.

Second, the many benefits that American capitalists sought and gained from other countries support the emphasis on expansionist motives. Conquests, occupations, and pressure from the United States expanded opportunities for trade and investment.

Before the Spanish-American War (1898), US holdings in Cuba totaled $50 million; by 1929 that sum had jumped to $1.5 billion.[42] Exchanges with the Philippines also boomed and focused increasingly on the United States. In 1895 only 13 percent of Filipino commerce was with the United States; by 1920 total shipments had increased tenfold, and two-thirds involved the United States. As occupiers of the Dominican Republican and Haiti, US forces collected customs duties and repaid American creditors. During these decades the American colossus elbowed out European investors. The Americans forced the British to renounce all rights to an isthmian canal and drove their firms from Central America. The state department ordered a British oil company to leave Costa Rica, remarking that the United States "considers it most important that only approved Americans should possess oil concessions in the neighborhood of the Panama Canal." US-backed dictators offered favorable conditions to American investors.[43]

After World War II the United States, now unmistakably the wealthiest, most powerful nation, sought to reshape trade and investment across the globe in ways that benefited American producers and financiers. "We are the giant of the economic world," Truman boasted in 1947. "Whether we like it or not, the future pattern of economic relations depends upon us."[44] The giant soon flexed its muscles. In announcing the "Truman doctrine" that year, the president noted that Britain, once the dominant power in southeastern Europe, could no longer preserve "internal order and security" in Greece and Turkey. Truman asked Congress for $400 million for the two countries, observing that without this measure, "Confusion and disorder might well spread throughout the entire Middle East."[45] The same imperative drove the Marshall Plan—a proposal designed to revive the European economy, check resurgent leftist parties, and not incidentally boost US exports. If America failed to act, Secretary of State George Marshall warned, "the consequences to the economy of the United States should be apparent to all." The United States provided over $12 billion to aid European recovery.[46]

Self-interest writ large also helps explain why the Americans supported the French in Indochina and increasingly became involved in the Vietnam War. American postwar policy focused on blocking left-leaning parties and keeping doors open for American investors. Policymakers accepted no shades of purple between the bright red of ruthless Communism and the true blue of free market capitalism. US leaders conflated nationalism, reform, and leftist doctrines and tarred all with the brush of Marxist-Leninist dogma. Policymakers grouped under the same red rubric various popular movements, including those in Guatemala, Nicaragua, Cuba, Iran, Chile, and Vietnam. Activists in these countries sinned in American eyes with their efforts to control their own economies and restrict foreign investors.

Guided by Secretary of State Acheson, the Truman administration rebuffed Ho Chi Minh's efforts to carve out a middle path. In discussions with the Chinese in 1944, Ho pointed to the coalition government he had established and stated, "I am a communist but what is important to me now is the independence and the freedom of my country, not communism. . . . I personally guarantee you that communism will not become a reality in Vietnam for another fifty years." He reiterated the same message after he arrived in Paris in 1946 to negotiate with the French. Ho observed that Vietnam might be ready for Communism in a half century, "but not now." He emphasized that the Vietnamese constitution was modeled on the American one and contained safeguards for private property.

"If the capitalists come to our country, it will be a good thing for them," Ho noted. "They will make money, but not as it was made in the old days. From now on it is fifty-fifty." Although some in the state department were open to those nuances, Acheson was not, remarking that the fact Ho Chi Minh was as much a "nationalist as a Commie is irrelevant. All Stalinists in colonial areas are nationalists." Ho, he stated, was an "outright Commie." One result of ignoring nationalism and local sources of unrest was the "domino thesis," which treated Communism as a contagion that emanated from the USSR and spread like a virus from one country to the next.[47]

Americans also backed the French in Vietnam because of concerns about European recovery. During the war FDR had mused about an independent Indochina. But US determination to rebuild a war-ravaged Europe argued against decolonization; progressive policies in the Third World could drive a wedge between the United States and its allies. "The essence" of the problem, the Central Intelligence Agency (CIA) explained, is "to satisfy the nationalist aspirations of colonial peoples while at the same time maintaining the economic and political stability of European colonial powers." In fact, there was no balancing the two goals: assistance to states like France had to prevail.[48] The same imperative applied to Japan, which served in the Far East (like West Germany in Europe) as a bulwark against the Soviet Union. Japanese prosperity, American policymakers asserted, required that the island nation maintain access to its traditional markets and sources of raw materials, including Vietnam. Assistant Secretary of the Army Tracy Vorhees asserted that "Japan's economic recovery depends upon keeping Communism out of Southeast Asia."[49] In April 1954, while the fateful battle at Dien Bien Phu raged, Eisenhower told a press conference that the loss of Vietnam would remove "in its economic aspects, that region that Japan must have as a trading area or Japan, in turn, will have only one place in the world to go—that is, toward the Communist areas in order to live."[50]

IV

The third reason that makes clear upper-class expansionists shaped US foreign policy (including the war in Vietnam) was the leadership role American manufacturers and investors played in guiding these initiatives.[51] Throughout these decades the boldest imperialists came from the financial and industrial centers of the North, the region stretching from the big cities of the Northeast, like Boston and New York, to Chicago in the Midwest. The most prominent critics of these policies hailed from the South and West. The Republicans, whose strength lay in the North, were the strongest supporters of the Spanish-American War and the acquisition of the Philippines. Theodore Roosevelt of New York and Henry Cabot Lodge of Massachusetts helped guide the party, while Democrats, backed by Western and Southern voters, opposed such imperialist ventures.[52] Similar divisions were evident in the clashes over entry into World War I and the battles between internationalists and isolationists in the 1930s.[53]

Northern business interests took the lead in crafting Cold War policies and, more particularly, in supporting the Vietnam War. This was not a case of shadowy figures in boardrooms pulling strings; there was no need for such clandestine influence because the key policymakers were themselves inextricably involved with big business. They were wealthy bankers like Averell Harriman, Paul Nitze, and Cyrus Vance, or corporate lawyers such as John

Foster Dulles, Clark Clifford, Dean Acheson, and Paul Warnke. Many in this tight circle were Harvard or Yale grads (Acheson, McGeorge Bundy, Nitze, Warnke, Vance, Walt Rostow, Robert McNamara, and Harriman) or Princeton alumni (Dulles, Kennan). Most of these individuals knew each other well. Harriman told an aide about Acheson: "To you he's the great Secretary of State. But to me he's the freshman I taught to row at Yale."[54]

Two examples illustrate the tight weave that bound together decision-makers and corporate America. Averell Harriman counseled four Democratic presidents from Roosevelt to Johnson. He oversaw the Lend-Lease program for FDR, took part in the Yalta Conference, served as ambassador to Moscow and the UK, and helped Truman launch the Marshall Plan. He was undersecretary of state during Kennedy's administration, and when Johnson opened negotiations with the North Vietnamese in 1968, Harriman headed the US delegation. Harriman was also one of the wealthiest individuals in the United States. The son of a railway baron, his holdings included a private bank, the Union Pacific and Southern Pacific railroads, the Polaroid Corporation, and Wells Fargo & Co. In the 1930s he chaired the Business Council for the Department of Commerce, and when Truman wanted to push through the Marshall Plan, Harriman brought together a group of prominent businessmen to advocate for the measure.[55]

John Foster Dulles was equally well connected to the business elite. Dulles, who specialized in international business, was a partner in the New York City law firm of Sullivan & Cromwell. During World War I he served on the War Industries Board, afterward he assisted Wilson at Versailles, and in the 1920s he oversaw German reparations. He helped draft the preamble to the UN charter in 1945, assisted Secretary of State Acheson in establishing postwar ties with Japan, and became Eisenhower's secretary of state in 1953. His law firm and family were deeply involved with corporate America. For example, the United Fruit Company retained Sullivan & Cromwell as its council and looked to Dulles and the State Department for relief when Guatemalan president Arbenz threatened to expropriate its unused lands. (In addition, John Foster's brother, Allen—who headed the CIA—had served on UFCO's board of directors.) The Dulleses enthusiastically supported the company's request and succeeded in toppling Arbenz.[56]

These advisers, like the business community they worked with, resolved to stop social change in Southeast Asia and regarded those rebellions as facets of aggressive, monolithic communism. Robert McNamara, who was plucked from the presidency of the Ford Motor Company to become Kennedy's secretary of defense, recalled the mindset of those days: "It seemed obvious that the Communist movement in Vietnam was closely related to the guerilla insurgencies in Burma, Indonesia, Malaya, and the Philippines during the 1950s. We viewed these conflicts not as nationalist movements—as they largely appear in hindsight—but as signs of a unified Communist drive for hegemony in Asia."[57] Successive presidents relied on these individuals for advice. The so-called Wise Men, a group that included Acheson, Harriman, Vance, and Clifford, regularly visited the White House, and until the end of 1967 most of these individuals reinforced calls for escalation. In 1965 Acheson told LBJ "he was wholly right on Vietnam," to which Johnson replied, "I am particularly strengthened by your support of our work in Vietnam, and I continue to feel that anything men of your standing can say to the country will be of great help."[58]

During the first months of 1968 these pillars of the financial and industrial establishment turned against the war. Mounting protests, lack of military progress, increased deaths, and soaring expenses all made clear that this was not a fight worth continuing. The first dissents had come even earlier. In 1966 Kennan, Eurocentric as were most of these men, suggested, "Certain areas of the world are more important than others."[59] The next year McNamara expressed his doubts in terms that would be familiar to anyone in business. He remarked that the war had not produced the desired "end products—broken enemy morale and political effectiveness." But for most of the Wise Men the turning point came in the spring of 1968. Acheson, Harriman, Clifford, Nitzke, Warnke, and Vance all told Johnson the time had come to de-escalate. "The establishment bastards have bailed out," Johnson reportedly sighed after a meeting with these advisers. They recognized that further escalation would wildly increase the national debt, heighten social dissension, and hurt the business climate.[60]

While the Wise Men joined the ranks of critics late in the day, many politicians who hailed from outside the Northern financial and industrialist heartland voiced objections much earlier. The most prominent doves came from the West and Midwest and in a few instances from the South. In 1962 Montana senator Mike Mansfield urged Kennedy to withdraw from Southeast Asia. In 1964 Wayne Morse (Oregon) and Ernest Gruening (Alaska) were the two senators who opposed the Gulf of Tonkin resolution. These dissenters were soon joined by Frank Church (Idaho), Mark Hatfield (Oregon), George McGovern (South Dakota), and George Aiken (Vermont). Within the White House challenges to Cold War orthodoxy came from Vice President Hubert Humphrey (Minnesota) and Undersecretary of State George Ball (Iowa). Also among the critics were four Southerners: William Fulbright (Arkansas), Al Gore Sr. (Tennessee), John Sherman Cooper (Kentucky), and Thruston

Morton (Kentucky).[61] During the Nixon years these doves again stood out for their opposition to the war. In 1970 the McGovern-Hatfield amendment called for an end to all military operations, while in 1971 the Cooper-Church amendment demanded American forces be withdrawn from Cambodia and Laos. Both proposals failed despite heartfelt pleas from the sponsoring senators.[62]

Two other groups of protestors, who stood well removed from the affluent advisers who encouraged LBJ, also condemned the war. College students, both from the White middle class and working class, became ever more outspoken in denouncing the conflict. Their marches and demonstrations in campuses across the country reflected both a concern for moral issues and a fear that the widening draft might end their student deferments.[63]

The other group that eventually turned against the war was African Americans. Many Blacks initially saw the armed forces as an opportunity for employment and advancement. But they also experienced the racism that characterized the services. African Americans were more likely to be placed in combat; in 1965, for example, Blacks comprised over 30 percent of the infantry on the front lines. They were less likely to lead troops, forming only 2 percent of the officer corps. Racial taunts were common; violent clashes took place between Whites and Blacks, with the Black troops invariably bearing the brunt of punishments. While most African Americans initially backed US participation, by 1968, with race riots at home, Martin Luther King's condemnation of the conflict, and mounting evidence of bias within the military, sentiment among African Americans moved decisively against participation.[64]

To return to the question that frames this essay: Why did the United States go to war in Vietnam? Not simply to block

Communism, although that rhetoric was pervasive in these years. Similar struggles had been waged earlier in the name of Christianity and later to promote freedom. Nor was it to encourage modernization, although that label was pasted onto several programs. Rather, the entanglement in Southeast Asia was part of a long-term resolve to create a world that was receptive to the interests of American manufacturers and investors.

6 Do "Waves" Explain the Women's Movement?

The course of American history, as the other essays in this volume suggest, was shaped by elite demands for economic growth and territorial expansion, with racism tightly woven into that imperative. But along with that *thesis* was an *antithesis*: the many protests that challenged and at times altered this path. The opposition came from abolitionists and union members, from farmers and critics of imperialism, from civil rights leaders and members of the LGBTQ community. One of the most important groups questioning the status quo was the women's movement. Their resistance and that of others played an important role in the *synthesis* that became the American story.

Often the women's movement has been viewed through the framework of waves. As early as 1968, the idea of a "second wave" had gained wide acceptance, with an article in the *New York Times* reporting, "Proponents call it the Second Feminist Wave, the first having ebbed after the glorious victory of suffrage."[1] Undoubtedly, the "second wave" is useful shorthand to refer to the resurgence of feminism in the 1960s and 1970s. The two waves have also become the way that many understand the entire women's movement. In a recent essay, Cornelia Dayton and Lisa Levenstein declare, "Nearly every U.S. history textbook and survey course discusses the growth of feminism, usually breaking it into a first wave of suffrage activism instigated by Susan B. Anthony and Elizabeth Cady Stanton and a second wave sparked by the publication of Betty Friedan's *The Feminine Mystique* in 1963." Researchers, however, divide over the utility of this concept, with advocates and opponents exchanging sharply worded volleys in scholarly publications.[2]

This chapter agrees with the critics who suggest that "waves" do more to distort than to clarify. Waves focus attention on two periods and exclude much that is happening outside those protests. The following pages suggest a more encompassing approach. This retelling, broadly chronological, incorporates the scholarship on the "first" and "second" waves. But it sets that material within the framework of four periods and suggests the extraordinary richness of the women's movement. It also makes clear that racial concerns repeatedly affected policies.

The First Era, 1800–1929: Three Strands of Activism

During the nineteenth and early twentieth centuries three braided strands of activism characterized protests by middle-class women.[3] The first strand emerged from "domesticity," the idea that women occupied a separate sphere, one with grave limitations but also important responsibilities. The second strand reflected the demand, voiced by many women, for independence and a stature equal with men. And the third was the struggle for suffrage. These three facets of the women's movement were distinct but at times overlapped and even blended into each other.

All three drew strength from the growth of the economy and the spread of education for middle-class girls and women. The new republic welcomed a surge of academies and seminaries established exclusively for women. Between 1790 and 1830 educators chartered 196 schools for women, and at least another 158 more opened between 1830 and 1860. Many of these institutions had rigorous curricula and high-minded ideals that influenced generations of students. Mary Lyon, who in 1837 founded Mount Holyoke Academy (it became a college in 1888), said her goal was "to turn the daughters who were acted upon into women capable of self-propelled action." Beginning in 1837 with Oberlin College, a few institutions of higher education opened their doors to women, and the numbers attending soared after the Civil War. Between 1870 and 1900 female enrollment in colleges skyrocketed, from eleven thousand to eighty-five thousand. Studies of prominent women make clear their strong educational backgrounds.[4]

I

Of the three strands, *benevolence* (the activities that emerged from the doctrine of domesticity) involved the most women. In 1842, decades after women launched the first charitable ventures, Catherine Beecher summarized this ideology in *A Treatise on Domestic Economy*. She began with *subordination*: "It is decided . . . she ["woman"] take a subordinate station, and that, in civil and political concerns, her interests be intrusted to the other sex, without her taking any part in voting, or in making or administering laws." Still, Beecher and others viewed domesticity as a striking advance over patriarchy. Women were now cherished for their nurturing and moral role. "In matters pertaining to the education of their children," Beecher declared, "in the selection and support of a clergyman, in all benevolent enterprises, and in all questions relating to morals or manners, they have a superior influence."[5] Historians vigorously debate whether the idea of two spheres was oppressive or liberating, but in important respects it was both.[6]

Beginning with the associations established in the late 1790s, benevolent activities evolved through several phases, with the common note that women spoke as defenders of the home and, more broadly, morality. During the first decades of the nineteenth century women came together in the cities and towns of the Northeast in their role as "moral mothers." These early societies assisted respectable, if needy, individuals and encouraged piety. For example, New York women established the Society for the Relief of Poor Widows with Small Children (1797); the Association for the Relief of Respectable, Aged, Indigent Females (1814); and the Female Sunday School Union (1816). Boston women founded, among other agencies, the Female Bible Society of Boston and Its Vicinity (1814) and the Fatherless and Widows' Society (1817).[7]

By the 1830s the objects of benevolence were no longer limited to "respectable" individuals, and tactics now broadened to include more involvement in the public sphere. The Boston Female Moral Reform Society (1835) addressed prostitution, as did the New-York Female Moral Reform Society (1834), which successfully lobbied the state assembly to make seduction a crime. Antislavery agitation also underscored these new dimensions. In the mid-1830s women in the Northeast formed female Anti-Slavery Societies; circulated petitions; and despite the disapproval of some male abolitionists, spoke to mixed audiences. In 1838 these women demonstrated their strength (and revealed the hostility they encountered) when they gathered in a Philadelphia convention. The assembly ended abruptly when a mob attacked and set fire to the hall.[8]

During the 1850s many female societies shifted their focus to establishing or strengthening institutions, and increasingly members of the various associations affirmed suffrage as a means to achieve their ends. In Philadelphia the Rosine Association sponsored a home "for the reformation, employment, and instruction of females, who had led immoral lives."[9] In New York City the American Female Guardian Society opened several industrial schools. Women's groups expanded the New Haven Orphan Asylum. Some reformers now called for suffrage, not as a natural right, but to further their benevolent goals. In so doing, they gently tugged the doctrine of domesticity beyond its original confines. In 1848 Amelia Bloomer attended the Seneca Falls meeting, the first public gathering that demanded the vote. But her focus was on the scourge of alcoholism and dress reform. As a leader of the Women's New York Temperance Society, she declared, "[T]he only way in which women can do any anything effectually in this cause is through the ballot-box." Other women demanded the vote to improve their children's education. Before the Civil War two states, Kentucky and Michigan, granted some women the right to vote on school taxes. Later in the century other states offered this carefully circumscribed privilege—an initiative that could be viewed as compatible with the doctrine of two spheres.[10]

The most important benevolent organization was the Woman's Christian Temperance Union, formally organized in 1874 at a convention in Cleveland. The driving force behind the WCTU, its programs, and its rapid expansion was Frances Willard, who was appointed national secretary at the Cleveland meeting and who served as president from 1879 until her death in 1898. Dues-paying membership climbed from 13,000 in 1876 to over 150,000 in the 1880s, making the WCTU larger than any of the suffrage associations. The organization soon moved beyond fighting saloons; it campaigned for the eight-hour day, the end of child labor, raising the age of consent, and prison reform. Willard formed a close association with the Prohibition Party and the Knights of Labor.[11]

Reflecting Willard's strong advocacy, the WCTU endorsed women's suffrage. For Willard, the ballot was needed to protect domestic values, not to assert an abstract right. A reporter, covering one of her speeches, observed: "[S]he thought it time that Woman, who is truest to God and our country by instinct and education, should have a voice at the polls." Using the slogan "Home Protection," she persuaded the National WCTU in 1881 to call for women's suffrage. Only in 1894 would language about the consent of the governed replace home protection.[12]

The WCTU was also important for the small but growing cohort of Southern Black middle-class women. Many of these individuals, born to freed parents, pursued the limited opportunities for higher education. Determined to demonstrate their respectability, they responded enthusiastically to the message Willard delivered to Black and White audiences. Typically, African American women formed their own WCTU chapters. While White women approved Willard's outreach ("Everywhere the Southern White people desired me to speak to the colored," she observed), they rejected integrated societies.[13]

In addition to their involvement in the WCTU, Black women supported a variety of benevolent organizations. In the Northern cities these agencies dated back to the 1820s and 1830s, when women (at times working with men) formed groups such as the New York African Mutual Instruction Society and the African Female Benevolent Society of Troy, New York. After the Civil War these societies expanded across the South. In the 1890s the various clubs came together in the National Federation of Afro-American Women and the National Association of Colored Women (whose motto was "lifting as we climb").[14]

The nineteenth century closed with one more important, benevolent reform: the settlement house movement. Responding to the flood of immigrants from eastern and southern Europe, middle-class women opened centers to assist the recent arrivals. Founders included Jane Addams, who started Hull House in Chicago (1889); Vida Scudder, who with other women established Denison House in Boston (1892); and Lillian Wald, who began the Henry Street Settlement in New York (1893). By 1900 over a hundred such houses welcomed newcomers.

Addams and the other "settlers" regarded the problems immigrants faced as transitory and similar to the difficulties that confronted the early pioneers. Optimism and a touch of noblesse oblige suffuse the writings of the well-off settlers.[15] In her memoir, *Twenty Years at Hull House* (1910), Addams observes, "Hull-House was soberly opened on the theory that the dependence of classes on each other is reciprocal." She continues: "I think that time has also justified our early contention that the mere foothold of a house, easily accessible, ample in space, hospitable and tolerant in spirit, situated in the midst of the large foreign colonies which so easily isolate themselves in American cities, would be in itself a serviceable thing for Chicago."[16] In most instances, the settlements did not extend their services to African Americans, who also had begun to move to these metropolises.[17]

The era of benevolent reform came to an end in the 1920s. Although temperance crusaders seemingly triumphed in 1919 with the Eighteenth Amendment, which prohibited the sale of alcohol, this experiment in social engineering proved to be a failure. Many defied the ban, and the measure was repealed in 1933. The Sheppard-Towner Act, one of few other reform measures launched during this socially conservative decade, was also short-lived. By providing public health nurses and training for midwives, it sought to improve maternity care and child care. Launched in 1921, the law was allowed to expire in 1929 after outcries condemning it as a socialist program.[18]

II

The second strand in the women's movement of the nineteenth and early twentieth centuries reflects the actions and words of individual women who were determined to realize their full potential. These women, with their exemplary lives, their essays and novels, often had an outsized influence on others. (The discussion includes a few male novelists whose female characters also had an important impact on readers.)

This story begins with the outspoken women of the 1830s and 1840s, a period before the so-called first wave began. Like other visitors, Frenchman Alexis de Tocqueville, who toured America in the 1830s, was impressed by the strong-minded women he met. He observed, "Long before the young American woman has reached marriageable age, the process of freeing her from her mother's care has started stage by stage. Before she has completely left childhood behind she already thinks for herself, speaks freely, and acts on her own. . . . [S]he is full of confidence in her own powers."[19] These bold women populate novels, works that from the first half of the century include James Fenimore Cooper's *The Last of the Mohicans* (1826), *The Deerslayer* (1841), and *The Chainbearer*

(1845).[20] The same independent spirit shines in Sarah Grimké's *Letters on the Equality of the Sexes* (1837), essays that challenge the tenets of domesticity. That doctrine, Grimké observes, "teaches women to regard themselves as a kind of machinery, necessary to keep the domestic engine in order, but of little value as the *intelligent* companions of men." Catherine Beecher sharply rebuked Grimké for these comments.[21]

Women came together in discussion groups that resembled, in some ways, the "consciousness raising" of the 1960s. Over the course of seven years, Margaret Fuller, whose magisterial *Woman in the Nineteenth Century* (1845) influenced many, presided over "Conversations" in different cities. One student who attended Fuller's gatherings reflected, "She spoke upon what woman could do—said she should like to see a woman everything she might be in intellect and character." Fuller also took pains to distinguish herself from Beecher, arguing that there was no "essential difference" between men and women.[22]

After midcentury a range of novels documented (if sometimes critically) the aspirational journeys individual women pursued. These works include Nathaniel Hawthorne's *The Blithedale Romance* (1852); *My Wife and I* (1871) by Harriet Beecher Stowe, who was Catherine's sister; and Henry James's *The Bostonians* (1886). Other novels profile women who sought to become doctors, a profession made possible after Elizabeth Blackwell enrolled in an American medical school in 1847. Nan, in Louisa May Alcott's *Jo's Boys* (1886), studies medicine, "for now, thanks to other intelligent women, colleges and hospitals were open to her." Anna Prince in Sarah Orne Jewett's *A Country Doctor* (1884) spurns marriage so she can get a medical degree. Other fictional women also blazed bold paths. Jo, the hero of Alcott's *Little Women* (1868–1869), is resolute in her determination to become a writer, even while her sisters lead more traditional lives.[23]

While these independent women supported suffrage, they criticized the single-minded pursuit of that goal—as well as benevolent reform. Jane Croly, who spoke at the inaugural meeting of the Ladies' Social Science Association in 1869, underscored the limitations of the vote: "The ballot is at best only one agency; it cannot do everything. It does not do everything for men."[24] Florence Kelley's critique was even more incisive. Educated at Cornell and in Switzerland and widely read, Kelley increasingly felt that both suffragists and maternalistic reformers were out of touch with an industrializing America. In 1885 when female carpet weavers went on strike in Yonkers, New York, Kelley was angered by the silence of the leading women's publications: "Now what *can* be the matter with the suffragists? Are they ignorant of the existence of the strike? And if so what a wretchedly narrow horizon they must have!" She expanded her arguments a few years later: "[T]he vital question is no longer between . . . the temperance, the white cross [i.e., Christianity] and the suffrage movements." Rather, "the question that forces itself upon us . . . is this: In the great strife of classes, in the life and death struggle that is rending society to its foundations, where do I belong?" Kelley moved to Chicago and joined Jane Addams at Hull House in her work with impoverished immigrants.[25]

During the 1890s and the first decades of the new century, still another influential group of independent women rethought feminism. Russian born anarchist Emma Goldman harshly criticized capitalism for subjugating women, noting that "women and children carried the heaviest burdens of our ruthless economic system." She denounced those who narrowly focused on the vote, and in an essay, "The Woman Suffrage Chameleon," mocked the suffragists who supported World War I just to advance their cause.[26] Charlotte Perkins Gilman, an acclaimed author and lecturer, agreed with Goldman that society oppresses women. In *Women and Economics* (1898) she argues that "progress ... will flow on smoothly and rapidly when both men and women stand equal in economic relation."[27] A third outspoken writer, Margaret Sanger, battled the laws that denied women's right to contraception. In 1914 she established a monthly journal, *The Woman Rebel*, "A Paper for the advancement of WOMAN'S FREEDOM." The magazine advocated for "birth control" (a term she coined) and socialism.[28]

Female novelists during these years also depicted bold, confident women. In *The Country of the Pointed Firs* (1896), Sarah Orne Jewett presents a community of self-reliant, caring women. Successful farmers, grain dealers, and hotel keepers are among the women who populate Willa Cather's *O Pioneers!* (1913) and *My Antonia* (1918). In *The Custom of the Country* (1913) and *Summer* (1917), Edith Wharton creates female protagonists who defy their narrow-minded neighbors. The repression that followed World War I, along with the violence and racism of the 1920s, brought this period of intellectual ferment to a close.[29]

III

The third strand of the nineteenth- and early twentieth-century women's movement was the struggle for suffrage (activism traditionally known as *first wave feminism*). The campaign began in 1848 with the convention at Seneca Falls, New York, where delegates demanded the right to vote. Annual meetings, calling for suffrage, continued throughout the 1850s. Recent historians, unlike the earliest chroniclers, emphasize the racism, xenophobia, and class bias that characterized the movement from its start. In arguing for elevating women, the Seneca Falls resolutions declared, "He [i.e., mankind] has withheld from her rights which are given to the most ignorant and degraded men—both natives and foreigners."[30]

After the Civil War the clash over race moved to the center of the story. The debate over enfranchising Black men roiled the American Equal Rights Association, formed in 1866. Elizabeth Cady Stanton and Susan B. Anthony denounced the proposed Fifteenth Amendment, which extended the vote to African American men but not women. At the climactic May 1869 meeting Stanton declared, "'Manhood suffrage' is national suicide and woman's destruction. . . . Think of Patrick and Sambo and Hans and Yung Tung, who do not know the difference between a monarchy and a republic, who cannot read the Declaration of Independence or Webster's spelling book, making laws for Lucretia Mott . . . [or] Susan B. Anthony."[31]

Disagreements over the Fifteenth Amendment shattered the American Equal Rights Association and led to the emergence of two new organizations: the National Woman Suffrage Association, headed by Stanton and Anthony, and the American Woman Suffrage Association, which endorsed Black male enfranchisement and was led by Lucy Stone and her husband, Henry Blackwell. Both groups backed state campaigns for suffrage and supported a national amendment. In 1890, with debates over the Fifteenth Amendment fading, they united to form the National American Woman Suffrage Association (NAWSA). Before 1900 success came only in the West, with Wyoming, Utah, Colorado, and Idaho granting women the vote.[32]

Race continued to be an important issue as the movement gathered strength in the decades before 1920. Since Seneca Falls, African American women, like Sojourner Truth, Mary Ann Shadd Cary, and Frances Ellen Watkins Harper, had called for both women's rights and racial justice. In 1866 Harper addressed the inaugural meeting of the American Equal Rights Association, stating that "we are all bound up together in one great bundle of humanity"— an admonition most women present did not accept.[33] This tension continued after 1900, as the new leaders of the NAWSA, Carrie Chapman Catt and Anna Howard Shaw, redoubled their efforts to win over White Southerners. The 1903 New Orleans convention excluded Blacks and allowed state associations to bar non-Whites. Racial politics entered into the planning for the Woman Suffrage Procession, a grand parade, organized by Alice Paul and held in March 1913, the day before President Wilson's inauguration. Southern delegates threatened to pull out if African Americans were included, leading to proposals to relegate Blacks to the end of the march. Only at the last moment were those plans scrapped.[34]

Success crowned these years of hard work. The NAWSA and the more radical National Woman's Party, which Paul founded in 1916, pressured President Wilson and other elected officials. The disparity between America's lofty wartime ideals and women's status argued for reform. In 1919 Congress approved the Nineteenth Amendment, and the next year the states ratified the measure.[35]

The suffrage campaign subsided in the 1920s, with race continuing to shape the women's movement. Relatively few women voted in the 1920 election (about 35 percent of those eligible, compared to 70 percent of the men), and they typically followed their husbands' leads. Southern states adopted regulations that purged African American women from the voter lists, just as similar ordinances two decades earlier had barred Black men. Alice Paul continued to lead the National Woman's Party and now campaigned for an Equal Rights Amendment. But she did little to build up a broad following and faced resistance from progressive leaders who felt the measure would imperil legislation protecting working women.[36] Paul was also indifferent to the pleas of Black women who hoped the party would defend their rights. She dismissed such issues as "race questions" unrelated to her goal of "political equality for women."[37]

The Second Era, 1930–1959: Advances and Retreats

Women recorded striking advances during the 1930s and the war years, but lost ground (at least in the fight for equal rights) after 1945. Two groups of women, who sometimes were at odds with each other, spearheaded the struggle during the Depression and World War II. One was the circle around Eleanor Roosevelt, whose influence reflected her support for women's issues, her concern for the less fortunate, and her marriage to a successful politician who became New York governor and then president of the United States. Many of the women linked to Roosevelt had earlier worked with each other. For example, Frances Perkins, Rose Schneiderman, and Pauline Newman were involved in the reforms that followed the Triangle Shirtwaist Fire of 1911. Eleanor, who joined the Women's Trade Union League in 1919, came to know many of these activists.[38]

Partly because of Eleanor's resolve, Franklin Roosevelt's administration included an unprecedented number of women, and the impact of those individuals was far reaching. FDR appointed Frances Perkins as secretary of labor, the first woman to hold a cabinet position. Perkins, who had worked with Franklin when he was governor, helped shape, among other measures, the National Recovery Administration (NRA), the Social Security Act, and the Fair Labor Standards Act. Perkins, in turn, put Rose Schneiderman on the NRA Labor Advisory Board. "Red Rose," as she was called (both because of her views and her hair), drafted labor codes that protected vulnerable men and women. "The code," Schneiderman explained about one such plan, "though not an ideal one, will go far toward making life and work for the tens of thousands of textile workers more humane and secure." Other associates of Perkins and Eleanor, for example, Pauline Newman and Frieda Miller, advised the Women's Bureau of the US Department of Labor, assisted the International Labor Organization, and served in New York State government.[39]

Another noteworthy friend of Eleanor Roosevelt was Mary Jane McLeod Bethune, the daughter of former slaves. Bethune had established a school in Florida and had led the National Urban League and the National Association of Colored Women. During the New Deal, as director of Negro Affairs in the National Youth Organization, she found positions for thousands of young African Americans. She also brought together a group of office holders into what became known as the "Black Cabinet." They pushed for more Black representation in government and the armed services. Southern members of Congress, however, blocked their plans to enact anti-lynching laws and end the poll tax.[40]

Perhaps surprisingly, ER's circle, including Perkins, Schneiderman, Newman, Miller, and Bethune, opposed the Equal Rights Amendment. Many had waged lengthy battles to improve working conditions for women and felt the amendment threatened those gains. Sex-specific laws, Perkins asserted, recognized "the need to safeguard the health and welfare of women workers for the sake of developing a healthy, happy, and competent national population."[41] Despite their own exemplary careers, these women celebrated maternalism. Eleanor Roosevelt remarked, "The normal woman feels that her home must come first and that if she falls in love and has children, this is the life which probably will bring her the greatest lasting happiness."[42]

Still, beginning in the mid-1930s calls for an Equal Rights Amendment grew louder. The boldness of New Deal reforms encouraged the campaign, as did the growing number of married women in the workforce, a development that undercut arguments about women as the "weaker sex." The National Woman's Party (which Eleanor called "a perfectly useless organization") continued to lead the charge. One of its leaders announced in 1936, "We have the best chance of winning Equal Rights now than we have ever had since the Amendment was first introduced." Advocates made their case in congressional hearings in 1938, noting that twenty-seven states still kept women from serving on juries, while others barred them from occupations like taxi driver.[43]

World War II strengthened the arguments for adopting the ERA. Fully 350,000 women served in the armed forces, and their proportion in the workforce soared. They became the mainstay of industries, such as defense, that had employed few women before the war. Their entry into traditionally male occupations challenged assertions that women needed "protective" legislation. One activist rejoiced, "The women are getting along extremely well. They are holding hundreds of jobs that were formerly supposed to be unsuitable to them. . . . And they are liking it."[44] Editorialists argued these patriotic individuals should be accorded full rights. Politicians responded, with the Senate Judiciary Committee endorsing the ERA in 1942 and 1943, as did both parties in their 1944 platforms. The high-water mark of this agitation came in 1946 when a majority of the Senate—although not the required two-thirds—supported the amendment.[45]

After 1945 the push for the ERA ground to a halt. Various groups within and outside Congress rallied against the measure. Returning GIs replaced women in factories and offices. Many individuals now focused on starting families, driving up the birthrate between 1946 and 1958. For women, the reigning symbol was no longer "Rosie the Riveter" but sitcom housewives like Harriet Nelson and June Cleaver.[46] Still, there was a twist in this reversion to domesticity. After a brief pause, women's participation in the workforce rose strongly. The postwar economy, dominated by service industries, needed women as secretaries, nurses, teachers, salespeople, and domestics. Calls for female labor, however, excluded the managerial posts some had held during the war. Women's earnings, compared to men's, declined after 1945, a slide unchecked until 1973.[47]

The Third Era, 1960–1989: Equal Rights and Consciousness Raising

Activism resumed in the 1960s, beginning the era traditionally called *second wave feminism*. During the next twenty-five years women recorded advances on two fronts: dismantling discriminatory laws and raising consciousness. A presidential initiative and three acts of Congress provided the foundation for a broad onslaught against oppressive practices. In 1961 President Kennedy established the Presidential Commission on the Status of Women. Lawmakers passed the Equal Pay Act in 1963, and in 1964 the Civil Rights Act, which included Title VII, prohibiting discrimination on the basis of sex, as well as race, religion, and national origin. The Voting Rights Act of 1965 banned the practices that had denied suffrage to African Americans, male and female, in much of the South.[48]

During the late 1960s and 1970s feminists pressured commissions, courts, and Congress to address discrimination and implement the measures just adopted. In 1966 Betty Friedan and a group of like-minded activists formed the National Organization for Women (NOW) to demand that officials take more forceful action. Ruth Bader Ginsburg, working with the American Civil Liberties Union, pursued similar goals. Ginsburg appeared before the Supreme Court six times in the 1970s, winning five of those cases and spearheading an assault against laws that privileged one sex over another. Another landmark victory (one not involving RBG) was *Roe v. Wade* (1973), affirming the right of women to have an abortion. In 1972 Congress further bolstered women's rights with Title IX of the Education Amendments. This addition to the Civil Rights Act banned discrimination based on gender in educational programs receiving federal funding.[49]

For NOW and its supporters, the adoption of the Equal Rights Amendment was to be the culmination of the campaign to remake the legal system. Congress had periodically discussed the amendment, which Alice Paul had championed in the 1920s. NOW endorsed the ERA in 1967, and in 1972 the two houses of Congress approved the amendment and sent it to the states for ratification. Initially the campaign went well, with thirty (of the required thirty-eight) states quickly ratifying the measure and an additional five adding their support by 1977. But the STOP ERA campaign checked that momentum and ultimately blocked ratification. Still, despite that setback, feminists could point to remarkable progress in their efforts to dismantle legal barriers.[50]

During these years (and earlier), other groups pushed for change, alongside the middle-class women who dominated NOW. Women in the International Union of Electrical Workers launched their fight against gender bias in the 1950s and pushed hard for the Equal Pay Act of 1963 and the enforcement of Title VII. The National Council of Churches (NCC), which represented more than thirty million Christians (with African Americans comprising one-fourth of the membership), had, since the 1940s, demanded justice for Blacks and women. Various women's caucuses within the NCC fought for abortion rights, same-sex relationships, nonsexist religious practices, and more women in the pulpit. Outspoken individuals within the American Civil Liberties Union advocated for women's rights in the 1950s and championed progressive measures, including the defense of lesbians, a step NOW resisted in its early years. NOW, whose membership reached 125,000 in 1978, is best viewed as one voice in a larger chorus.[51]

Activists also focused on consciousness raising, an initiative that soon led to other demands. Beginning in the late 1960s women came together in small groups, gatherings that reflected their discontent with the male-dominated antiwar and New Left movements. The publication and popularity of Friedan's *The Feminine Mystique* spurred these efforts. Among the other books widely discussed were works by Shulamith Firestone, Germaine Greer, and Kate Millett.[52] A series of national organizations sought to capture and focus that energy—and to do so more fully than NOW could. Gloria Steinem and others in 1971 founded the Women's Action Alliance (WAA), and in 1972 *Ms. Magazine*. The WAA drafted a far-ranging agenda, one that addressed racism and poverty, as well as promoting women's rights.[53]

Race roiled the protests of these years, much as it had disrupted the movement in the nineteenth and early twentieth centuries. Middle-class White women dominated the groups formed in the late 1960s and early 1970s. Wini Breines notes that White feminists "harbored a political image of universal community that made little sense to women who were not like us."[54] African American and Chicana women resented such assumptions. Black activist Pauli Murray tried to slow NOW's support for the ERA, fearing that a movement "confined almost solely to 'women's rights' without strong bonds with other movements toward human rights . . . might develop into a head on collision with Black civil rights and other struggles." As the result of these clashes, African American and Latina women formed their own organizations, ones that fought both racism and sexism.[55]

The Fourth Era, 1990–Present: Two Cheers for the Women's Movement

The decades since 1990 have been ones of striking accomplishments, but also setbacks that make clear full equality remains a distant goal. The demand for women's rights now enjoys widespread support. By the 1990s about 65 percent of women and almost 60 percent of men told pollsters they endorsed women's demands. Approval of *feminism* rose as well; in 2020 some 61 percent of women agreed that feminism defined them.[56]

Women have recorded noteworthy advances in the workplace. In 1968 women earned only 2 percent of dental degrees, 4 percent of law degrees, and about 8 percent of MDs. By the mid-1990s these percentages had risen, respectively, to 37, 43, and 42 percent. More generally, the proportion of women in the workforce climbed from

40 to 60 percent between the 1960s and 1990s. Changing attitudes and the stagnation in men's wages encouraged women to scale these heights. Middle-class couples needed two incomes to maintain their standard of living. Similar concerns spurred college enrollment; in the 1980s women surpassed men in degrees awarded.[57]

More women achieved prominence in local, state, and national governments, with the most significant advances coming in the new century. Groups like EMILY's List, a political action committee backed by middle- and upper-income donors, accelerated these changes. Since its founding in 1985, the fund has raised $240 million to elect pro-choice Democratic women. The proportion of women in the US House and Senate rose from 5 percent in 1987–1989, to 16 percent in 2005–2007, to nearly 28 percent in 2021–2023. In that recent Congress, the House seated 154 women, including 123 Democrats, who comprise 41 percent of party members in the chamber.[58]

Feminists also organized the Women's March on January 27, 2017, the largest women-led protest in history. Over 470,000 people came to the capital, and an estimated five to seven million individuals took part in demonstrations across the United States and around the world. Donald Trump's election provoked the march, which took place the day after his inauguration. What is remarkable is how quickly the protest came together, from a single Facebook post to the creation of an organizing committee, to the formation of volunteer groups, to the many arrangements needed to make the event a success. One organizer noted with pride that the "Women's March movement was able to activate and mobilize hundreds of thousands of first-time activists." The platform advocated pay equality for men and women; endorsed LGBTQ rights; and declared its support for unions, civil rights, the environment, and reproductive freedom.[59]

Racial tension, an inextricable part of the women's movement since its inception, surfaced as well in the Washington march. Conflict emerged despite the prominence of women of color among the organizers and the condemnation of racism that was part of the "Unity Principles." Many Black activists saw such statements as lip service in a society where even well-intentioned White women were complicit in oppression. Roxane Gay remarked, "It took... the election of a white supremacist to motivate women, en masse, to march.... Somehow, the mass incarceration of black men, the state-sanctioned murders of black men and women by law enforcement, the pay gap between white women and women of color... and so many other issues were not drastic enough to inspire the kind of outrage seen in... the Women's March." Some African American feminists chose not to attend; others announced on social media that White women should "check their privilege." The racial divide evident in the 1840s was still present in the 2010s.[60]

Two other aspects of this reinvigorated feminism are noteworthy. One was the "Me Too" movement, which dates from 2006 and activist Tarana Burke's social media posts denouncing the sexual assaults on vulnerable women. The campaign gained national prominence in 2017 with the introduction of the Twitter hashtag #MeToo and the shocking revelations about film producer Harvey Weinstein.[61] A second important development was the new emphasis on *intersectionality*. Kimberlé Crenshaw, a Black law professor, introduced the term in 1989 to emphasize that women have multiple "identities," involving questions of gender, race, and class. Women across the globe, particularly in academic forums, have used the concept as a springboard for analysis.[62]

If extraordinary progress has been made, the early 2020s are not yet the moment for a victory lap. Support for feminism varies along partisan lines, with 75 percent of Democratic women and only 42 percent of Republican women saying the term describes them.[63] The proportion of women in the workforce, which had climbed since the 1950s, peaked at 60 percent in 1999 and has gradually declined. At least in part the slowdown in the participation rate reflected the absence of government programs such as maternity leave and child care, common in other wealthy countries. Women's work remains undervalued; in 2021 women received only 82 cents for every dollar earned by men. Women also remain badly under-represented on corporate boards and in C-suite offices.[64] The rise of misogynistic rhetoric during the Trump presidency and the *Dobbs* decision in June 2022 reversing *Roe v. Wade* marked serious set-backs. A *New York Times* survey (conducted just before the Supreme Court ruled) revealed many dispirited activists. Letty Pogrebin, one of the founders of *Ms. Magazine*, commented: "My feelings are of frustration and rage and deep disappointment when I look at how far we've slid back on two things: reproductive rights and non-sex-ist child rearing and education."[65] The story of the women's movement presented here is unquestionably one of significant advances. But it is also the account of a journey that still has far to go.

To return to the question that opens this essay—"Do waves explain the women's movement?" —the answer must be a resound-ing *No*. The focus on a "first wave" and "second wave" highlights two campaigns. But it ignores the actions of many people who, over the course of more than two centuries, worked hard to improve the lives of American women. More broadly, the story of the women's movement illustrates how dissenters and crusaders in many areas labored to make the nation a better place for all.

7 *Why Do So Many Americans Passionately Support Trump?*

Donald Trump's election in November 2016 surprised many people, including Trump himself. As favorable returns poured in during election night, Trump admonished family members who urged him to celebrate. "Don't tell me that if we haven't really won," he said. "I want to know for sure."[1] Since that evening, politicians, reporters, and social scientists have labored to explain Trump's victories in 2016 and 2024 and his continuing popularity despite his lack of prior experience in elective office, numerous scandals, disdain for the Republican establishment, attacks on democratic norms, two impeachments, scurrilous comments about women and other groups, and a felony conviction. Analysts point to Trump's ability to inspire his followers, the hard times many Americans face, urban crime, the influx of immigrants, an electoral system that gives undue weight to rural voters, and the influence of Fox News.[2]

This essay argues that at the heart of Trump's extraordinary, sustained support are the voters who coalesced around their sense of White Christian identity. Other individuals cast their ballots for Trump, particularly in 2024, when his coalition broadened. But the loyalty of this core group defines the MAGA ("Make America

Great Again") movement and shapes Trump's messaging. These individuals push back against the (perceived) threats from those who challenge the world they cherish. Their antagonists include outspoken Blacks, immigrants, LGBTQ advocates, feminists, condescending liberals, and secularists. While economic problems matter to many of his followers, racial concerns and cultural issues remain most important.

Three developments explain the large, passionate bloc of Trump supporters, who came together in 2016. One is the long history of racialized appeals to Whites, campaigns that date from the Civil War, intensified in the 1960s, and culminated in the 2010s. The second development is the transformation of the Democrats from a party that relied on the working class to one that curried favor with the coastal elites and championed socially progressive measures. This change cut adrift a large group of less wealthy voters. The third and most immediate cause is the election of Barack Obama. The ascension of a Black man to the highest office in the country highlighted for many citizens all they felt was wrong with the direction the United States was taking.

The coalition supporting Trump is fervent in its convictions and, seemingly, unshakable in its loyalty. These individuals elevated Trump in 2016, delivered seventy-four million votes in his unsuccessful 2020 bid for reelection, and made him president again in 2024. His most ardent backers disdain the democratic process, rejecting court orders and unfavorable results, and they push back against mainstream science with its assertions about vaccine mandates and global warming. They rage against the flood of immigrants, welfare recipients, pro-choice groups, and gun control advocates, as well as against "woke" teachers and trans activists. Trump has transformed the Republican Party and, if his coalition continues to hold, which seems likely, this bloc of angry voters will fundamentally change the American political system.

I

Since the Civil War, race has played an important role in shaping partisan loyalties. Once split between Democrats and Whigs, White Southerners became unwavering Democrats after 1865, broadcasting their dislike of the Republicans, the party of emancipation. By the same measure, African Americans, many of whom could vote in the South between Reconstruction and the turn of the century, applauded the party of Lincoln. Blacks in the North, most of whom were enfranchised by the Fifteenth Amendment, shared those loyalties. Except in a few states, the right to vote was limited to men before the adoption of the Nineteenth Amendment in 1920.

Republicans, however, found they could create a winning coalition without Southern Whites. Between Lincoln's inauguration in 1861 and 1933 when Franklin Roosevelt entered office, Republicans controlled the Senate for sixty-two of those seventy-two years and dominated the House. The manufacturing heartland voted Republican, as did the major cities, with a few notable exceptions, such as New York and Boston.[3]

Like an imposing statue knocked from its plinth, the Republican colossus was rudely pushed aside in the elections of 1932 and 1936, and another durable entity, the New Deal coalition, set in its place. The wheel had turned. During the sixty-two years from 1933 to 1995, Democrats controlled the House for fifty-eight years and held sway in the Senate as well.

Attitudes toward race left their imprint on the coalition that emerged in the 1930s. The victory of FDR and the Democrats returned the South to power. Controlling a crucial bloc of votes, Southerners scuttled legislation that attacked discrimination. An anti-lynching bill quietly died after congressmen from Dixie warned that if Roosevelt signed the measure, "it will ruin him in the Southern states." Coming from the poorest part of the nation, these politicians welcomed federal spending—but only if Washington limited the funds directed to African Americans. White Southerners did not want federal money unsettling long-established social relations. Reflecting that demand, the Social Security Act of 1935 excluded farmworkers and maids, two categories that accounted for more than 60 percent of regional Black employment. The NAACP opposed the bill, arguing that it was "like a sieve with holes just big enough for the majority of Negroes to fall through." States also retained control over welfare payments and provided lower amounts to Blacks or simply rejected their claims.[4]

Despite blatant discrimination in welfare in the South and in the mortgages underwritten by the Federal Housing Administration throughout the country, African Americans backed the Democrats in the 1936 election and would remain one of the party's most loyal constituencies. For the first time since Reconstruction, Blacks benefited from government programs. Swedish sociologist Gunnar Myrdal explained the contradictions involved: "Negroes get fewer benefits, in relation to their needs, than do Whites. Nevertheless, since they are so much poorer than Whites, their representation on the relief rolls usually exceeds their proportion in the population." Individuals in the administration, including Eleanor Roosevelt, reached out to prominent African Americans, inviting them to public events.[5] The inclusion of both Blacks and racist Southern Whites made the Democratic Party an inherently unstable amalgam. That tension would not be resolved until the new millennium, when White Southerners, after decades of wavering, joined Republican ranks.

Still, class was more important than race in shaping the New Deal coalition. Social welfare legislation and the National Labor Relations Act of 1935 aided workers, and more generally, bolstered support among the less wealthy. Unions and working people became mainstays of the Democratic Party. As a result, cities, which as a group had leaned Republican, now moved solidly into the Democratic column.[6]

II

Efforts to use race to draw Whites away from the Democratic Party emerged soon after Roosevelt's death, with dissent initially centered in the Lower South. Disaffected Whites resented the advances Blacks recorded after World War II. In 1948 Truman integrated the armed forces. In 1954 the Supreme Court in *Brown v. Board of Education of Topeka* struck down the doctrine of "separate but equal"—dissolving the legal underpinnings for segregated schools. The Montgomery Bus Boycott of 1955–1956 challenged segregation in one important city.

Between 1948 and 1960 politicians in the Deep South fretted publicly about these changes. The dissident Democrats leading the charge did not rush into the Republican fold, although the GOP at times benefited from these protests. Most observers regarded the parties as similar in their tepid support for civil rights. In 1948 disgruntled Whites in Louisiana, Mississippi, Alabama, and South Carolina delivered their state's electoral votes to the "Dixiecrat" candidate, Strom Thurmond. Anger was expressed in 1952 and

1956, although no candidates were fielded. In 1960 Harry Byrd, a conservative Democrat, brandished the same states' rights slogans and gained the electoral votes of Mississippi and Alabama.[7] Still, this dissension was only a prelude to the politics of race that would soon emerge.

The civil rights movement intensified in the 1960s and, with strong government support, recorded significant gains. Among the protests were the sit-ins, which began at Woolworth's in Greensboro, North Carolina, in 1960; the Freedom Rides in 1961; the March on Washington in 1963; and Freedom Summer in 1964, which focused on voter registration in Mississippi.[8] In response, lawmakers, led by President Johnson, adopted a series of far-reaching measures. The Civil Rights Act of 1964 banned discrimination in public facilities, while the Voting Rights Act of 1965 removed the barriers that disenfranchised African Americans across the South. Black voting soared in the old Confederacy. Other Great Society measures addressed gaps in the New Deal welfare programs—and did so without excluding African Americans. The Social Security Act of 1965 funded Medicare for older Americans, while Medicaid assisted welfare recipients. These initiatives, and related acts like the Food Stamp program and Head Start for preschoolers, helped the poorest Americans, and particularly Blacks. The proportion of African Americans living below the poverty line fell from 55.1 percent in 1959 to 33.5 percent in 1968.[9]

These initiatives stirred up a hornet's nest of resentment in the South and across the nation. After LBJ signed the Civil Rights Act, an aide asked him why he looked so troubled. "I think we just delivered the South to the Republican Party for a long time to come," he replied. That prediction was premature by about forty years, but the 1964 election would be the last time a majority of Whites voted

Democratic. And only in one subsequent election (Jimmy Carter in 1976) would the Democrats sweep the South.[10]

George Wallace's campaigns for the presidency in 1964, 1968, and 1972 revealed the new politics of race. Few Americans could doubt where Wallace stood on civil rights. In his January 1963 inaugural address as governor he declared, "Segregation now! Segregation tomorrow! Segregation forever!" That June, in an event watched by a large television audience, Wallace stood at the door to the University of Alabama to block the admission of Black students. In 1964, however, when he launched the first of his three runs at the presidency, Wallace discarded the overt racism that discomfited many Northerners otherwise sympathetic to his views. Indeed, when a reporter later asked him about his inaugural speech, Wallace explained, "I made mistakes in the sense that I should have clarified my position more. I was never saying anything that reflected upon black people, and I'm very sorry that it was taken that way."[11]

Wallace's public remarks may have been scrubbed of hateful epithets, but his point of view remained clear. He became one of the first and most proficient practitioners of what Ian López calls "dog whistle politics." Few of the raucous, mostly male audience packed into Madison Square Garden in October 1968 were fooled by his disclaimer, "I'm not talking about race," when he went on to declare, "Anarchy prevails today in the streets of the large cities." He condemned fair housing laws, bussing for integration, and funding for those who might become rioters.[12] Wallace's identitarian politics suggested the pattern of many future campaigns. He exalted the "producers," the "beauticians, the truck drivers, the office workers, the policemen and the small businessmen." He mocked liberals, the "hypocrites who send your kids half-way across town while they have their chauffeur drop their children off at private schools." More broadly, Wallace appealed to those individuals (as the journalist Pete Hamill observed) who "want to return to a time in America when you lived in the same house all of your life and knew everybody you would ever care to know on the street where you were born."[13] Many were receptive to this message. In 1968, the highwater mark for his popularity, Wallace received almost ten million votes as well as the electoral support of five Southern states.

The lesson of Wallace's campaigns—the broad appeal of coded racism—was not lost on other politicians. Richard Nixon, who vied with Wallace in 1968, carefully targeted his law-and-order ads, gloating that one such announcement "hits it right on the nose. . . . [I]t's all about law and order and those damn Negro-Puerto Rican groups out there."[14] His close adviser, John Ehrlichman, explained that Nixon discussed crime and housing in terms that allowed a voter to "avoid admitting to himself that he was attracted by a racist appeal."[15]

Ronald Reagan mined the same vein in his successful 1980 and 1984 runs for the presidency. His stump speech detailed the misdeeds of a "Chicago welfare queen," who has "eighty names, thirty addresses, [and] twelve Social Security cards. . . . She's got Medicaid, getting food stamps, and she is collecting welfare under each of her names." Often, she drove a Cadillac. Reagan also explained that the food stamp program was helping "some young fellow ahead of you to buy a T-bone steak," while "you were waiting in line to buy hamburger." On occasion, Reagan slipped and described the young man as a "strapping young buck," a veiled reference to African Americans.[16]

Reagan's other actions illuminate the recurrent patterns of identitarian politics. Like Wallace, he celebrated an earlier, untroubled time. His "Morning in America" campaign ads depicted small-town America with its picket fences, parades, and friendly neighbors. The counterpart of attacks on welfare was tax breaks for the elite. Reagan lowered the top marginal tax rates from 70 to 28 percent, saving the rich hundreds of millions of dollars. Billionaires applauded politicians like Reagan who focused on race rather than class.[17] Reagan's anti-Black animus was evident in his decision to reinvigorate the "War on Drugs," which Nixon had launched in 1971. Despite comparable levels of drug use among Whites and African Americans, arrests of Blacks soared during the 1980s, climbing from twice to ten times the rate for Whites.[18]

George H. W. Bush, who had been Reagan's vice president, similarly resorted to "dog whistle" appeals in his successful 1988 campaign for the presidency. Although Bush had been a moderate Republican, he eagerly tied his opponent, Michael Dukakis, to Willie Horton, an African American criminal. As governor of Massachusetts, Dukakis had approved a weekend furlough for Horton, who stabbed a man and raped his fiancée. Pollsters confirmed that those ads, more than any other single factor, led to Dukakis's defeat. In office, Bush expanded the incarceration of young Black men, opposed affirmative action, and retreated on civil rights enforcement.[19]

Bill Clinton showed that Democrats too could attract those angry White voters. From one vantage, Clinton's ability to please warring groups seems almost magical. He reached out to African Americans, appearing with activist Jesse Jackson and playing the saxophone on the Arsenio Hall show. Toni Morrison called him the "first black president." But at the same time Clinton successfully courted the disgruntled Whites who had cheered Wallace and Reagan, winning at least seven Southern states in each of his elections. At a gathering hosted by Jackson, he pointedly criticized the Black rap artist, Sister Souljah, for her anti-White rhetoric. He interrupted his campaign to oversee the execution of Ricky Ray Rector, a mentally impaired Black man, commenting, "I can be nicked a lot, but no one can say I'm soft on crime." As president, he oversaw "tough on crime" laws that dramatically expanded the prison population and created disparate sentences for crack cocaine (used by Blacks) and powder cocaine (used by Whites). His 1996 welfare reform act limited eligibility to five years, banned anyone convicted of a felony drug offense, and provided incentives for states to remove individuals from the rolls—all steps that disproportionately hurt African Americans.[20]

Still, despite the prejudice broadcast by a series of politicians, realignment around race and other cultural issues did not come until the 2010s. The failure of the Republican firebrand Pat Buchanan illustrates how the political establishment held firm in the 1990s. Buchanan championed views similar to those Trump would later espouse.[21] He railed against immigrants—the "millions of undocumented aliens [who] break our laws, cross our borders, and demand social benefits paid for with the tax dollars of American citizens." He condemned the liberal doctrines forced upon schoolchildren ("Their minds are being poisoned against their Judeo-Christian heritage") and called for an "America first" foreign policy. He promised "to make our Country America the beautiful again."[22] But Buchanan was unable to break the grip traditional Republicans had on the party. George H. W. Bush defeated him in the 1992 presidential primaries, as did Bob Dole in the

1996 balloting. In 2000 Buchanan ran as the Reform Party candidate and received 0.4 percent of the popular vote. Only with the anger and resentment that followed Obama's election did voters coalesce in a party that elevated a populist demagogue.[23]

III

A second development paved the way for the new alignment that, ultimately, would elect Trump. Democrats moved away from their reliance on the working class, drew closer to the elites on the coast, and gradually became the advocates of socially progressive causes. As Trump supporters would describe this change, the Democrats became the party of affluent, politically correct, secular-minded, condescending liberals. That trend put into play a large group of less wealthy White voters who traditionally had supported the Democrats.

Initially, unions and big city bosses were remarkably influential in the Democratic Party that had emerged in the 1930s. But their power lessened markedly with the reforms adopted in 1972. Delegations attending that year's convention had to adhere to guidelines shaped by gender, race, and age. No provisions were made for unions or the working class, and the party gradually drifted toward a more business-friendly outlook. The reformed Democratic Party favored candidates—like George McGovern in 1972, Walter Mondale in 1984, and Michael Dukakis in 1988—who were progressive on social issues but less appealing to broader constituencies. Those three presidential hopefuls were roundly defeated in both the popular and electoral votes.[24]

The Democratic Party also fielded two winning candidates— Jimmy Carter and Bill Clinton. They muted their position on race, distanced themselves from the working class, and embodied the reformed party's new pro-business outlook. Upset by Watergate and the messy unwinding of the Vietnam War, voters elevated Jimmy Carter in 1976. Carter smoothed his ascent by reassuring fellow Southerners that he would be cautious in pursuing integration. He proved himself a "new" Democrat by turning a cold shoulder to appeals from labor, cutting taxes for the rich, bailing out the Chrysler corporation, and deregulating the airline industry.[25]

As president, Bill Clinton reaffirmed the new orientation of the party, announcing, "The era of big government is over." His leanings had long been clear: before running for office, Clinton chaired the Democratic Leadership Council, a centrist advisory group. His administration backed away from helping the poor but did not end assistance to big business. While eliminating welfare programs and fumbling an attempt at expanding health care (with a proposal that catered to special interests), Clinton lowered capital gains taxes and deregulated telecoms. He pleased the financial community by repealing the Glass-Steagall Act, a New Deal measure that separated commercial and investment banking. Quashing that law led to speculative ventures and, eventually, to the Great Recession of 2008–2009. Clinton also pushed for the North American Free Trade Agreement, arguing it would benefit workers. In fact, NAFTA allowed manufacturers to move plants to Mexico and cut American jobs.

With his appeal to professionals and high-income earners, Clinton helped redraw party lines, a process that would culminate in Trump's election. The coastal elites (and kindred spirits in cities such as Chicago and Denver) became a particular source of party strength. California, which had voted Republican in every election save one (1964) between 1952 and 1988, now moved firmly into the

Democratic column. These new affluent partisans benefited from globalization and a skewed income distribution that favored the top few percent. Many drew their wealth from financial services and the tech sector. At the same time, poorer White Americans, once loyal to the party of the New Deal, increasingly felt adrift, unsure which politicians to support.[26]

The Democrats also carved out a more progressive approach to social issues—positions that enraged future Trump supporters. The party of the Kennedys and Clinton supported women's issues, while Republicans following Ronald Reagan's lead opposed the Equal Rights Amendment and abortion rights. Clinton sought to end the long-standing ban on gays in the military (although his compromise proposal, "Don't Ask, Don't Tell," satisfied no one). But these "progressive" policies never included raising taxes on the rich or seriously addressing the needs of impoverished communities.

Still, at the beginning of the new millennium party lines were not as deeply etched as they would become after 2016. White voters with only a high school education, a group that would become a mainstay of the Trump coalition, divided equally between Democrats and Republicans. Many traditional Republicans served in Congress and occupied statehouses. In the mid-1990s, for example, 23 percent of Republicans were more liberal than the median Democrat. (By 2014 that figure would plummet to 4 percent, and with Trump those few apostates would disappear.)[27] Nor did dramatic change occur during George W. Bush's two terms (2001–2009). In those years, as polls and studies of congressional voting reveal, Republicans became slightly more moderate than they had been in the 1990s. Bush's "compassionate conservatism" included the expansion of Medicare and education reform.

However, with the attacks of 9/11 and the wars launched against two Middle Eastern countries, a new group, Muslims, was added to the list of those most hated.[28]

IV

The election of Barack Obama was the third and most immediate reason for the creation of the coalition that carried Trump into office. For many, the first Black president was both an unfortunate reality and a symbol of everything going wrong in the nation. Obama's presidency (2009–2017) helped transform a loose conglomeration of disgruntled White voters, not tightly affiliated with one party, into a larger, angrier group, firmly allied with the Republicans and resolute in its defense of White identity and Christian values.

In some respects, Obama was a "new" Democrat in the tradition of Carter and Clinton. He surrounded himself with advisers drawn from Wall Street, extended the tax cuts he inherited from Bush, and bailed out the bankers whose greed and shady practices precipitated the Great Recession. He was the first Democratic president to receive more donations from Wall Street than his Republican opponent. He also took a hard line on immigration, expelling over 1.4 million undocumented individuals.[29]

But for many White Christian voters, Obama also embodied all that was unsettling about the "New Democrats." The new president endorsed same-sex marriage and the full acceptance of gays in the military. Although many saw him as the "Deporter-in-Chief," Obama also created a special, protected status for the "Dreamers," the more than six hundred thousand undocumented immigrants brought to the United States as children. At times he displayed the condescension that alienated many disgruntled Whites. During the 2008 campaign he castigated his opponents, saying it was not surprising that "they get bitter, they cling to guns or religion or antipathy toward people who aren't like them or anti-immigrant sentiment or anti-trade sentiment as a way to explain their frustrations." Many falsely believed that his admission to Harvard reflected the affirmative action that pushed minorities to the front of the line. Finally, Obama, acting at times like an old-school Democrat, favored initiatives, like the Affordable Care Act, that rewarded the "undeserving."[30]

The volcanic rage directed toward Obama and his policies erupted soon after he entered office. On February 19, 2009, a month after the inauguration, CNBC television reporter Rick Santelli denounced Obama's proposed aid to homeowners facing foreclosure. Quietly ignoring the millions given to bankers and the questionable practices of those financiers, Santelli focused on the individuals who had missed mortgage payments. He declared, "The government is rewarding bad behavior!" and invited viewers to protest with a "tea party."[31] Eight days later rallies occurred in forty cities, while still larger gatherings convened on Tax Day, April 15. A thousand Tea Party groups formed. It was as if lightning had struck the floor of a parched forest, igniting a conflagration. The Tea Partiers were the shock troops of the new movement. While about two hundred thousand people attended the various meetings, polls show that (depending on the question asked) between 18 and 30 percent of Americans supported their views—percentages that should be doubled if the focus is on the Republican Party. Among those applauding these protests, although few joined the Tea Party, were poorer Whites with no more than a high school education. Many of them lived in rural areas or in smaller towns.

Tea Partiers advocated for many issues, but the movement is best understood as the defense of a White, Christian identity that was (they felt) increasingly under attack. Members were well aware of the demographic changes that threatened the dominance of churchgoing White people. Non-Hispanic Whites, who had comprised 75.6 percent of the population in 1990, were only 63.8 percent of the total in 2010, and that freefall, it was clear, would continue. Any understanding of this protest must rely on two excellent books: Theda Skocpol and Vanessa Williams's *The Tea Party and the Remaking of Republican Conservatism* (2012) and Arlie Hochschild's *Strangers in Their Own Land: Anger and Mourning on the American Right—a Journey to the Heart of Our Political Divide* (2016). These authors spent many months and, in Hochschild's case, years, attending meetings and speaking at length to protesters. They tell similar stories.[32]

Obama represented everything that angered the Tea Partiers. He was part of the liberal elite that sneered at them. One Louisianan told Hochschild, "Oh, liberals think that Bible-believing Southerners are ignorant, backward, rednecks, losers. They think we're racist, sexist, homophobic, and maybe fat." Many wondered if, with his Kenyan father, he was even American; his years of schooling in Indonesia suggested he was Muslim rather than Christian. They resented his assistance to the undeserving. One individual, after assuring Skocpol and Williams, "I am not a racist," explained that Obama is "a socialist" who "got a lot of it from his father."[33]

Only indirectly did economic grievances propel the movement. The fading of the American dream, declining economic mobility, and rising inequality did not lead these Republicans to criticize the very rich or large companies. Members of the Tea Party were usually older adults, often in comfortable circumstances, though not wealthy. They directed the anger that came from narrowing opportunities at the groups they felt were "cutting in line," not at the inequities of capitalism.[34]

The relationship between the Tea Party and billionaire backers like the Koch family was complex. David Koch and Charles Koch helped fund the movement, and the protesters welcomed that support. Through FreedomWorks, Americans for Prosperity, and Tea Party Patriots, the Kochs sought to channel this dissent toward their goals, which included ending environmental regulations, shrinking the government ("down to the size where it could be drowned in a bathtub," as Grover Norquist said), cutting taxes, and restricting the right to vote. Advocates like Norquist and politicians such as Paul Ryan of Wisconsin enthusiastically endorsed this ideology. Tea Partiers agreed with much of the Kochs' free market agenda but dissented in one important area: they wanted Social Security and Medicare strengthened, not weakened. They considered themselves "deserving" recipients of that government largesse. Another magnate—Rupert Murdoch—through his ownership and management of Fox News also had an outsized influence on the Tea Party. Far and away the most watched network, Fox did more than report on events—it helped plan and publicize them. Its distortions of Obama's programs intensified Tea Party anger.[35]

Along with unsettling demographic trends and the presence of Obama in the White House, what made Tea Partiers feel like "strangers in their own land" was the perception that government had shunted them aside to help the undeserving. Favors offered to minorities raised taxes and relegated White men to the back of the line. One man told Hochschild, "I don't like the government paying unwed mothers to have a lot of kids, and I don't go for affirmative action."[36] Like other Tea Partiers, he had stories about privileged Blacks collecting government payments. Many felt the issue was a moral one: hard work, not the dole, should be the path to success. A Tea Party bumper sticker announced, "You are not ENTITLED to what I have EARNED." For similar reasons they despised illegal immigrants and refugees. While women were active in the Tea Parties, most members—55 to 60 percent—were men and denounced programs that advantaged women.[37]

For many Tea Partiers, deeply held Christian beliefs only compounded their alienation. In a 2010 poll almost 40 percent of members described themselves as evangelical Christians, and their voices frequently dominated local meetings. These believers decried the growing tolerance shown to same-sex couples and transgender individuals, the widespread access to abortion, and the rise of secularism. One woman noted, "There are fewer and fewer white Christians like us," while another complained, "science has become a religion." Tea Partiers clung to the truths they had known since childhood and would not be bullied by so-called experts. They substituted conspiracies for the explanations put forth by the mainstream press.[38]

Tea Party members trod a careful line on race. They avoided racial epithets directed against Blacks (they were less scrupulous in discussing Muslims and Mexicans) and welcomed African American speakers who shared their views. Still, as George Wallace showed, racism does not require offensive language. Often drawing upon personal observations, Tea Partiers argued Blacks were poor because they had a "plantation mentality," avoided hard work, and had too many children. They dismissed the idea that discrimination hindered African Americans. The truly disadvantaged group, they asserted, was White people.[39]

The Tea Partiers and the many Republicans who sympathized with their views triumphed in the 2010 elections. They gained sixty-three seats in the House of Representatives and wrested control of twenty state legislatures from the Democrats. As a result, in much of the country Republicans controlled the redistricting that followed the 2010 census, drawing partisan maps that locked in their gains. The new assemblies took up a wish list of social legislation, such as restrictions on abortion.[40]

Still, on a national level few seemed to be listening. The Democrats had moved steadily to the left (at least on social issues), while the Republican nominees for president—John McCain and Mitt Romney—hewed too close to the center. No one spoke for these discontented, hardworking citizens, no one . . . until the candidacy of Donald Trump.[41]

V

The developments that structure this essay suggest the extraordinary possibility for change that lurked within the political order in 2016—but it took Trump to bring together and animate that large bloc of disgruntled voters. To recapitulate: first, for many years politicians had used racist appeals to gain the votes of those who feared the encroachment of minorities. Second, the Democrats cut their working-class allies adrift, catered to the coastal elites, and became ever more politically correct. Third, the election of a Black president, along with adverse demographic trends, deeply distressed a large swath of voters. Still, forging a winning coalition required a leader with the racist views, rhetorical skills, and political genius of Donald Trump (although his critics might gasp at those words).

Trump, with his victories in 2016 and 2024 and his strong showing in 2020, transformed the Republican Party. He changed it from an organization whose leaders were at home in America's country clubs to one dominated by White Christian nationalists. The two aspects of the new MAGA coalition—its ideology and base of support—are closely connected but can be teased apart for the sake of analysis.

A shared approach to race was the most important concern that brought together Trump's following. Trump was well positioned to lead this group: racism was a recurrent theme in his career. In 1974 when the Justice Department sued the Trumps for discriminating against Blacks in the apartment buildings they owned, Donald Trump, as spokesman for the family firm, angrily denied the charges and countersued the government. Ultimately, the Trumps agreed to change their practices. In 1989 after four Blacks and one Hispanic youth were arrested for raping a White woman in Central Park, Trump took out full-page ads calling for the death penalty. He was unconvinced when DNA evidence overturned the convictions in 2002 and incensed when New York City paid restitution to the five. Trump did not originate the "birther" claim that Obama was born outside the United States, but he did more than any individual to spread the lie.[42]

The 2016 Republican primary underscored the importance of White identity in forging new party lines. Pundits confidently predicted Trump could never defeat the sixteen other more experienced candidates who contested the Republican nomination. But one by one they fell away, including the last three standing: John Kasich, Marco Rubio, and Ted Cruz. Polling shows that the voters who condemned immigrants, disliked Muslims, and blamed Black poverty on lack of effort shunned Kasich and Rubio, had lukewarm

TABLE 3. Views of Those Supporting the Presidential Candidates in 2020

	Percent Agreeing with Statements	
Statement	Biden Voters	Trump Voters
Racism is an enduring part of society.	85	28
White people have advantages because of their skin.	86	18
The Democratic Party is trying to replace the current electorate with people from poorer countries.	9	66

Source: University of Massachusetts Amherst, "CRT & Race in America," Dec. 2021 national poll, https://polsci.umass.edu/toplines-and-crosstabs-december-2021-national-poll-crt-race-america.

feelings about Cruz, and propelled Trump to victory. No attribute correlated more fully with support for Trump than the belief that Whites were a threatened group.[43]

A 2021 survey, presented in table 3, underscores the continuing strength of racism in defining the two parties.

Trump's attacks on non-White immigrants amplified these prejudices. During the 2016 campaign Trump declared that the Mexicans crossing the border are "bringing crime. They're rapists." His blunt solution: "I will build a great, great wall. . . . And I will have Mexico pay for that wall."[44] Shortly after entering office in 2017, Trump banned arrivals from seven predominantly Muslim countries—an order that the courts forced him to modify. He complained about "having all these people from shithole countries come here," singling out Haiti, Africa, and El Salvador, and suggesting, "we should have more people from Norway."[45] (Much like his embrace of Norwegians, Trump welcomed Afrikaners, a group of White farmers who, he claimed, were the victims of "unjust and immoral practices" by the Black majority in South Africa.)[46] Rants against these unwanted arrivals became the centerpiece of his rallies. Undocumented immigrants, he stated, were "poisoning the blood of our country."[47] Haitians were a particular object of his scorn. In 2024 he spread false information about Springfield, Ohio, a town that experienced a large influx of Haitian immigrants. "In Springfield," he announced, "they're eating the dogs, the people that came in. They're eating the cats."[48]

These racial views were also evident in Trump's attacks on school curricula and in his relentless efforts, during his second term, to root out DEI (diversity, equity, and inclusion) initiatives from every level of the government. He did not see those programs as ones that widened opportunities for groups that had historically faced discrimination. Rather, he judged "DEI hires" (typically, women and people of color) as inherently inferior. With no evidence except his biases, he blamed wildfires in California and a plane crash in the Potomac on individuals elevated by those programs. He declared that the Federal Aviation Administration had "determined that the work force was too white."[49]

Trump also embraced a set of "culture war" issues, making clear the MAGA coalition reflected the values of White *Christian* nationalists. When contemplating his presidential bid, Trump had his staff monitor conservative talk radio. They reported that "the GOP base was frothing over a handful of issues," particularly abortion. Even before the 2016 campaign Trump switched from pro-choice to pro-life. Evangelicals were delighted when he appointed three conservative judges, carefully vetted by the Federalist Society, to the Supreme Court. The results were what Trump hoped for and his followers had long desired. The tribunal limited access to abortion by overturning *Roe v. Wade*, expanded protections for Christian prayers, and struck down restrictions on gun ownership.[50] Trump also joined his voice to those denouncing transgender individuals. "[T]here are only two genders: male and female," he announced in his 2025 inauguration.[51]

Not surprisingly for a party that wanted to return to an imaginary past ("Make America Great Again") and restricted the right of women to control their bodies, MAGA voters supported a leader who was unabashedly misogynistic and celebrated hypermasculinity. Trump's harsh comments about women preceded his presidential campaigns. In the *Access Hollywood* tapes, recorded in 2005 but released in October 2016, he bragged: "And when you're a star, they let you do it . . . . Grab them by the p---y. You can do anything."[52] Trump insulted both men and women, but he more often focused on appearance in criticizing women. In his first campaign he railed against Carly Fiorina, who also sought the nomination. He said, "Look at that face. Would anyone vote for that?" More than twenty women complained about his unwanted advances. In 2023 E. Jean Carroll, who took Trump to court over sexual abuse, won an $83 million defamation suit. In 2024 he made clear his patriarchal outlook, vowing to be a "protector" of women, adding, "Well, I'm going to do it, whether the women like it or not."[53] Trump's fascination with tough, "real" men was the counterpart of his misogyny. The wrestler Hulk Hogan, who dramatically ripped off his shirt to reveal a MAGA slogan, spoke at the 2024 Republican National Convention. Ultimate Fighting Championship CEO Dana White shared the stage with Trump after the 2024 victory.[54]

Unmoored from the groups that once dominated the GOP, Trump abandoned the party's traditional views on the economy. In 2016 he attacked both old-line Republicans and Democrats, like the Clintons, for backing the North American Free Trade

Agreement and the Trans-Pacific Partnership Agreement. He labeled NAFTA "the single worst trade deal ever approved in this country," arguing that the agreement hurt workers.[55] The broad popularity of that contention pleased his followers and forced Democrats to reconsider their position. His bold, simplistic solutions to the country's economic problems attracted many voters. In 2016 he declared that he would raise taxes on the rich and take on Big Pharma, which was "getting away with murder."[56] His proposals in 2024 were still more extensive. Cutting taxes, he declared, would spur growth. Deporting immigrants would solve the housing crisis. High tariffs would revive American manufacturing.[57]

In fact, Trump's policies disproportionately helped the rich. After he took office in 2017, he did not fight Big Pharma or stop the export of jobs overseas. His 2017 tax cut overwhelmingly benefited the top few percent, while adding trillions to the deficit. Tariffs, which ultimately are a tax on consumers, burden the poor, who spend most of their income, more than the rich, who proportionately save more. His Labor Department reduced funding for workplace safety and restricted the ability of workers to sue. His pro-business leanings were also reflected in his choices of billionaires for administrative posts. In 2024 he solicited campaign funds from oil companies, promising them more drilling. He praised Elon Musk for firing workers, calling him the "greatest cutter."[58]

Trump's foreign policy broke from the expansionism of post–World War II presidents, but in two wildly different ways. On the one hand, he despised traditional alliances, viewing NATO in transactional terms and harshly criticizing those allies who did not pay their share of defense costs. When his military advisers explained that America's presence around the Pacific would help him sleep at night, he replied: "I sleep like a fucking baby at night. I don't need anything out there."[59] His reverence for strong men tugged him away from the country's long-standing partnerships. Trump admires rulers such as Vladimir Putin, Xi Jinping, Kim Jong-un, Viktor Orbán, and Recep Erdoğan—who share his dislike of liberal democracy and progressive measures.[60] On the other hand, Trump's bluster was reminiscent of an earlier, imperialist era. In 2025 he called on the US to seize the Panama Canal ("vital to our country") and Greenland (for "national security purposes"), and did not rule out taking military action to accomplish those goals. He suggested using economic pressure to make Canada the fifty-first state.[61]

Hand in hand with Trump's dramatic recasting of Republican ideology was his transformation of the party's voting base. The realignment Trump presided over in 2016–2020 (if it lasts) is comparable to the shifts in party structure in 1856–1860 and 1932–1936. In each case, while there are continuities with older voting patterns, a new order emerged.

One key component of that shift was the movement of less wealthy White Americans into the Republican Party. These individuals, who had once been New Deal stalwarts, had gradually drifted away from the party of FDR. By the early 2000s these voters consistently backed neither party. They often favored Republicans but liked Bill Clinton's flair and Obama's "audacity of hope." With Trump's nomination, poorer Whites became the bedrock of the recast GOP, in 2020 comprising over half of all Republican voters.

A 2021 Pew analysis of the Republican coalition labels the most outspoken members of this group the "Populist Right" and suggests those partisans comprised 25 percent of MAGA voters. Typically these individuals came from rural areas and small towns and had no more than a high school education. They denounced globalization, resented trade deals, and favored higher corporate taxes. But even more than economic policies, social conservatism attracted them. Increasingly, their rage focused on immigrants and people of color who (they felt) took jobs from deserving White Christians.[62]

A second group—the "Faith and Flag Conservatives"—also played a prominent role in the MAGA coalition, and like the Populist Right formed about a quarter of Trump voters. These individuals had long been aligned with the GOP, and their commitment to the party only increased with Trump's ascent. The Faith and Flag Conservatives are largely evangelical Christians; many had been Tea Party members. The group is passionate about cultural issues, including abortion and school prayer. They furiously oppose trans rights, restrictions on gun ownership, and school curricula that hint at "critical race theory." They agree with the Populist Right about immigrants, Blacks, and the threats faced by White Americans, but do not criticize big business.[63] While they urge the government to reduce transfers to the "undeserving," they fiercely defend their own entitlement payments. Trump defied Republican orthodoxy and courted these individuals by declaring he would "Save Medicare, Medicaid and Social Security without cuts."[64] These two groups comprise the most passionate group of Trump supporters; they turn out for primary contests and are the most active campaigners in general elections.

The remaining half of Trump voters are less fervently committed to Trump's agenda, although still sympathetic to his efforts to seal the border and purge "woke" doctrines. Important numerically, most view Reagan, not Trump, as the ideal president. Many are small town or rural folk, have been lifelong Republicans, or are professionals whose loyalties date back to the days when the Republicans commanded much of the upper middle class. Along with these individuals, who have steadfastly backed the GOP, millions of voters in 2024 swung to Trump because of the promises he made about combating inflation and improving the economy. Thanks to this groundswell, the popular vote for Trump increased from 46.1 percent in 2016 and 46.8 percent in 2020 to 49.8 percent in 2024.[65]

Corporate titans, including oil executives like the Kochs and tech billionaires such as Peter Thiel and Elon Musk, comprise a small but influential element within the party. Their relations with Trump are largely transactional; some who registered mild dissent during his first administration courted him after his 2024 victory, when his mandate was stronger and his attacks on enemies more ruthless. They hope that their newfound enthusiasm and large donations will mean government contracts, fewer regulations, lower taxes, and more generally favorable treatment.[66] The array of billionaires in his cabinet and attending his 2025 inauguration attests to the increased importance of the very rich in his second administration. Trump has assembled the unlikely coalition that marks modern Populist regimes: he heads a party that dispenses favors to the top few percent while securing the support of the less wealthy.

The groups *abandoning* the Republicans illustrate the other part of the realignment of 2016–2020. The wealthiest third of Americans, who long had supported the GOP, are now Democrats. College graduates, traditionally divided in their loyalties, overwhelmingly cheered Biden and Harris. In many respects, the new makeup of the two parties has turned the New Deal alignment on its head.[67]

Other lines of division are also present and bring the MAGA coalition into sharper focus. Since Ronald Reagan's presidency a gender gap has shaped politics, with women more likely to favor the Democrats and men the Republicans. With Trump that split has widened and become a chasm that divides most groups, including Black, White, and Hispanic voters, as well as age and wealth strata. While White women favored Trump, they did so by far smaller margins than White men.[68] Race continues to matter. Even with Trump's gains in 2024, Black men and women overwhelmingly backed the Democrats. The same pattern held for Hispanic men and women, except in 2024, when a majority of Hispanic men voted for Trump. In 2020 non-Whites (Blacks, Hispanics, and "others") comprised 15 percent of Republican voters and 39 percent of Democrats.[69] Age was also a factor. Far more than any age cohort, young voters (eighteen to twenty-nine) applauded the Democrats, a leaning that held, if narrowly, in 2024.[70]

The 2024 election sheds light on the realigned parties. Trump's victory—he won the popular vote and the electoral college, while his party gained the Senate and retained control of the House—was part of a global wave of anti-incumbency. Inflation and the lingering effects of the pandemic angered electorates everywhere. Polls show that for American voters the economy (39 percent) was the top issue, far ahead of immigration (21 percent), or abortion (11 percent). Assessing the problems facing homeowners and businesspeople, most economists condemn Trump's solutions: massive deportations, high tariffs, and tax cuts that favor the rich. But his impassioned presentation of these ideas during the campaign and his focus on the hardships people experienced proved a winning strategy. These "issues" did not fundamentally reshape party lines, but they added an important group to the MAGA loyalists.[71]

By contrast, the Democrats lost ground in 2024 and have wandered far from the days of FDR's New Deal and LBJ's Great Society, when their party platforms excited a wide swath of voters. The Affordable Care Act ("Obamacare") adopted in 2010 was the rare recent example of an impactful, long-lived Democratic social program. Kamala Harris campaigned on democracy and the preservation of reproductive rights, issues that did not speak to the concerns of a hotel worker in Las Vegas who could barely afford groceries and had given up the dream of buying a house. The Democrats have a progressive wing, but it does not shape party policies. A member of that group, Senator Bernie Sanders, acerbically noted: "It should come as no great surprise that a Democratic Party which has abandoned working class people would find that the working class has abandoned them."[72] The Democratic Party may have had the better position on democracy, climate change, abortion, trans rights, gun control, religious freedom, sexism, and racism. But in an election that turned on the economy, that platform had grave shortcomings.

The rise of Trump can be viewed within the book's framework. Racism, a large part of his appeal, has long been integral to the American story. Since the 1960s African Americans have recorded noteworthy gains, even if those advances have not eradicated prejudice or inequality. The triumph of Trump and the MAGA coalition suggests the slowing or even reversal of those advances. Trump's opposition to the expansionist imperatives of Cold War America is also significant, although his blustering foreign policy pronouncements make his course unclear. If Trump does back away from intervening around the globe, the US and other nations will benefit. Expansionism, a central theme of US history, has had a very mixed legacy.[73]

Conclusion and Acknowledgments

As recent battles over school curricula, books, monuments, and public holidays make clear, history matters. How we view the past shapes how we regard the present. It helps us discern the roots of current problems and pursue necessary changes. Despite fierce disagreements over race, most Americans, in both red and blue states, learn a version of history that emphasizes high ideals and progress. The Revolution is about "liberty," the Civil War about "freedom." The grave challenges Americans have faced, such as slavery; the disenfranchisement of Blacks, women, and less wealthy Whites (those groups overlap); and the lack of civil rights for African Americans, have been solved or are being addressed in the stately march to a "more perfect union." If America has erred in some foreign ventures, the country generally is a force for good in the world.

This book challenges those myths and suggests a different narrative. It argues that at the heart of the American story are the demands of affluent citizens for economic growth and territorial expansion. This dynamic underlay the two events—the Revolution and the Civil War—that provide the foundation for the United States. An expansion-minded group, led by individuals like George

Washington and Benjamin Franklin, emerged in the colonies by the mid-eighteenth century. Before 1763 they campaigned against the French and their Indian allies; after 1763, working toward the same goal—a mighty New World "empire"—they fought the British. Independence was a stepping stone and the Constitution a key achievement in realizing their vision—but for these leaders, growth had no bounds. While some Revolutionaries spoke about human rights, such high-minded values remained subordinate in an elitist patriarchal society. Southerners were unbending in their demands for the protection of slavery, a policy accepted by the North and sanctified in the Constitution. Racism was enshrined in the founding documents.

Similar motives—the demand for expansion—brought on the Civil War. During the first half of the nineteenth century, quarrels between Northerners and Southerners about slavery led not to war but to compromise, because strong economic ties bound the country together. That amity dissolved after midcentury, when shifts in the economy transformed the two sections. Planters and small farmers in the cotton states, particularly in their southern reaches, saw more keenly than ever the need for new territories to survive. At the same time shifting patterns of trade created in the North a self-confident regional power with its strength in New England and around the Great Lakes. That bloc had its own agenda for growth and little interest in sectional bargains.

As in the Revolution, high ideals—emancipation and equality— remained far less important than the self-interested agenda of expansion. Ending slavery was not a Northern aim until a year into the fighting, when it became a practical step in winning the war. During Reconstruction the victorious Republicans gave only half-hearted and short-lived support to the freedpeople. Northern politicians shunned land reform, allowed a repressive system of sharecropping to emerge, and made little effort to check White rage. At the end of the century Northerners stood by while White Southerners disenfranchised Blacks, erasing the last vestige of post–Civil War progress. Together the Revolution and Civil War confirmed racism as the corollary of the obsession with growth.

Challenging the Myths of US History explores the country that emerged from those two foundational events. In many respects, the expansionists of 1776 and 1861 were extraordinarily successful. These leaders, and the many who shared their views, transformed a nation that began as a ragged group of colonies hugging the Atlantic into a prosperous continental empire. Wars and diplomacy enlarged that territory to include Alaska, Hawaii, Puerto Rico, and, between 1898 and 1946, the Philippines. After the Civil War, entrepreneurs with strong support from the national and state governments built a powerful industrial nation. Successive waves of immigrants came to a country that served as a beacon for the oppressed and poor. Until recently, the US provided its citizenry with the highest standard of living in the world and the greatest social mobility.

But territorial spread and an opportunity to rise are not the only noteworthy outcomes that emerged from a country where growth was the prime directive. The toxic combination of expansionism and racism shaped the hundred years' war the new nation waged against Native peoples, campaigns that some historians label genocide.[1] American *conquistadors* expelled the Mexicans from lands they had long settled. They recruited Chinese immigrants to build the transcontinental railroad and then cut off that flow when the labor was no longer needed. Overseas, military actions and covert interventions, launched with shifting justifications and tinged with racism, served the needs of upper-class Americans far more than local populations. The results were disastrous for countries across the globe, including in Southeast Asia, the Middle East, and the Western Hemisphere.

Racism, an intrinsic part of the expansionist nation, had a far-reaching impact on American society. Every essay notes the impact of that bias, including most notably the discussion of homicides, the women's movement, and the course of American politics leading to the election of Donald Trump.

Still, there was another side to the American story. That was the determination of reformers to restrain the excesses of a society whose drive for growth often came at the expense of the less privileged. Protests shaped the path of development. Among those working for a more just society were abolitionists, labor organizers, farmers, foreign policy critics, civil rights activists, supporters of social welfare programs, and LGBTQ advocates. This book notes those campaigns and examines one closely: the women's rights movement. Any full evaluation of America's history must recognize those crosscurrents and acknowledge the promise as well as the perils of the path the nation has embarked upon.

.   .   .

Writing these seven essays has been a voyage of discovery, one that involved revisiting familiar places as well as exploring distant locales. In that quest I've benefited not only from the books and articles listed in the notes, but also from a remarkable group of individuals who generously provided guidance. Many of the scholars who assisted me I like to think of as good friends, individuals I've known for decades, although we see each other only occasionally, chiefly at conferences. Fortunately, friendship never muted their incisive critiques, and I'm deeply in debt for their close readings. This group includes Anne Boylan, Paul Buhle, David Chanoff, Boyd Cothran, Daniel Crofts, Woody Holton III, Melvyn Leffler, Bernard Lightman, Roger Lowenstein, Michael McDonnell, Arthur Redding, Randolph Roth, Frank Towers, David Waldstreicher, Gavin Wright, Karin Wulf, and Rosemarie Zagarri. Another set of readers tested these arguments and helped me keep my presentations clear, sensible, and accessible. In this group are Jamie Cameron, Aaron Davis, Robert Douglas, Mike Egnal, Ron Knowles, Neil Mather, Tim Nau, Charles Novogrodsky, George Weider, and Jamie Zeppa.

I am grateful to my editor, Niels Hooper, at University of California Press, for his support and guidance. I sought out Niels because of his long-standing engagement with books that offer a critical perspective on the American past, and I am honored to be included in the list of authors he has worked with.

Finally, as always, my family has been a wonderful source of support. My two sons, Bart and Ben, thoughtfully (and kindly) critique my writing. My wife, Judith Humphrey, is always the first person to read my drafts; they are released to the world only once they pass muster with her. Judith, Ben, Bart, and their families, including our four grandchildren, make a still greater contribution: they remind me of the inimitable joys of the present and the importance of a fuller understanding of the past for the generations to come.

Notes

Preface

1. Kevin Sullivan and Lori Rozsa, "DeSantis Doubles down on Claim That Some Blacks Benefited from Slavery," *Washington Post*, July 22, 2023, https://www.washingtonpost.com/politics/2023/07/22/desantis-slavery-curriculum/.

2. David Walstreicher, *Slavery's Constitution: From Revolution to Ratification* (New York: Hill & Wang, 2009); Robert G. Parkinson, *Thirteen Clocks: How Race United the Colonies and Made the Declaration of Independence* (Chapel Hill: University of North Carolina Press, 2021); Tamika Nunley, "Slavery and the Political Touchstones of a Young Republic," *William and Mary Quarterly*, 79.1 (2022): 135–144. Sean Wilentz, in *No Property in Man: Slavery and Antislavery at the Nation's Founding* (Cambridge, MA: Harvard University Press, 2018), offers a dissenting viewpoint.

3. Seth Cotlar, "The Contemporary Resonance of the Nation's Founding Arguments," *William and Mary Quarterly*, 78.4 (2021): 721–726.

1. Is There Progress in the Study of US History?

1. For the debate over the scientific method, see Thomas Kuhn, *The Structure of Scientific Revolutions*, 4th ed. (Chicago: University of Chicago Press, 2012); Robert Nola and Howard Sankey, *Theories of Scientific Method: An Introduction* (Stocksfield, UK: Acumen, 2007); Ronald A. Brown and Alok Kumar, "The Scientific Method: Reality or Myth?," *Journal of College Science Teaching*,

42.4 (2013): 10–11; Clyde Freeman Herreid, "The Scientific Method Ain't What It Used to Be," *Journal of College Science Teaching*, 39.6 (2010): 68–72.

2. Helge Kragh, *Cosmology and Controversy: The Historical Development of Two Theories of the Universe* (Princeton, NJ: Princeton University Press, 1996).

3. On an epistemological level, this chapter considers progress in history much like progress in science: the movement toward a fuller and more accurate understanding of reality. That quest, by its very nature, is unending, and as the text makes clear, is a more difficult pursuit in the field of history than in the sciences. See the discussion in Peter Novick, *That Noble Dream: The "Objectivity Question" and the American Historical Profession* (New York: Cambridge University Press, 1988), esp. 1–17, 415–468.

4. Oscar Handlin and Mary Handlin, "The Origins of the Southern Labor System," *William and Mary Quarterly*, 7.2 (1950): 199–222; Winthrop Jordan, *White over Black* (Chapel Hill: University of North Carolina Press, 1968), 71–82; Philip D. Morgan, *Slave Counterpoint: Black Culture in the Eighteenth-Century Chesapeake* (Chapel Hill: University of North Carolina Press, 1998), 8–18; Rebecca Anne Goetz, "Rethinking the 'Unthinking Decision': Old Questions and New Problems in the History of Slavery and Race in the Colonial South," *Journal of Southern History*, 75.3 (2009): 599–612; Michael Guasco, *Slaves and Englishmen: Human Bondage in the Early Modern Atlantic World* (Philadelphia: University of Pennsylvania Press, 2014): 195–226.

5. Abraham Lincoln, Speech, July 10, 1858, in *Collected Works of Abraham Lincoln*, ed. Roy P. Basler, 8 vols. (New Brunswick, NJ: Rutgers University Press, 1953–55), 2: 501.

6. Lincoln, "Last Public Address," Apr. 11, 1865, in *Collected Works*, 8: 403.

7. Fourth debate with Stephen A. Douglas, Sept. 18, 1858, in *Collected Works*, 3: 145–146.

8. Eric Foner, "Lincoln and Colonization," in *Our Lincoln: New Perspectives on Lincoln and His World*, ed. Eric Foner (New York: W. W. Norton, 2008), 135–166.

9. James Oakes, "Natural Rights, Citizenship Rights, States' Rights, and Black Rights: Another Look at Lincoln and Race," in *Our Lincoln*, 109–134; Eric Foner, *The Fiery Trial: Abraham Lincoln and American Slavery* (New York: W. W. Norton, 2010); James M. McPherson, *Abraham Lincoln and the Second American Revolution* (New York: Oxford University Press, 1991), 43–64; Marc Egnal, *Clash of Extremes: The Economic Origins of the Civil War* (New York: Hill

and Wang, 2009), 227–233; Stephen B. Oates, *With Malice Toward None: The Life of Abraham Lincoln* (New York: Harper & Row, 1977); David H. Donald, *Lincoln* (New York: Simon & Schuster, 1995).

10. Albert Einstein and Leopold Infeld, *The Evolution of Physics: From Early Concepts to Relativity and Quanta*, new ed. (1938; New York: Simon & Schuster, 1961), 263.

11. Howard N. Rabinowitz, "More Than the Woodward Thesis: Assessing the Strange Career of Jim Crow," *Journal of American History*, 75.3 (1988): 842–856; C. Vann Woodward, "Strange Career Critics: Long May They Persevere," *Journal of American History*, 75.3 (1988): 857–868.

12. For the links between scientific method and history, see David A. Hollinger, "T. S. Kuhn's Theory of Science and Its Implications for History," *American Historical Review*, 78.2 (1973): 370–393; Thomas L. Haskell, "Objectivity Is Not Neutrality: Rhetoric vs. Practice in Peter Novick's *That Noble Dream*," *History and Theory*, 29.2 (1990): 129–157; Raymond Martin, "The Essential Difference between History and Science," *History and Theory*, 36.1 (1997): 1–14; Raymond Martin, "Progress in Historical Studies," *History and Theory*, 37.1 (1998): 14–39.

13. Frances FitzGerald, *America Revised: History Schoolbooks in the Twentieth Century* (1979; New York: Vintage Books, 1980), 59–89. A striking exception to prevailing views was W. E. B. DuBois, *Black Reconstruction in America* (1935; New York: Atheneum, 1969).

14. FitzGerald, *America Revised*, 29–40; Joseph Moreau, *Schoolbook Nation: Conflicts over American History Textbooks from the Civil War to the Present* (Ann Arbor: University of Michigan Press, 2003), 137–174; Kyle Ward, *History in the Making: An Absorbing Look at How American History Has Changed in the Telling over the Last 200 Years* (New York: The New Press, 2006).

15. George Rawick, *From Sundown to Sunup: The Making of the Black Community* (Westport, CT: Greenwood Publishing, 1972); John W. Blassingame, *The Slave Community: Plantation Life in the Antebellum South* (New York: Oxford University Press, 1972); Eugene Genovese, *Roll, Jordan, Roll: The World the Slaves Made* (New York: Pantheon Books, 1974); Herbert G. Gutman, *The Black Family in Slavery and Freedom, 1750–1925* (New York: Vintage Books, 1976); Lawrence W. Levine, *Black Culture and Black Consciousness: Afro-American Folk Thought from Slavery to Freedom* (New York: Oxford University Press, 1977); Peter Kolchin, "Slavery in United States Survey Textbooks," *Journal of*

American History, 84.4 (1998): 1425–1438; Drew Faust et al., "Interchange: The Practice of History," *Journal of American History*, 90.2 (2003): 585.

16. Thomas C. Holt, "Reconstruction in United States History Textbooks," *Journal of American History*, 81.4 (1995): 1641–1651; Van Gosse, "Consensus and Contradiction in Textbook Treatments of the Sixties," *Journal of American History*, 82.2 (1995): 659, 664–665. Many of the advances in the writing of African American history come from the work of Black scholars. See Jacqueline Goggin, *Carter G. Woodson: A Life in Black History* (Baton Rouge: Louisiana State University Press, 1993); John Hope Franklin, *Mirror to America: The Autobiography of John Hope Franklin* (New York: Farrar, Straus and Giroux, 2005).

17. Cornelia H. Dayton and Lisa Levenstein, "The Big Tent of U.S. Women's and Gender History: A State of the Field," *Journal of American History*, 99.3 (2012): 793–817; Linda M. Ambrose, Jenny Barker Devine, and Jeannie Whayne, "Revisiting Rural Women's History," *Agricultural History*, 89.3 (2015): 380–387; Crystal N. Feimster, "The Impact of Racial and Sexual Politics on Women's History," *Journal of American History*, 99.3 (2012): 822–826; Mary E. Frederickson, "Going Global: New Trajectories in U.S. Women's History," *The History Teacher*, 43.2 (2010): 169–189; Tamar W. Carroll, "Revisiting Second Wave Histories: New Chronologies, Geographies, and Appraisals," *Journal of Women's History*, 31.3 (2019): 136–146.

18. Ned Blackhawk, "Look How Far We've Come: How American Indian History Changed the Study of American History in the 1990s," *OAH Magazine of History*, 19.6 (2005): 13–17; Susan Sleeper-Smith et al., eds., *Why You Can't Teach United States History without American Indians* (Chapel Hill: University of North Carolina Press, 2015); Philip J. Deloria, "Indigenous/American Pasts and Futures," *Journal of American History*, 109.2 (2022): 255–270.

19. Ned Blackhawk, *The Rediscovery of America: Native Peoples and the Unmaking of U.S. History* (New Haven, CT: Yale University Press, 2023), 1–13; Donald L. Fixico, ed., *Rethinking American Indian History* (Albuquerque: University of New Mexico Press, 1997); Alyssa Mt. Pleasant et al., "Materials and Methods in Native American and Indigenous Studies: Completing the Turn," *William and Mary Quarterly*, 53.2 (2018): 207–236; Jean M. O'Brien, *Firsting and Lasting: Writing Indians out of Existence in New England* (Minneapolis: University of Minnesota Press, 2010).

20. Pekka Hämäläinen, *The Comanche Empire* (New Haven, CT: Yale University Press, 2008); Pekka Hämäläinen, *Lakota America: A New History of Indigenous Power* (New Haven, CT: Yale University Press, 2019); Daniel K. Richter, *The Ordeal of the Longhouse: The Peoples of the Iroquois League in the Era of European Colonization* (Chapel Hill: University of North Carolina Press, 1992); Jennifer Nez Denetdale, *Reclaiming Diné History: The Legacies of Navajo Chief Manuelito and Juanita* (Tucson: University of Arizona Press, 2007); Katrina Jagodinsky, *Legal Codes and Talking Trees: Indigenous Women's Sovereignty in the Sonoran and Puget Sound Borderlands, 1854-1946* (New Haven, CT: Yale University Press, 2016).

21. J. Samuel Walker, "The Origins of the Cold War in United States History Textbooks," *Journal of American History*, 81.4 (1995): 1652-1661.

22. George Chauncey, *Gay New York: Gender, Urban Culture, and the Making of the Gay Male World, 1890-1940* (New York: Basic Books, 1994); Rachel Hope Cleves, "'What, Another Female Husband?': The Prehistory of Same-Sex Marriage in America," *Journal of American History*, 101.4 (2015): 1055-1081; Martin B. Duberman, Martha Vicinus, and George Chauncey Jr., eds., *Hidden from History: Reclaiming the Gay and Lesbian Past* (New York: New American Library, 1989).

23. Faust et al., "Interchange," 576-611; Stephen Tuck, "The New American Histories," *The Historical Journal*, 48.3 (2005): 811-832, esp. 816-819.

24. Richard White, "American Environmental History: The Development of a New Historical Field," *Pacific Historical Review*, 54.3 (1985): 297-335; Paul S. Sutter, "The World with Us: The State of American Environmental History," *Journal of American History*, 100.1 (2013): 94-119; Alfred W. Crosby, "The Past and Present of Environmental History," *American Historical Review*, 100.4 (1995): 1177-1189; Douglas C. Sackman, ed., *A Companion to American Environmental History* (Malden, MA: Wiley-Blackwell, 2010); Mark Fiege, *The Republic of Nature: An Environmental History of the United States* (Seattle: University of Washington Press, 2013).

25. Paul K. Longmore and Lauri Umansky, eds., *The New Disability History: American Perspectives* (New York: New York University Press, 2001); Kim E. Nielsen, *A Disability History of the United States* (Boston: Beacon, 2012).

26. Peter Charles Hoffer, *Sensory Worlds in Early America* (Baltimore, MD: Johns Hopkins University Press, 2003); Richard C. Rath, *How Early America*

Sounded (Ithaca, NY: Cornell University Press, 2003); Gerald J. Fitzgerald and Gabriella M. Petrick, "In Good Taste: Rethinking American History with Our Palates," *Journal of American History*, 95.2 (2008): 392–404; Connie Y. Chiang, "The Nose Knows: The Sense of Smell in American History," *Journal of American History*, 404–416.

27. Gary J. Kornblith, "Venturing into the Civil War, Virtually: A Review," *Journal of American History*, 88.1 (2001): 145–151; Tara McPherson, "Why Are the Digital Humanities So White? or Thinking About the Histories of Race and Computation," in *Debates in the Digital Humanities*, ed. Matthew K. Gold (Minneapolis: University of Minnesota Press, 2012), 139–160; Heidi Kurvinen, "Toward Digital Histories of Women's Suffrage Movements," in *Digital Histories: Emergent Approaches within the New Digital History*, ed. Mats Fridlund et al. (Helsinki: Helsinki University Press, 2020), 149–159; Marc Egnal, "The Evolution of the US Novel: A Statistical Approach," *Social Science History*, 37.2 (2013): 231–254.

28. Gary Nash et al., *History on Trial: Cultural Wars and the Teaching of the Past* (New York: Alfred A. Knopf, 1997), 149–277, quotes on 192, 232; John Patrick Diggins, "The National History Standards," *The American Scholar*, 65.1 (1996): 495–522; William Cronon et al., "History Forum: Teaching American History," *The American Scholar*, 67.1 (1998): 91–106.

29. Eric Foner, *The Story of American Freedom* (New York: W. W. Norton, 1998). For criticisms of that narrative, see David Blight, introduction to *Teaching Hard History: American Slavery*, Southern Poverty Law Center, 2018, 7–8, https://www.splcenter.org/20180131/teaching-hard-history; James W. Loewen, *Lies My Teacher Told Me: Everything Your American History Textbooks Got Wrong*, 2nd ed. (New York: Simon & Schuster, 2017).

30. James H. Merrell, "Second Thoughts on Colonial Historians and American Indians," *William and Mary Quarterly*, 69.3 (2012): 451–512; Michael Witgen, "Rethinking Colonial History as Continental History," *William and Mary Quarterly*, 69.3 (2012): 527–530. Two important works recast American history: Pekka Hämäläinen, *Indigenous Continent: The Epic Contest for North America* (New York: Liveright, 2022); and Blackhawk, *Rediscovery of America*.

31. Richard Rothstein, *The Color of Law: A Forgotten History of How Our Government Segregated America* (New York: Liveright Publishing, 2017), 64–67, quote on 65.

32. "Criminal Justice Fact Sheet: NAACP," May 24, 2021, https://www.naacp.org/criminal-justice-fact-sheet/; "Trends in U.S. Corrections," The Sentencing Project, May 17, 2021, https://www.sentencingproject.org/publications/trends-in-u-s-corrections/. These generalizations about textbooks hold for most survey texts, but there are regional variations—particularly in dealing with modern racial concerns (and less so in retelling the origins of the Revolution and Civil War). The major publishers modify their texts in keeping with state directives. Still, liberal California remains an outlier, while Texas establishes the norm. For example, books distributed in California mention "redlining" (which excluded Blacks from government housing assistance), but texts offered in most of the country do not. See "Two States, Eight Textbooks: Two American Stories," *New York Times*, Jan. 12, 2020, https://www.nytimes.com/interactive/2020/01/12/us/texas-vs-california-history-textbooks.html; Jill Cowan, "What California History Textbooks Tell Us," *New York Times*, Jan. 14 and Feb. 6, 2020, https://www.nytimes.com/2020/01/14/us/textbooks-history-california-texas.html.

33. Nikole Hannah-Jones, "Lead Essay," *New York Times Magazine*, Aug. 14, 2019, https://www.nytimes.com/interactive/2019/08/14/magazine/black-history-american-democracy.html; Jake Silverstein, "We Respond to the Historians Who Critiqued the 1619 Project," *New York Times Magazine*, Dec. 29, 2019, https://www.nytimes.com/2019/12/20/magazine/we-respond-to-the-historians-who-critiqued-the-1619-project.html.

34. Adam Serwer, "The Fight Over the 1619 Project Is Not About the Facts," *The Atlantic*, Dec. 23, 2019, https://www.theatlantic.com/ideas/archive/2019/historians-clash-1619-project/604093/; Philip W. Magness, "The 1619 Project Debate: A Bibliography," Jan. 3, 2020, American Institute for Economic Research, https://www.aier.org/article/the-1619-project-debate-a-bibliography/. See the video exchange between Glenn Loury and John McWhorter, https://bloggingheads.tv/videos/57295. McWhorter, an African American linguist, is critical of the 1619 Project. So is another Black scholar, Daryl Michael Scott. See "The 74 Interview," Mar. 22, 2022, www.the74million.org/article/the-74-interview-howard-historian-daryl-scott-on-grievance-history-the-1619-project-and-the-possibility-that-we-rend-ourselves-on-the-question-of-race/.

35. Jake Silverstein, "An Update to the 1619 Project," *New York Times Magazine*, Mar. 11, 2020, https://www.nytimes.com/2020/03/11/magazine/an-update-to-the-1619-project.html.

36. Silverstein, "We Respond." Alex C. Lichtenstein, in "1619 and All That," *American Historical Review*, 125.1 (2020): xv–xxi, makes concessions to the critics as part of a similar defense.

37. Allen C. Guelzo, *City Journal*, Dec. 8, 2019, https://www.city-journal .org/1619-project-conspiracy-theory.

38. Tom Mackaman, "An Interview with Historian James McPherson on the New York Times' 1619 Project," World Socialist Web Site, Nov. 14, 2019, https://www.wsws.org/en/articles/2019/11/14/mcph-n14.html.

39. Tom Mackaman, "An Interview with Historian James Oakes on the New York Times' 1619 Project," World Socialist Web Site, Nov. 18, 2019, https://www.wsws.org/en/articles/2019/11/18/oake-n18.html.

40. Tom Mackaman, "An Interview with Historian Gordon Wood on the New York Times' 1619 Project," World Socialist Web Site, Nov. 28, 2019, https://www.wsws.org/en/articles/2019/11/14/mcph-n14.html. Also see the analysis in David Waldstreicher, "The Hidden Stakes of the 1619 Controversy," *Boston Review*, Jan. 24, 2020, http://bostonreview.net/race-politics/david -waldstreicher-hidden-stakes-1619-controversy; and Leslie Harris, "I Helped Fact-Check the 1619 Project. The Times Ignored Me," *Politico*, March 6, 2020, https://www.politico.com/news/magazine/2020/03/06/1619-project-new -york-times-mistake-122248.

41. DeSantis quoted in Arelis R. Hernández and Griff Witte, "Texas Bill to Ban Teaching of Critical Race Theory . . . ," *Washington Post*, June 2, 2021; Stephen Sawchuk, "What Is Critical Race Theory, and Why Is It Under Attack?," *Education Week*, May 18, 2021; Matthew Karp, "History as End: 1619, 1776, and the Politics of the Past," *Harper's Magazine*, July 2021, https://harpers.org /archive/2021/07/history-as-end-politics-of-the-past-matthew-karp/.

2. Why the American Revolution?

1. Merrill Jensen, *The Articles of Confederation: An Interpretation of the Social-Constitutional History of the American Revolution, 1774–1781* (Madison: University of Wisconsin Press, 1940); *The New Nation: A History of the United States during the Confederation, 1781–1789* (New York: Knopf, 1950).

2. Charles Cohen, "The 'Liberty or Death' Speech: A Note on Religion and Revolutionary Rhetoric," *William and Mary Quarterly*, 38.4 (1981): 702–717.

3. Carl L. Becker, *The History of Political Parties in the Province of New York, 1760-1776* (1909; Madison: University of Wisconsin Press, 1968), 22.

4. Gordon S. Wood, "Rhetoric and Reality in the American Revolution," *William and Mary Quarterly*, 23.1 (1966): 11.

5. Edmund S. Morgan and Helen M. Morgan, *The Stamp Act Crisis: Prologue to Revolution*, rev. ed. (New York: Collier Books, 1963), 369.

6. Bernard Bailyn, "The Central Themes of the American Revolution: An Interpretation," in *Essays on the American Revolution*, ed. Stephen G. Kurtz and James H. Hutson (New York: W. W. Norton, 1973), 13; Wood, "Rhetoric and Reality," 26.

7. Paul H. Smith, "The American Loyalists: Notes on Their Organization and Numerical Strength," *William and Mary Quarterly*, 25.2 (1968): 259-277, quote on 260n.

8. On the relationship between my arguments and the work of the Progressive historian Charles Beard, see Marc Egnal, *A Mighty Empire: The Origins of the American Revolution*, with a new preface (1988; Ithaca, NY: Cornell University Press, 2010), 2-3; Marc Egnal and Joseph A. Ernst, "An Economic Interpretation of the American Revolution," *William and Mary Quarterly*, 3rd ser., 29 (1972): 3-32.

9. Jesse Lemisch, "Jack Tar in the Streets: Merchant Seamen in the Politics of Revolutionary America," *William and Mary Quarterly*, 25.3 (1968): 371–407; Staughton Lynd, *Class Conflict, Slavery and the United States Constitution: Ten Essays* (Indianapolis, IN: Bobbs-Merrill, 1967).

10. Most recent work on the Revolution either accepts the broad outlines of the neo-Whig argument or avoids a close examination of causes (suggesting the question has been solved). See, for example, Patrick Griffin, "De-decentering the Narrative: The Case for a Vast 1776," *William and Mary Quarterly*, 78.2 (2021): 229-234; Michael D. Hattem, "Revolution Lost? Vast Early America, National History, and the American Revolution," *William and Mary Quarterly*, 78.2 (2021): 269-274; Caitlin Fitz, *Our Sister Republics: The United States in an Age of American Revolutions* (New York: W. W. Norton/Liveright Publishing, 2016); Holger Hoock, *Scars of Independence: America's Violent Birth* (New York: Crown Publishing, 2017); T. H. Breen et al., "The Revolution at 250: A Conversation," *Journal of the Early Republic*, 44.4 (2024): 513-579.

11. Michael A. McDonnell, "Men Out of Time: Confronting History and Myth," *William and Mary Quarterly*, 68.4 (2011): 644-648; Gary Nash, *The Unknown American Revolution: The Unruly Birth of Democracy and the Struggle to Create America* (New York: Penguin Books, 2005); Morgan and Morgan, *Stamp Act Crisis*, 160-186.

12. May 1, 1766, *Journals of Captain John Montressor*, New York Historical Society *Collections*, 14 (1881), 363; Patricia U. Bonomi, *A Factious People: Politics and Society in Colonial New York* (New York: Columbia University Press, 1971), 221-222.

13. Marjoleine Kars, *Breaking Loose Together: The Regulator Rebellion in Prerevolutionary North Carolina* (Chapel Hill: University of North Carolina Press, 2002).

14. Woody Holton, *Forced Founders: Indians, Debtors, Slaves and the Making of the American Revolution in Virginia* (Chapel Hill: University of North Carolina Press, 1999), 164-171; Michael A. McDonnell and Woody Holton, "Patriot vs. Patriot: Social Conflict in Virginia and the Origins of the American Revolution," *Journal of American Studies*, 34 (2000): 231-256; Kars, *Breaking Loose Together*.

15. Egnal, *Mighty Empire*, 271-327. Peter Linebaugh and Markus Rediker, in *The Many-Headed Hydra: The Hidden History of the Revolutionary Atlantic* (Boston: Beacon Press, 2000), 211-247, explore the complex relationship between the common folk and wealthy revolutionaries.

16. Randolph, May 29, 1787, Gerry, May 31, 1787, Madison, June 26 1787, *The Records of the Federal Convention of 1787*, ed. Max Farrand, 4 vols. (1937; New Haven, CT: Yale University Press, 1987), 1: 26-27, 48, 423; Jackson Turner Main, *The Antifederalists: Critics of the Constitution, 1781-1788* (1961; New York: W. W. Norton, 1974), 1-71; Edward Countryman, *The American Revolution*, rev. ed. (New York: Hill and Wang, 2003), 113-165.

17. Jackson Turner Main, in *Political Parties Before the Constitution* (Chapel Hill: University of North Carolina Press, 1973), details divisions. Neo-Whig historians frequently cite the conclusions in Forrest McDonald, *We the People: The Economic Origins of the Constitution* (Chicago: University of Chicago Press, 1958), to show that Americans were not divided along class lines in the 1780s. An examination of McDonald's evidence, however, supports the alignments spelled out in Main. See also Saul Cornell, *The Other Founders: Anti-Federalism and the Dissenting Tradition in America, 1788-1828* (Chapel Hill: University of North Carolina Press, 1999).

18. Richard Henry Lee to Catherine Macauley, Nov. 29, 1775, quoted in Holton, *Forced Founders*, 158-159.

19. Peter H. Wood, "'Liberty Is Sweet': African-American Freedom Struggles in the Years Before White Independence," in *Beyond the American Revolution: Explorations in the History of American Radicalism*, ed. Alfred F. Young (DeKalb: Northern Illinois University Press, 1993), 149-184; Chernoh M. Sesay Jr., "The Revolutionary Roots of Slavery's Abolition in Massachusetts," *New England Quarterly*, 87.1 (2014): 99-131; Winthrop D. Jordan, *White over Black: American Attitudes Toward the Negro, 1550-1812*, 2nd ed. (1968; Chapel Hill: University of North Carolina Press, 2012), 269-311; David Waldstreicher, *Slavery's Constitution: From Revolution to Ratification* (New York: Hill and Wang, 2009); James A. Levernier, "Phillis Wheatley (ca. 1753-1784)," *Legacy*, 13.1 (1996): 65-75.

20. Rosemarie Zagarri, *Revolutionary Backlash: Women and Politics in the Early American Republic* (Philadelphia: University of Pennsylvania Press, 2007); Sara T. Damiano, "Writing Women's History Through the Revolution: Family Finances, Letter Writing, and Conceptions of Marriage," *William and Mary Quarterly*, 74.4 (2017): 697-728; Mary Beth Norton, *Liberty's Daughters: The Revolutionary Experience of American Women, 1750-1800* (Boston: Little, Brown, 1980); Linda K. Kerber, *Women of the Republic: Intellect and Ideology in Revolutionary America* (Chapel Hill: University of North Carolina Press, 1980); Judith Apter Klinghoffer and Lois Elkis, "'The Petticoat Electors': Women's Suffrage in New Jersey, 1776-1807," *Journal of the Early Republic*, 12.2 (1992): 159-193; Joel Perlmann and Dennis Shirley, "When Did New England Women Acquire Literacy?," *William and Mary Quarterly*, 48.1 (1991): 50-67; Cathy N. Davidson, *Revolution and the Word: The Rise of the Novel in America*, expanded ed. (New York: Oxford University Press, 2004), 1-56, quotes Adamson 185.

21. Matthew Kruer, *Time of Anarchy: Indigenous Power and the Crisis of Colonialism in Early America* (Cambridge, MA: Harvard University Press, 2021); Joaquín Rivaya-Martínez, "The Unsteady Comanchería: A Reexamination of Power in the Indigenous Borderlands of the Eighteenth-Century Greater Southwest," *William and Mary Quarterly*, 80.2 (2023): 251-286; Margaret Ellen Newell, "'The Rising of the Indians'; or, The Native American Revolution of (16)'76," *William and Mary Quarterly*, 80.2 (2023): 287-324; Nancy Shoemaker, "Settler Colonialism: Universal Theory or English Heritage?" *William and Mary Quarterly*, 76.3 (2019): 369-374.

22. Ned Blackhawk, *The Rediscovery of America: Native Peoples and the Unmaking of U.S. History* (New Haven, CT: Yale University Press, 2023), 106–210; Colin G. Calloway, *The American Revolution in Indian Country: Crisis and Diversity in Native American Communities* (New York: Cambridge University Press, 1995); Jim Piecuch, *Three Peoples, One King: Loyalists, Indians, and Slaves in the Revolutionary South, 1775–1782* (Columbia: University of South Carolina Press, 2008); James H. O'Donnell, *Southern Indians in the American Revolution* (Knoxville: University of Tennessee Press, 1973); Richard White, *The Middle Ground: Indians, Empires, and Republics in the Great Lakes Region, 1650–1815* (New York: Cambridge University Press, 1991).

23. Staughton Lynd and David Waldstreicher, in "Free Trade, Sovereignty, and Slavery: Toward an Economic Interpretation of American Independence," *William and Mary Quarterly*, 68.4 (2011): 605–607, discuss the "imperial school" and the midcentury origins of the Revolution. Lawrence Henry Gipson, "The American Revolution as an Aftermath of the Great War for Empire, 1754–1763," *Political Science Quarterly*, 65.1 (1950): 86–104; Fred Anderson, *Crucible of War: The Seven Years' War and the Fate of Empire in British North America, 1754–1766* (New York: Vintage Books, 2000).

24. Franklin to Peter Collinson, May 9, 1753, *The Papers of Benjamin Franklin*, ed. Leonard W. Labaree et al. (New Haven, CT: Yale University Press, 1959–), 4: 486.

25. Austin & Laurens to James Cowles, Aug. 20, 1755, in *The Papers of Henry Laurens*, ed. Philip M. Hamer et al. (Columbia: South Carolina Historical Society, 1968–), 1: 321.

26. Milton M. Klein, ed., *The Independent Reflector; or, Weekly Essays on Sundry Important Subjects More Particularly Adapted to the Province of New-York, by William Livingston* (Cambridge, MA: Harvard University Press, 1963), 443.

27. Austin & Laurens to Devonsheir, Reeve, & Lloyd, Aug. 20, 1755, in *Papers of Henry Laurens*, 1: 322.

28. Lawrence Washington to unknown, Nov. 7, 1749, quoted in Moncure D. Conway, *Barons of the Potomack and the Rappahannock* (New York: The Grolier Club, 1892), 275.

29. "The Humble Petition of Several of the Inhabitants of the Corporation . . . of Albany," ca. Oct. 1735, Rutherfurd Collection, 2: 139, New York Historical Society.

30. Philip Livingston to Jacob Wendell, Jan. 14, 1746, quoted in Bonomi, *Factious People*, 100–101; Thomas Elliot Norton, *The Fur Trade in Colonial New York, 1686–1776* (Madison: University of Wisconsin Press, 1974), 181.

31. *The Autobiography of Benjamin Franklin*, ed. Leonard W. Labaree et al. (New Haven, CT: Yale University Press, 1964), 145.

32. John W. Tyler, *Smugglers and Patriots: Boston Merchants and the Advent of the American Revolution* (Boston: Northeastern University Press, 1986); C. C. Goen, *Revivalism and Separatism in New England, 1740–1800: Strict Congregationalists and Separate Baptists in the Great Awakening* (New Haven, CT: Yale University Press, 1962); Christopher M. Jedrey, *The World of John Cleveland: Family and Community in Eighteenth-Century New England* (New York: W. W. Norton, 1979).

33. Sir Lewis Namier, *The Structure of Politics at the Accession of George III*, 2nd ed. (London: Macmillan, 1957), frontispiece.

34. Jonathan Mayhew, *Two Discourses, Oct. 25, 1759*, quoted in Charles W. Akers, *Called unto Liberty: A Life of Jonathan Mayhew, 1720–1766* (Cambridge, MA: Harvard University Press, 1964), 135–136.

35. John Adams to Nathan Webb, Oct. 12, 1755, in *Papers of John Adams*, ed. Robert Taylor et al. (Cambridge, MA: Harvard University Press, 1977–), 1: 5.

36. Franklin, *Poor Richard's Almanack*, 1750, in *Papers of Benjamin Franklin*, 3: 441.

37. John A. Schutz, *William Shirley: King's Governor of Massachusetts* (Chapel Hill: University of North Carolina Press, 1961), 88–96, quote on 90; Thomas Hutchinson, *History of the Colony and Province of Massachusetts-Bay*, ed. Lawrence S. Mayo, 3 vols. (Cambridge, MA: Harvard University Press, 1936), 2: 329n.

38. Thomas Hancock, 1746, quoted in W. T. Baxter, *The House of Hancock: Business in Boston, 1724–1775* (Cambridge, MA: Harvard University Press, 1945), 102.

39. Thomas Hutchinson to Israel Williams, Apr. 24, 1759, Israel Williams Papers, Massachusetts Historical Society.

40. William Smith, *The History of the Late Province of New-York from Its Discovery to the Appointment of Governor Colden, in 1762* (New York: New-York Historical Society, 1829), 2: 207.

41. Gov. Lyttleton to Board of Trade, June 19, Dec. 6, 1756, June 11, 1757, South Carolina Public Records, 27: 107–111, 201–204, 278–289.

42. Egnal, *Mighty Empire*, 1–2; Richard White, *The Middle Ground: Indians, Empires, and Republics in the Great Lakes Region, 1650–1815* (New York: Cambridge University Press, 1991), 307–309; Pauline Maier, *From Resistance to Revolution: Colonial Radicals and the Development of American Opposition to Britain, 1765–1776* (New York: Knopf, 1972).

43. Charles Thomson to Cook, Lawrence, & Co., Nov. 9, 1765, in *Revolutionary Papers, The Thomson Papers 1765–1816* (New York: New-York Historical Society, 1878), 1: 8.

44. "A Virginia Planter" to the Committee of Merchants in London, June 6, 1766, in *The Papers of George Mason, 1725–1792*, ed. Robert A. Rutland, 2 vols. (Chapel Hill: University of North Carolina Press, 1970), 1: 70.

45. William Livingston, *New York Gazette*, Apr. 11, 1768, quoted in Carl Bridenbaugh, *The Spirit of '76: The Growth of American Patriotism Before Independence, 1607–1776* (New York: Oxford University Press, 1975), 137.

46. Thomas Hutchinson to Mr. Robertson, Dec. 28, 1773, quoted in James K. Hosmer, *The Life of Thomas Hutchinson: Royal Governor of the Province of Massachusetts Bay* (1896; New York: Da Capo Press, 1972), 304.

47. Christopher Gadsden to James Pearson, Feb. 20, 1766, "Two Letters by Christopher Gadsden, February 1766," *South Carolina Historical Magazine*, ed. Robert M. Weir, 75 (1974): 174–175.

48. Thomas Jefferson, *A Summary View of the Rights of British America*, 1774, in *Tracts of the American Revolution, 1763–1776*, ed. Merrill Jensen (Indianapolis, IN: Bobbs-Merrill, 1967), 261, 275–276.

49. Virginia Nonimportation Resolves, May 17, 1769, in *The Papers of Thomas Jefferson*, ed. Julian Boyd et al. (Princeton, NJ: Princeton University Press, 1950–), 1: 28; Lynd and Waldstreicher, "Free Trade," 597–630; Holton, *Forced Founders*, 77–90; Egnal, *A Mighty Empire*, 126–149, 161–166, 185–189, 208–212; Marc Egnal, *New World Economies: The Growth of the Thirteen Colonies and Early Canada* (New York: Oxford University Press, 1998), 25–117.

50. Hutchinson, *History of Massachusetts*, 3: 355; Hosmer, *Life of Thomas Hutchinson*, 229.

51. Egnal, *Mighty Empire*, 170–189, 303–315.

52. Benjamin Franklin, June 28, 1787, in *Records of the Federal Convention*, 1: 451.

53. Garry Wills, *Inventing America: Jefferson's Declaration of Independence* (New York: Vintage Books, 1978), 167–255.

54. Thomas Paine, "Common Sense," 1776, in *Thomas Paine: Representative Selections with Introduction, Bibliography and Notes*, ed. Harry H. Clark (New York: American Book Company, 1944), 3.

3. What Caused the Civil War?

1. For the exchange with Zappa, see *Crossfire*, Mar. 28, 1986, https://www.youtube.com/watch?v=pnbvsfw3ttA.

2. Contemporary Civil War scholarship is a rich field, but at its core is an emphasis on slavery as the cause of the conflict. In his historiographical survey, Michael E. Woods observes that "[p]ublic statements by preeminent historians reaffirmed that slavery's centrality had been proven beyond a reasonable doubt," "What Twenty-First-Century Historians Have Said About the Causes of Disunion: A Civil War Sesquicentennial Review of the Recent Literature," *Journal of American History*, 99.2 (2012): 415–439, quote on 415. Edward L. Ayers remarks that "[s]lavery and freedom remain the keys to understanding the war," in *What Caused the Civil War? Reflections on the South and Southern History* (New York: W. W. Norton, 2005), 128; and Daniel Feller states bluntly, "Slavery brought on the Civil War," in "Libertarians in the Attic, or A Tale of Two Narratives," *Reviews in American History*, 32.2 (2004): 184–195, quote on 184. See also Frank Towers, "Partisans, New History, and Modernization: The Historiography of the Civil War's Causes, 1861–2011," *Journal of the Civil War Era*, 1.2 (2011): 237–264.

3. Lincoln to Alexander H. Stephens, Dec. 22, 1860, in *The Collected Works of Abraham Lincoln*, ed. Roy P. Basler, 9 vols. (New Brunswick, NJ: Rutgers University Press, 1953–1955), 4: 160.

4. Feller, "Libertarians in the Attic," 184–195. Clint Smith, *How the Word Is Passed: A Reckoning with the History of Slavery Across America* (New York: Little, Brown, 2021), illuminates the outlook of neo-Confederates.

5. Pew Research Center, "Civil War at 150: Still Relevant, Still Divisive," Apr. 8, 2011, https://www.people-press.org/2011/04/08/civil-war-at-150-still-relevant-still-divisive/; "Lots of Americans Don't Think Slavery Caused the Civil War," *Washington Post*, Nov. 1, 2017, https://www.washingtonpost.com/news/monkey-cage/wp/2017/11/01/lots-of-americans-dont-think-slavery-caused-the-civil-war/; "Poll: Americans Divided over Whether Slavery Was the Civil War's Main Cause," *Washington Post*, Aug. 6, 2015, https://

www.washingtonpost.com/news/education/wp/2015/08/06/poll-americans
-divided-over-whether-slavery-was-the-civil-wars-main-cause/.

6. James Oakes, *The Scorpion's Sting: Antislavery and the Coming of the Civil War* (New York: W. W. Norton, 2014); Charles Dew, *Apostles of Disunion: Southern Secession Commissioners and the Causes of the Civil War* (Charlottesville: University Press of Virginia, 2001). James McPherson blurbs Oakes's book, stating, "If any reader still questions whether the Civil War was all about slavery, this book overcomes all doubts."

7. Oakes, *Scorpion's Sting*, 13, 14.

8. Oakes, *Scorpion's Sting*, 50.

9. Dew, *Apostles of Disunion*, 1–2, 14–16.

10. Dew, *Apostles of Disunion*, 62.

11. James Tallmadge, Feb. 16, 1819, *Annals of Congress* (House), 15th Cong., 2nd Sess., 1204.

12. William Darlington, Feb. 16, 1820, *Annals of Congress* (House), 16th Cong., 1st Sess., 1375.

13. I draw much of this account from my book, *Clash of Extremes: The Economic Origins of the Civil War* (New York: Hill and Wang, 2009).

14. Bruce Levine, "'The Vital Element of the Republican Party,' Antislavery, Nativism, and Abraham Lincoln," *Journal of the Civil War Era*, 1.4 (2011): 481–505; "1848 United States presidential election," Wikipedia, https://en.wikipedia.org/wiki/1848_United_States_presidential_election; "1852 United States presidential election," Wikipedia, https://en.wikipedia.org/wiki/1852_United_States_presidential_election.

15. In many respects, the Constitution of 1787 reflected the first great sectional compromise. The clash over Missouri brought a new intensity to this debate. See Mathew Mason, *Slavery and Politics in the Early American Republic* (Chapel Hill: University of North Carolina Press, 2006).

16. Stephen A. Douglas, March 13, 1850, *Congressional Globe*, 31st Cong., 1st Sess., App., 365; Calhoun toast, Nov. 8, 1845, in *The Papers of John C. Calhoun*, ed. Robert L. Meriwether et al., 28 vols. (Columbia: University of South Carolina Press, 1959–), 22: 271.

17. Charles Sumner, Speech, June 28, 1848, in *Charles Sumner: His Complete Works*, intro. George F. Hoar, 20 vols. (1900; New York: Negro University Press, 1969), 2: 233.

18. Calhoun to Charles Tait, Oct. 26, 1820, in *Papers of John Calhoun*, 5: 413.

19. John Michael Rozett, "The Social Bases of Party Conflict in the Age of Jackson: Individual Voting Behavior in Greene County, Illinois, 1838–1848" (PhD diss., University of Michigan, 1974); Paul Goodman, "The Social Basis of New England Politics in Jacksonian America," *Journal of the Early Republic*, 6.1 (1986): 23–58; Frank Otto Gatell, "Money and Party in Jacksonian America: A Quantitative Look at New York City's Men of Quality," *Political Science Quarterly*, 82.2 (1967): 235–252.

20. William Seward, "The Election of 1848," Oct. 26, 1848, in *The Works of William H. Seward*, ed. George E. Baker, 3 vols. (New York: Redfield, 1853), 3: 299; Eric Foner, *The Fiery Trial: Abraham Lincoln and American Slavery* (New York: W. W. Norton, 2010), 51–53.

21. Madison Kuhn, "Economic Issues and the Rise of the Republican Party in the Northwest (PhD diss., University of Chicago, 1940); John C. Clark, *The Grain Trade in the Old Northwest* (Urbana: University of Illinois Press, 1966); William Cronon, *Nature's Metropolis: Chicago and the Great West* (New York: W. W. Norton, 1991), 64–70; George Rogers Taylor, *The Transportation Revolution, 1815–1860* (New York: Holt, Rinehart and Winston, 1962), 75–103.

22. Robert Toombs, May 27, 1858, *Congressional Globe*, 35th Cong., 1st Sess., App. 477.

23. Charles Stuart, July 28, 1854, *Congressional Globe*, 33rd Cong., 1st Sess., App. 1159.

24. John Wentworth, Jan. 6, 1854, *Congressional Globe*, 33rd Cong., 1st Sess., 139.

25. Truman Smith, Aug. 23, 1852, *Congressional Globe*, 32nd Cong., 1st Sess., App. 1135–1137.

26. Manisha Sinha, *The Slave's Cause: A History of Abolition* (New Haven, CT: Yale University Press, 2016); David W. Blight, *Frederick Douglass: Prophet of Freedom* (New York: Simon & Schuster, 2018).

27. *New-York Tribune*, Oct. 15, 1856, quoted in Eric Foner, *Free Soil, Free Labor, Free Men: The Ideology of the Republican Party Before the Civil War* (New York: Oxford University Press, 1970), 116.

28. Quoted in Kuhn, "Economic Issues," 129.

29. John E. Coleman, *The Disruption of Pennsylvania Democracy, 1848–1860* (Harrisburg: Pennsylvania Historical and Museum Commission, 1975), 103–110, quote on 108.

30. Horace Greeley to R. M. Whipple, April [?], 1860, quoted in James L. Huston, *The Panic of 1857 and the Coming of the Civil War* (Baton Rouge: Louisiana State University Press, 1987), 237.

31. John Sherman, May 27, 1858, *Congressional Globe*, 35th Cong., 1st Sess., 2431; John Sherman, Jan. 18, 1858, *Congressional Globe*, 35th Cong., 1st Sess., 326.

32. *New York Times*, May 18, 1860.

33. John C. Calhoun, "The Southern Address," 1849, in *The Works of John C. Calhoun*, ed. Richard K. Crallé, 6. vols. (New York: D. Appleton, 1883), 4: 290.

34. Milledgeville *Southern Recorder*, Aug. 29, 1843, quoted in Larry Keith Menna, "Embattled Conservatism: The Ideology of the Southern Whigs" (PhD diss., Columbia University, 1991), 173.

35. Perry quoted in Lillian A. Kibler, *Benjamin F. Perry: South Carolina Unionist* (Durham, NC: Duke University Press, 1946), 302–303.

36. Jefferson Davis, Speech at Jackson, Nov. 4, 1857, in *The Papers of Jefferson Davis*, ed. Haskell M. Monroe Jr. and James T. McIntosh, 10 vols. (Baton Rouge: Louisiana State University Press, 1971–1999), 6:157.

37. Hilliard M. Judge to Calhoun, Apr. 29, 1849, in *Papers of John Calhoun*, 26: 385.

38. Herschel Johnson to Calhoun, July 20, 1849, in *Papers of John Calhoun*, 26: 509.

39. *Charleston Mercury*, Nov. 3, 1860, quoted in *Southern Editorials on Secession*, ed. Dwight L. Dumond (1931; Gloucester, MA: Peter Smith, 1964), 204.

40. Constitution of the Confederate States, Mar. 11, 1861, https://avalon.law.yale.edu/19th_century/csa_csa.asp.

41. *Vicksburg Daily Whig*, Jan. 18, 1860, in *Southern Editorials*, 14-15.

42. S. D. Cabaniss to Governor Andrew Moore, quoted in Ollinger Crenshaw, *The Slave States in the Presidential Election of 1860* (1945; Gloucester, MA: Peter Smith, 1969), 255–256.

43. Richard N. Current, *Lincoln's Loyalists: Union Soldiers from the Confederacy* (Boston: Northeastern University Press, 1992), 84–104, 213–215.

44. Daniel W. Crofts, *Reluctant Confederates: Upper South Unionists in the Secession Crisis* (Chapel Hill: University of North Carolina Press, 1989), 351.

45. Current, *Lincoln's Loyalists*; Frank Towers, *The Urban South and the Coming of the Civil War* (Charlottesville: University of Virginia Press, 2004).

46. John Sherman, Feb. 10, 1863, *Congressional Globe*, 37th Cong., 3rd Sess., 843.

47. Roger Lowenstein, *Ways and Means: Lincoln and His Cabinet and the Financing of the Civil War* (New York: Penguin, 2022).

48. William Gillette, *Retreat from Reconstruction, 1869-1879* (Baton Rouge: Louisiana State University Press, 1979), 304.

4. Homicidal Nation

1. Rod Aya, "Norbert Elias and the 'The Civilizing Process,'" *Theory and Society*, 5.2 (1978): 219-228; Douglas Lee Eckberg, "Estimates of Early Twentieth-Century U.S. Homicide Rates: An Econometric Forecasting Approach," *Demography*, 32.1 (1995): 1-3; Eric H. Monkkonen, "Homicide in Los Angeles, 1827-2002," *Journal of Interdisciplinary History*, 36.2 (2005): 168-169; Eric Monkkonen, "Homicide: Explaining America's Exceptionalism," *The American Historical Review*, 111.1 (2006): 76-94.

2. William E. Hollon, *Frontier Violence: Another Look* (New York: Oxford University Press, 1974); Elizabeth Pleck, *Domestic Tyranny: The Making of Social Policy against Family Violence from Colonial Times to the Present* (New York: Oxford University Press, 1987); David Peterson del Mar, *Beaten Down: A History of Interpersonal Violence in the West* (Seattle: University of Washington Press, 2002); Ely Aaronson, *From Slave Abuse to Hate Crime: The Criminalization of Racial Violence in American History* (New York: Cambridge University Press, 2014).

3. Randolph Roth, *American Homicide* (Cambridge, MA: Harvard University Press, 2009), 17-23, quote on 18; Randolph Roth, "Emotions, Facultative Adaptation, and the History of Homicide," *The American Historical Review*, 119.5 (2014): 1529-1546.

4. Richard Maxwell Brown, *Strain of Violence: Historical Studies of American Violence and Vigilantism* (New York: Oxford University Press, 1975), vii.

5. Roth, *American Homicide*, 56, 352-356.

6. Carol Anderson, *The Second: Race and Guns in a Fatally Unequal America* (New York: Bloomsbury Publishing, 2021), 5-60.

7. Eric H. Monkkonen, "Homicide in New York, Los Angeles and Chicago," *Journal of Criminal Law and Criminology*, 92.3/4 (2002): 809-822.

8. Data from "Gun Law and Policy: Firearms and Armed Violence, Country by Country," GunPolicy.org, International Firearm Injury Prevention and Policy, https://www.gunpolicy.org/; see also Philip J. Cook and Harold A. Pollack, "Reducing Access to Guns by Violent Offenders," *RSF: The Russell Sage Foundation Journal of the Social Sciences*, 3.5 (2017): 3–8.

9. Cook and Pollack, "Reducing Access," 2–36. The 2015 National Firearms Survey determined that individual gun owners had on average 4.9 guns in 2015, a significant increase since the 1970s, according to Cook and Pollack (6). Recent figures on households that have guns range from 37 to 45 percent; Lydia Saad, "What Percentage of Americans Own Guns?," Gallup, Nov. 13, 2020, https://news.gallup.com/poll/264932/percentage-americans-own-guns.aspx, suggests 44 percent. See also Statistica Research Department, "Gun Ownership in the U.S., 1972–2020," Statista, https://www.statista.com/statistics/249740/percentage-of-households-in-the-united-states-owning-a-firearm/. International figures are from Aaron Karp, "Estimating Global Civilian-held Firearms Numbers: Briefing Paper," Small Arms Survey, June 2018, http://www.smallarmssurvey.org/fileadmin/docs/T-Briefing-Papers/SAS-BP-Civilian-Firearms-Numbers.pdf.

10. James Alan Fox and Marianne W. Zawitz, "Homicide Trends in the United States," Bureau of Justice Statistics, http://bjs.ojp.usdoj.gov/content/pub/pdf/htius.pdf; Alfred Blumstein and Richard Rosenfeld, "Explaining Recent Trends in U.S. Homicide Rates," *Journal of Criminal Law and Criminology*, 88.4 (1998): 1175–1216; Jeffrey Fagan and Daniel Richman, "Understanding Recent Spikes and Longer Trends in American Murders," *Columbia Law Review*, 117.5 (2017): 1235–1296.

11. United States v. Miller, 307 U.S. 174, 59 S. Ct. 816 (1939), LexisNexis, https://www.lexisnexis.com/community/casebrief/p/casebrief-united-states-v-miller-238853368; Anthony Fleming, Dylan S. McLean and Raymond Tatalovich, "Debating Gun Control in Canada and the United States," *World Affairs*, 181.4 (2018): 352; Cook and Pollack, "Reducing Access," 17–20.

12. Elliott Currie, *A Peculiar Indifference: The Neglected Toll of Violence on Black America* (New York: Metropolitan Books, 2020), 216–223; Cook and Pollack, "Reducing Access," 18–20

13. Glenn Kessler, "What Research Shows on the Effectiveness of Gun-Control Laws," *Washington Post*, May 27, 2022, https://www.washingtonpost

.com/politics/2022/05/27/what-research-shows-effectiveness-gun-control
-laws/; Michael Siegel, "The Impact of State-Level Firearms Laws on Homicide Rates by Rate/Ethnicity," Office of Justice Programs, April 2020, https://
www.ojp.gov/pdffiles1/nij/grants/254669.pdf.

14. Cook and Pollack, "Reducing Access," 10–17, 25–26.

15. Glenn Kessler, "Biden's Claim That the 1994 Assault-Weapons Law
'Brought Down' Mass Shootings," *Washington Post*, Mar. 24, 2021, https://www
.washingtonpost.com/politics/2021/03/24/bidens-claim-that-1994-assault
-weapons-law-brought-down-mass-shootings/ evaluates the impact of the
1994 law.

16. Cook and Pollack, "Reducing Access," 4–9; Kessler, "Biden's Claim";
FBI Reports, https://ucr.fbi.gov/crime-in-the-u.s; FBI, Crime Data Explorer,
https://crime-data-explorer.app.cloud.gov/pages/explorer/crime/shr.

17. Jill Lepore, *In the Name of War: King Philip's War and the Origins of American Identity* (New York: Vintage Books, 1998), 3–18; Ibram X. Kendi, *Stamped
from the Beginning: The Definitive History of Racist Ideas in America* (New York:
Nation Books, 2016), 17–45; Patrick Wolf, "Settler Colonialism and the Elimination of the Native," *Journal of Genocide Research* (Dec. 2006): 387–409; Jeff
Benvenuto et al., "Colonial Genocide in Indigenous North America," in *Colonial Genocide in Indigenous North America*, ed. Andrew Woolford et al. (Durham, NC: Duke University Press, 2014), 1–25; Michael Witgen, *An Infinity of
Nations: How the Native New World Shaped Early America* (Philadelphia: University of Pennsylvania Press, 2012).

18. Ned Blackhawk, *The Rediscovery of America: Native Peoples and the
Unmaking of U.S. History* (New Haven, CT: Yale University Press, 2023), 73–105;
Roth, *American Homicide*, 27–80; Randolph Roth, *American Homicide Supplemental Volume* (May 2010), https://cjrc.osu.edu/research/interdisciplinary
/hvd/ahsv, tables 1–11; Randolph Roth, "Yes We Can: Working Together
Toward a History of Homicide That Is Empirically, Mathematically, and The-
oretically Sound," *Crime, Histoire & Sociétés/Crime, History & Societies*, 15.2
(2011): 131–145. In this instance, homicide rates are calculated for adults and
exclude population and murder data for those age fifteen and younger. See
also the chapters in Susan Sleeper-Smith, Jeffrey Ostler, and Joshua L Reid,
eds., *Violence and Indigenous Communities: Confronting the Past and Engaging
the Present* (Evanston, IL: Northwestern University Press, 2021).

19. Peter C. Mancall, "Disappointment, Grievance, and Violence in Early Virginia," *William and Mary Quarterly*, 80.3 (2023): 465-472; Paul Musselwhite, Peter C. Mancall, and James Horn, eds., *Virginia 1619: Slavery and Freedom in the Making of English America* (Chapel Hill: University of North Carolina Press, 2019); James D. Rice, "War and Politics: Powhatan Expansionism and the Problem of Native American Warfare," *William and Mary Quarterly*, 77.1 (2020): 3-32.

20. Roth, *American Homicide*, 81-104; Roth, *American Homicide Supplemental*, tables 1-21. Many of the colonial-era homicide figures are estimates extrapolated from small samples. Still, the sources suggest good reasons for trusting these figures, even if the final numbers may be imprecise. See Roth, *American Homicide*, 477-495; Roth, *American Homicide Supplemental Volume: Homicide Estimates*, Oct. 2009, https://cjrc.osu.edu/sites/cjrc.osu.edu/files/AHSV-Homicide-Estimates.pdf.

21. Blackhawk, *Rediscovery of America*, 211-249; Jeffrey Ostler, *Surviving Genocide: Native Nations and the United States from the American Revolution to Bleeding Kansas* (New Haven, CT: Yale University Press, 2019), 383-387; Claudio Saunt, *Unworthy Republic: The Dispossession of Native Americans and the Road to Indian Territory* (New York: W. W. Norton, 2020); Susan Sleeper-Smith, *Indigenous Prosperity and American Conquest: Indian Women of the Ohio River Valley, 1690-1792* (Chapel Hill: University of North Carolina, 2018); Lisa Ford, *Settler Sovereignty: Jurisdiction and Indigenous People in America and Australia, 1788-1836* (Cambridge, MA: Harvard University Press, 2010); Allan Greer, *Property and Dispossession: Natives, Empires, and Land in Early Modern North America* (New York: Cambridge University Press, 2018).

22. Randolph Roth, Michael D. Maltz, and Douglas L. Eckberg, "Homicide Rates in the Old West," *Western Historical Quarterly*, 42.2 (2011): 192; Clare V. McKanna, *Race and Homicide in Nineteenth-Century California* (Reno: University of Nevada Press, 2002); Jason E. Pierce, *Making the White Man's West: Whiteness and the Creation of the American West* (Boulder: University Press of Colorado, 2016), 214-216, 228-231.

23. Roth, *American Homicide*, 360-364, 372-374; Randolph Roth, "Guns, Murder, and Probability: How Can We Decide Which Figures to Trust?," *Reviews in American History*, 35.2 (2007): 170-171; Pierce, *White Man's West*, 217-218, 232-235, quote on 233; Benjamin Madley, *An American Genocide: The*

United States and the California Indian Catastrophe (New Haven, CT: Yale University Press, 2016).

24. Blackhawk, *Rediscovery of America*, 250–288; Roth, *American Homicide*, 360–387; Pierce, *White Man's West*, 210, 235–240; Erika Lee, "The Chinese Exclusion Example: Race, Immigration, and American Gatekeeping, 1882–1924," *Journal of American Ethnic History*, 21.3 (2002): 36–62; Erika Lee, *At America's Gates: Chinese Immigration during the Exclusion Era, 1882–1943* (Chapel Hill: University of North Carolina Press, 2003); Manu Karuka, *Empire's Tracks: Indigenous Nations, Chinese Workers, and the Transcontinental Railroad* (Oakland: University of California Press, 2019).

25. Laura J. Arata, "Terror and Tourism: Lynching, Legend, and the Montana Vigilantes," *Pacific Northwest Quarterly*, 106.4 (2015): 183–198; Richard Maxwell Brown, "Western Violence: Structure, Values, Myth," *Western Historical Quarterly*, 24.1 (1993): 9–11; Pierce, *White Man's West*, 219–222; John W. Davis, *Wyoming Range War: The Infamous Invasion of Johnson County* (Norman: University of Oklahoma Press, 2010); Alan Trachtenberg, *The Incorporation of America: Culture and Society in the Gilded Age* (New York: Hill and Wang, 1982).

26. Brown, "Western Violence," 4–20; Roth, *American Homicide*, 380–383; Robert R. Dykstra, "Overdosing on Dodge City," *Western Historical Quarterly*, 27.4 (1996): 505–514.

27. Roth, Maltz, and Eckberg, "Homicide Rates in the Old West"; "Murder Rates: State and Regional Murder Statistics Show No Correlation between Use of the Death Penalty and Reduced Crime," Death Penalty Information Center, https://deathpenaltyinfo.org/facts-and-research/murder-rates; "Crime in the United States," FBI Criminal Justice Information Services Division, 2014, https://ucr.fbi.gov/crime-in-the-u.s/2014/crime-in-the-u.s.-2014/tables/table-5. Deadwood is in present-day South Dakota.

28. Richard Maxwell Brown, *No Duty to Retreat: Violence and Values in American History and Society* (New York: Oxford University Press, 1991), 3–36, quotes on 3, 27, 34; Brown, "Western Violence," 4–20.

29. "Crime in the United States," FBI Criminal Justice Information Services Division, 2019, https://ucr.fbi.gov/crime-in-the-u.s/2019/crime-in-the-u.s.-2019/tables/table-43; "Crime in the United States," FBI Criminal Justice Information Services Division, 2013, https://ucr.fbi.gov/crime-in-the-u.s/2013/crime-in-the-u.s.-2013/offenses-known-to-law-enforcement/expanded

-homicide/expanded_homicide_data_table_6_murder_race_and_sex_of_vicitm _by_race_and_sex_of_offender_2013.xls; Fox and Zawitz, "Homicide Trends in the United States," http://bjs.ojp.usdoj.gov/content/pub/pdf/htius.pdf; Roth, *American Homicide Supplemental Volume*; "U.S. Murder/Homicide Rate 1990–2021," Macrotrends, https://www.macrotrends.net/countries/USA/united-states/murder-homicide-rate. Siegel, "State-Level Firearms Laws," 1, notes that in 2017 Blacks comprised 59 percent of those killed by firearms.

30. Statista, "Number of Murder Victims in the United States in 2020, by Race/Ethnicity and Gender," https://www.statista.com/statistics/251877/murder-victims-in-the-us-by-race-ethnicity-and-gender/; Currie, *Peculiar Indifference*, 19–45, and passim; James Forman Jr., *Locking Up Our Own: Crime and Punishment in Black America* (New York: Farrar Straus & Giroux, 2017).

31. Marvin E. Wolfgang and Franco Ferracuti, *The Subculture of Violence: Towards an Integrated Theory in Criminology*, trans. from the Italian (London: Tavistock Publications, 1967), 158; Currie, *Peculiar Indifference*, 79–140.

32. Lauren J. Krivo, Ruth D. Peterson, and Danielle C. Kuhl, "Segregation, Racial Structure, and Neighborhood Violent Crime," *American Journal of Sociology*, 114.6 (2009): 1765–1802; Elizabeth Griffiths, "Race, Space, and the Spread of Violence Across the City," *Social Problems*, 60.4 (2013): 491–512; Ruth D. Peterson and Lauren J. Krivo, *Divergent Social Worlds: Neighborhood Crime and the Racial-Spatial Divide* (New York: Russell Sage Foundation, 2010); Julie A. Phillips, "White, Black, and Latino Homicide Rates: Why the Difference?," *Social Problems*, 49.3 (2002): 349–373. Phillips provides the estimates for the differences in homicides rates accounted for by the environment (363–366).

33. James L. Greer, "Historic Home Mortgage Redlining in Chicago," *Journal of the Illinois State Historical Society*, 107.2 (2014): 204–233; Paige Glotzer, *How the Suburbs Were Segregated: Developers and the Business of Exclusionary Housing, 1890–1960* (New York: Columbia University Press, 2020).

34. Neil Bhutta et al., "Disparities in Wealth by Race and Ethnicity in the 2019 Survey of Consumer Finances," *FEDS Notes*, Board of Governors of the Federal Reserve System, Sept. 28, 2020, https://doi.org/10.17016/2380-7172 .2797; "Homeownership Rates Show That Black Americans Are Currently the Least Likely Group to Own Homes," *USA Facts*, July 28, 2020, https://usafacts .org/articles/homeownership-rates-by-race/; Ira Katznelson, *When Affirmative*

Action Was White: An Untold History of Racial Inequality in Twentieth-Century America (New York: W. W. Norton, 2005), 113–143.

35. See, for example, the debate over Edward E. Baptist, *The Half Has Never Been Told: Slavery and the Making of American Capitalism* (New York: Basic Books, 2014), particularly the multiple reviews in the *Journal of Economic History*, 75.3 (2014): 919–931.

36. Roth, *American Homicide*, 94–104, 147–176; Randolph Roth, *American Homicide Supplemental Volume: American Homicides* (Historical Violence Database, Criminal Justice Research Center, Ohio State University, May 2010), tables 6, 12, 13, 15, 16, https://cjrc.osu.edu/sites/cjrc.osu.edu/files/AHSV -American-Homicides-5-2010.pdf; Walter Johnson, *River of Dark Dreams: Slavery and Empire in the Cotton Kingdom* (Cambridge, MA: Harvard University Press, 2013), 209–243; Baptist, *Half Has Never Been Told*, 111–144; and Thavolia Glymph, *Out of the House of Bondage: The Transformation of the Plantation Household* (New York: Cambridge University Press, 2008), 25–31, all detail the violent nature of slavery.

37. James M. Denham and Randolph Roth, "Why Was Antebellum Florida Murderous? A Quantitative Analysis of Homicide in Florida, 1821–1861," *Florida Historical Quarterly*, 86.2 (2007): 216–239; Roth, *American Homicide*, 206–271.

38. Jeff Forret, *Slave against Slave: Plantation Violence in the Old South* (Baton Rouge: Louisiana State University Press, 2015); John Ernest, *A Nation within a Nation: Organizing African-American Communities Before the Civil War* (Chicago: Ivan R. Dee, 2011); Dylan C. Penningroth, *The Claims of Kinfolk: African American Property and Community in the Nineteenth-Century South* (Chapel Hill: University of North Carolina Press, 2003).

39. Eric Foner, *Reconstruction: America's Unfinished Revolution, 1863–1877* (New York: Harper & Row, 1988), 110–118, 281–291, quotes on 114, 118; Glymph, *Out of the House of Bondage*, 210–226.

40. Foner, *Reconstruction*, 119–123, 425–444, quotes on 120, 121.

41. Foner, *Reconstruction*, 524–553, 569–575, quote on 574; Melinda Meek Hennessey, "Racial Violence during Reconstruction: The 1876 Riots in Charleston and Cainhoy," *South Carolina Historical Magazine*, 86.2 (1985): 100–112; Gilles Vandal, "Black Violence in Post-Civil War Louisiana," *Journal of Interdisciplinary History*, 25.1 (1994): 45–64; Roth, *American Homicide*,

347-353; Anderson, *The Second*, 86-101; Elaine Frantz Parsons, *Ku-Klux: The Birth of the Klan during Reconstruction* (Chapel Hill: University of North Carolina Press, 2015).

42. Stephen Hahn, *A Nation Under Our Feet: Black Political Struggles in the Rural South from Slavery to the Great Migration* (Cambridge, MA: Harvard University Press, 2003), 412-451; Crystal N. Feimster, *Southern Horrors: Women and the Politics of Rape and Lynching* (Cambridge, MA: Harvard University Press, 2009); Chris M. Messer, "The Tulsa Race Riot of 1921: Toward an Integrative Theory of Collective Violence," *Journal of Social History*, 44.4 (2011): 1217-1232; Allen D. Grimshaw, "Actions of Police and the Military in American Race Riots," *Phylon*, 24.3 (1963): 271-289; Cameron McWhirter, *Red Summer: The Summer of 1919 and the Awakening of Black America* (New York: Henry Holt, 2011).

43. Douglas A. Blackmon, *Slavery by Another Name: The Re-Enslavement of Black Americans from the Civil War to World War II* (New York: Anchor Books, 2008), 4; Edward L. Ayers, *Vengeance and Justice: Crime and Punishment in the Nineteenth-Century American South* (New York: Oxford University Press, 1984); Matthew J. Mancini, *One Dies, Get Another: Convict Leasing in the American South, 1866-1928* (Columbia: University of South Carolina Press, 1996); David M. Oshinsky, *"Worse Than Slavery": Parchman Farm and the Ordeal of Jim Crow Justice* (New York: Simon & Schuster, 1996); Brandon Jett, "'The Most Murderous Civilized City in the World': Patterns of Homicide in Jim Crow Memphis, 1917-1926," *Tennessee Historical Quarterly*, 74.2 (2015): 104-127; Anderson, *The Second*, 99-106. See also Daryl Michael Scott's views on the impact of the Thirteenth Amendment, at https://darylmichaelscott.com/current-project/.

44. Jeffrey S. Adler, "Murder, North and South: Violence in Early-Twentieth-Century Chicago and New Orleans," *Journal of Southern History*, 74.2 (2008): 305.

45. "'The Most Murderous Civilized City in the World': Patterns of Homicide in Jim Crow Memphis, 1917-1926," *Tennessee Historical Quarterly*, 74.2 (2015): 107-108; Jett, "Most Murderous," 107-108.

46. Khalil Gibran Muhammad, *The Condemnation of Blackness: Race, Crime, and the Making of Modern America* (Cambridge, MA: Harvard University Press, 2010), quote on xvii (new preface, 2019).

47. John Gramlich, "The Gap between the Number of Blacks and Whites in Prison Is Shrinking," Pew Research Center, Apr. 30, 2019, https://www

.pewresearch.org/short-reads/2019/04/30/shrinking-gap-between-number
-of-blacks-and-whites-in-prison/.

48. United States Commission on Civil Rights, "Examining the Race Effects of Stand Your Ground Laws," Feb. 2020, p. 16, https://www.usccr.gov/files /pubs/2020/04-06-Stand-Your-Ground.pdf; Stephanie Jones-Rogers, "Police Shootings: How Many More Must Perish Before We See Justice?" *The Berkeley Blog*, July 26, 2017, https://blogs.berkeley.edu/2017/07/27/stephanie-jones -rogers-police-exonerations-history-of-slavery/; NAACP, "Criminal Justice Fact Sheet," 2020, https://www.naacp.org/criminal-justice-fact-sheet/; "Police Shootings Database 2015–2022," *Washington Post*, May 6, 2020, https://www .washingtonpost.com/graphics/investigations/police-shootings-database/.

49. Elizabeth Hinton, *America on Fire: The Untold Story of Police Violence and Black Rebellion Since the 1960s* (New York: Liveright Publishing, 2021), quote on 14; Vandal, "Black Violence"; Roth, *American Homicide*, 387–430; FBI Crime Statistics, 2018, https://ucr.fbi.gov/crime-in-the-u.s/2018/crime-in -the-u.s.-2018/topic-pages/tables/expanded-homicide-data-table-6.xls; John Dollard, *Caste and Class in a Southern Town*, 3rd ed. (Garden City, NY: Doubleday Anchor Books, 1949), 267–287; Isabel Wilkerson, *Caste: The Origins of Our Discontents* (New York: Random House, 2020); Currie, *Peculiar Indifference*, 79–133; Sheldon Hackney, "Southern Violence," *The American Historical Review*, 74.3 (1969): 906–925.

50. Hinton, *America on Fire*, 13, quotes Koen.

51. Thomas C. Holt, *The Movement: The African American Struggle for Civil Rights* (New York: Oxford University Press, 2021); Taylor Branch, *Parting the Waters: America in the King Years, 1954–1963* (New York: Simon & Schuster, 1988). See also Robert Gebeloff et al., "How the Pandemic Reshaped American Gun Violence," *New York Times*, May 14, 2024, https://www.nytimes.com /interactive/2024/05/14/us/gun-homicides-data.html. The essay emphasizes the continuing racial component of gun violence.

5. Why Did the United States Fight in Vietnam?

1. George C. Herring, *America's Longest War: The United States and Vietnam, 1950–1975* (New York: Wiley, 1979), x; David L. Anderson, "No More Vietnams: Historians Debate the Policy Lessons of the Vietnam War," in *The War That*

Never Ends: New Perspectives on the Vietnam War, ed. David L. Anderson and John Ernst (Lexington: University Press of Kentucky, 2007), 13–33.

2. Mark Philip Bradley, in "Legacies of the Vietnam War," *Journal of American History*, 93.2 (2006): 472.

3. Luu Doan Huynh, in "Legacies of the Vietnam War," 474.

4. Fredrik Logevall, *Embers of War: The Fall of an Empire and the Making of America's Vietnam* (New York: Random House, 2013), 112–118, 234–235; George C. Herring, *America's Longest War: The United States and Vietnam, 1950–1975*, 5th ed. (New York: McGraw-Hill, 2014), 31.

5. Dwight D. Eisenhower, Press Conference, Apr. 7, 1954, in Fredrik Logevall, *The Origins of the Vietnam War* (Harlow, UK: Pearson Education, 2001), 102.

6. David Brinkley and Chet Huntley interview, Sept. 9, 1963, https://www.jfklibrary.org/sites/default/files/2018-07/JFKandVietnamLessonPlan.pdf.

7. "Military Advisers in Vietnam, 1963," https://www.jfklibrary.org/sites/default/files/2020-05/Military%20Advisors%20in%20Vietnam%20Lesson%202020.pdf; Logevall, *Origins of the Vietnam War*, 42.

8. Johnson, Speech at Johns Hopkins University, Apr. 7, 1965, http://www.lbjlibrary.org/exhibits/the-presidents-address-at-johns-hopkins-university-peace-without-conquest.

9. Richard Nixon, "The 'Silent Majority' Speech on the Vietnam War," Nov. 3, 1969, https://www.c-span.org/video/?153819-1/president-nixons-silent-majority-speech-vietnam-war.

10. Herring, *America's Longest War*, 5th ed., 277–331.

11. Platt Amendment, Mar. 2, 1901, https://www.ourdocuments.gov/doc.php?flash=false&doc=55&page=transcript.

12. William McKinley, "President McKinley at the Home Market Club, Boston, Mass," *Christian Science Sentinel*, Feb. 23, 1899, https://sentinel.christianscience.com/shared/view/axgppsxx5c; "The Great Bugbear Is Dead," *New York Times*, Feb. 18, 1899, https://nyti.ms/3Fr8tFE. Kelvin Santiago-Valles, in "'Still Longing for de Old Plantation': The Visual Parodies and Racial National Imaginary of US Overseas Expansionism, 1898-1903," *American Studies International*, 37.3 (1999): 18–43, discusses the racial dimensions of these conquests.

13. Robert W. Rydell, *All the World's a Fair: Visions of Empire at American International Expositions, 1876–1916* (Chicago: University of Chicago Press, 1994), 154–183; Richard Kennedy, "Rethinking the Philippine Exhibit at the

1904 St. Louis World's Fair," in Smithsonian Institution, *Smithsonian Folklife Festival* (1998), 41–44; McKinley, "Home Market Club," Feb. 23, 1899.

14. Stanford M. Lyman, "The 'Yellow Peril' Mystique: Origins and Vicissitudes of a Racist Discourse," *International Journal of Politics, Culture, and Society*, 13.4 (2000): 683–747.

15. John H. Coatsworth, "What For?," *ReVista: Harvard Review of Latin America* (Summer 2005), https://revista.drclas.harvard.edu/book/export/html/316831.

16. Roosevelt Corollary, from Annual Message to Congress, Dec. 6, 1904, https://www.ourdocuments.gov/doc.php?flash=false&doc=56&page=transcript.

17. Woodrow Wilson, "Fourteen Points," Jan. 8, 1918, https://millercenter.org/the-presidency/presidential-speeches/january-8-1918-wilsons-fourteen-points.

18. Franklin Roosevelt, First Inaugural Address, Mar. 4, 1933, https://millercenter.org/the-presidency/presidential-speeches/march-4-1933-first-inaugural-address.

19. Walter LaFeber, *Inevitable Revolutions: The United States in Central America*, 2nd ed. (New York: W. W. Norton, 1983), 107.

20. LaFeber, *Inevitable Revolutions*, 119.

21. Dwight D. Eisenhower, "The Eisenhower Doctrine," Jan. 5, 1957, https://millercenter.org/the-presidency/presidential-speeches/january-5-1957-eisenhower-doctrine.

22. LaFeber, *Inevitable Revolutions*, 157–162, quote on 159; Walter LaFeber, "The Tension between Democracy and Capitalism during the American Century," *Diplomatic History*, 23.2 (1999): 277–278; Gabriel Kolko, *Confronting the Third World: United States Foreign Policy, 1945–1980* (New York: Pantheon Books, 1988), 163–164.

23. *A Report to the National Security Council* (NSC 68), Apr. 14, 1950, 4, https://info.publicintelligence.net, US-NSC-68.

24. Blanche Wiesen Cook, "The Impact of Anti-Communism in American Life," *Science & Society*, 53.4 (1989/1990): 470–475; Cyndy Hendershot, *Anti-Communism and Popular Culture in Mid-Century America* (Jefferson, NC: McFarland, 2003); Arthur Redding, *Turncoats, Traitors, and Fellow Travelers: Culture and Politics of the Early Cold War* (Jackson: University Press of Mississippi, 2008), 3–36.

25. Avi Wolfman-Arent, "Red Tape: The Untold Stories of Philadelphia's 1950s Teacher Purge," June 16, 2022, https://whyy.org/episodes/schooled -red-tape-the-untold-stories-of-philadelphias-1950s-teacher-purge/; Mary C. Brennan, *Wives, Mothers, and the Red Menace: Conservative Women and the Crusade against Communism* (Boulder: University Press of Colorado, 2008), 13–30; Stuart J. Foster, *Red Alert! Educators Confront the Red Scare in American Public Schools, 1947–1954* (New York: P. Lang, 2000), 1–10.

26. Edward S. Herman and Noam Chomsky, *Manufacturing Consent: The Political Economy of the Mass Media* (New York: Pantheon Books, 1988), 169–252. Herman and Chomsky borrowed the idea of the "manufacture of consent" from Walter Lippmann (xi).

27. Bill Clinton, Remarks at the Brandenburg Gate, July 12, 1994, https:// millercenter.org/the-presidency/presidential-speeches/july-12-1994-remarks -brandenburg-gate.

28. Bill Clinton, Address on Bosnia, Nov. 27, 1995, https://millercenter.org /the-presidency/presidential-speeches/november-27-1995-address-bosnia.

29. George W. Bush, Address on the U.S. Response to the Attacks of September 11, Sept. 22, 2001, https://millercenter.org/the-presidency/presidential -speeches/september-22-2001-address-us-response-attacks-september-11.

30. Barack Obama, Speech on Strategy in Afghanistan and Pakistan, at US Military Academy, West Point, NY, Dec. 1, 2009, https://millercenter.org /the-presidency/presidential-speeches/december-1-2009-speech-strategy -afghanistan-and-pakistan.

31. Donald Trump, Remarks at the UN General Assembly, Sept. 24, 2019, https://millercenter.org/the-presidency/presidential-speeches/september-24 -2019-remarks-united-nations-general-assembly.

32. Nils Gilman, "Modernization Theory, the Highest Stage of American Intellectual History," in *Staging Growth: Modernization, Development, and the Global Cold War*, ed. David Engerman et al. (Amherst: University of Massachusetts Press, 2003), 47–80, quote on 56.

33. David Ekbladh, "Profits of Development: The Development and Resources Corporation and Cold War Modernization," *The Princeton University Library Chronicle*, 69.3 (2008): 487–506, quotes on 490, 496.

34. W. W. Rostow, *The Stages of Economic Growth: A Non-Communist Manifesto* (Cambridge, UK: Cambridge University Press, 1960), 1, 2.

35. Michael E. Latham, *Modernization as Ideology: American Social Science and Nation-Building in the Kennedy Era* (Chapel Hill: University of North Carolina Press, 2000), 69–149.

36. Johnson, Speech at Johns Hopkins University.

37. Michael E. Latham, "Redirecting the Revolution? The USA and the Failure of Nation-Building in South Vietnam," *Third World Quarterly*, 27.1 (2006): 27–41, quote on 34; Latham, *Modernization as Ideology*, 151–207.

38. Latham, "Redirecting the Revolution?," 36.

39. Gabriel Kolko, *Vietnam: Anatomy of War, 1940–1975* (1986; London; Unwin Paperbacks, 1987), 72.

40. Marilyn B. Young, *The Vietnam Wars, 1945–1990* (New York: Harper-Collins, 1991), ix.

41. Odd Arne Westad, "Introduction: Reviewing the Cold War," in *Reviewing the Cold War: Approaches, Interpretations, and Theory*, ed. Odd Arne Westad, Nobel Symposium 107 (Lysebu, Norway, 1998), 1–23, quote on 10.

42. Cheryl A. Rubenberg, "US Policy Toward Nicaragua and Iran and the Iran-Contra Affair: Reflections on the Continuity of American Foreign Policy," *Third World Quarterly*, 10.4 (1988): 1485.

43. LaFeber, *Inevitable Revolutions*, 57; Kris James Mitchener and Marc Weidenmier, "Empire, Public Goods, and the Roosevelt Corollary," *Journal of Economic History*, 65.3 (2005): 658–692; Allan E. S. Lumba, *Monetary Authorities: Capitalism and Decolonization in the American Colonial Philippines* (Durham, NC: Duke University Press, 2022), 147–54.

44. Harry S. Truman, Address on Foreign Economic Policy, Mar. 6, 1947, https://www.trumanlibrary.gov/library/public-papers/52/address-foreign-economic-policy-delivered-baylor-university.

45. Harry S. Truman, Truman Doctrine Speech, Mar. 12, 1947, https://avalon.law.yale.edu/20th_century/trudoc.asp.

46. Dean Acheson, *Present at the Creation: My Years in the State Department* (New York: W. W. Norton, 1969), 232–235; George Marshall, "Marshall Calls on European Countries to Organize for U.S. Aid," June 1947, https://www.nationalarchives.gov.uk/education/resources/cold-war-on-file/marshall-on-marshall-plan/.

47. Logevall, *Embers of War*, 57–58, 105–131, 170–174, 250–259, quotes on 105, 172, 259.

48. Melvyn P. Leffler, "The Inevitable Tragedy: The United States Embroilment in Vietnam," *Leidschrift*, 19.2 (2004): 58; Logevall, *Embers of War*, 89.

49. Leffler, "Inevitable Tragedy," 62; Acheson, *Present at the Creation*, 228-231.

50. Eisenhower, Press Conference, Apr. 7, 1954, in Logevall, *Origins of the Vietnam War*, 101-102.

51. Joseph A. Fry, in "Place Matters: Domestic Regionalism and the Formation of American Foreign Policy," *Diplomatic History*, 36.3 (2012): 451-482, provides an overview of the relevant literature.

52. David Turpie, "'Howling Upon the Scent of Another Victim': Senator Edward W. Carmack, the Philippine Issue, and Southern Opposition to Imperialism," *Tennessee Historical Quarterly*, 68.4 (2009): 411-432; Harold Baron, "Anti-Imperialism and the Democrats," *Science & Society*, 21.3 (1957): 222-239, quote on 234; Joseph A. Fry, *Dixie Looks Abroad: The South and U.S. Foreign Relations, 1789-1973* (Baton Rouge: Louisiana State University Press, 2002), 117-138; Paola E. Coletta, "McKinley, the Peace Negotiations, and the Acquisition of the Philippines," *Pacific Historical Review*, 30.4 (1961): 341-350.

53. Fry, *Dixie Looks Abroad*, 139-260; LaFeber, *Inevitable Revolutions*, 49-54; Report of the Special Committee on Investigation of the Munitions Industry (The Nye Report), US Congress, Senate, 74th Cong., 2nd Sess., February 24, 1936, 3-13, https://www.mtholyoke.edu/acad/intrel/nye.htm; John Edward Wiltz, "The Nye Committee Revisited," *The Historian*, 23.2 (1961): 211-233; Marc C. Johnson, "Franklin D. Roosevelt, Burton K. Wheeler, and the Great Debate: A Montana Senator's Crusade for Non-intervention Before World War II," *Montana: The Magazine of Western History*, 62.4 (2012): 3-22, 91-93; Dewey W. Grantham Jr., "The Southern Senators and the League of Nations, 1918-1920," *North Carolina Historical Review*, 26.2 (1949): 187-205.

54. Walter Isaacson and Evan Thomas, *The Wise Men: Six Friends and the World They Made: Acheson, Bohlen, Harriman, Kennan, Lovett, McCloy* (New York: Simon & Shuster, 1986), passim, 681.

55. Rudy Abramson, *Spanning the Century: The Life of W. Averell Harriman, 1891-1986* (New York: William Morrow, 1992), passim.

56. LaFeber, *Inevitable Revolutions*, 117-122.

57. Robert S. McNamara, *In Retrospect: The Tragedy and Lessons of Vietnam* (New York: Times Books. 1995), 31.

58. Isaacson and Thomas, *Wise Men*, 651.

59. Joseph A Fry, *Debating Vietnam: Fulbright, Stennis, and Their Senate Hearings* (Lanham, MD: Rowman & Littlefield, 2006), 43.

60. Herring, *America's Longest War*, 224.

61. The majority of White Southern politicians were hawks—standing to the right of the "Wise Men." They lacked the global vision and balance of the Northern establishment. See the discussion in Fry, *Dixie Looks Abroad*, 222–223, 284–289; and Fry, *Debating Vietnam*, 18–22, 85–149.

62. Kyle Longley, "Congress and the Vietnam War: Senate Doves and Their Impact on the War," in *The War That Never Ends: New Perspectives on the Vietnam War*, ed. David L. Anderson and John Ernst (Lexington: University Press of Kentucky, 2007), 289–310.

63. Robert C. Cottrell, *The Activist 1960s: Striving for Political and Social Empowerment in America* (Jefferson, NC: McFarland, 2023); Melvin Small, *Antiwarriors: The Vietnam War and the Battle for America's Hearts and Minds* (Washington, DC: Scholarly Resources, 2002); H. Bruce Franklin, *Vietnam and Other American Fantasies* (Amherst: University of Massachusetts Press, 2000), chap. 3.

64. Gerald F. Goodwin, *Race in the Crucible of War: African American Servicemen and the War in Vietnam* (Amherst: University of Massachusetts Press, 2023), 1–151; Natalie Kimbrough, *Equality or Discrimination? African Americans in the U.S. Military During the Vietnam War* (Lanham, MD: University Press of America, 2007); James E. Westheider, *Fighting on Two Fronts: African Americans and the Vietnam War* (New York: New York University Press, 1997).

6. Do "Waves" Explain the Women's Movement?

1. Martha W. Lear, "The Second Feminist Wave," *New York Times*, Mar. 10, 1968, https://timesmachine.nytimes.com/timesmachine/1968/03/10/90032 407.pdf?pdf_redirect=true&ip=0.

2. Cornelia H. Dayton and Lisa Levenstein, "The Big Tent of U.S. Women's and Gender History: A State of the Field," *Journal of American History*, 99.3 (2012): 793–817, quote on 807; Tamar W. Carroll, "Revisiting Second Wave Histories: New Chronologies, Geographies, and Appraisals," *Journal of Women's History*, 31.3 (2019): 136–146. Kathleen A. Laughlin, Julie Gallagher, Dorothy Sue Cobble, Eileen Boris, Premilla Nadasen, Stephanie Gilmore, and Leandra

Zarnow, in "Is It Time to Jump Ship? Historians Rethink the Waves Metaphor," *Feminist Formations*, 22.1 (2010): 76–135, show more sympathy to the ideas of waves. See also Nancy A. Hewitt, "Feminist Frequencies: Regenerating the Wave Metaphor," *Feminist Studies*, 38.3 (2012): 658–680; Jo Reger, "Finding a Place in History: The Discursive Legacy of the Wave Metaphor and Contemporary Feminism," *Feminist Studies*, 43.1 (2017): 193–221.

3. Although it is difficult to discern a "woman's movement" before 1800, there were protests. Notable recent works on that era include Kirsten Sword, *Wives Not Slaves: Patriarchy and Modernity in the Age of Revolutions* (Chicago: University of Chicago Press, 2021); Edith Gelles, "Revolutionary Women," *William and Mary Quarterly*, 76.2 (2019): 313–317; Sara T. Damiano, "Writing Women's History Through the Revolution: Family Finances, Letter Writing, and Conceptions of Marriage," *William and Mary Quarterly*, 74.4 (2017): 697–728; Alejandra Dubcovsky, "The Great Power of Native Women," *William and Mary Quarterly*, 80.4 (2023): 740–744.

4. Miriam H. Berlin, "The Education of Women: A Tale of Developing Autonomy and Expanding Choices," *Change*, 18.2 (1986): 50–55, quote on 51; Kabria Baumgartner, *In Pursuit of Knowledge: Black Women and Educational Activism in Antebellum America* (New York: New York University Press, 2019); Mary Kelley, *Learning to Stand and Speak: Women, Education, and Public Life in America's Republic* (Chapel Hill: University of North Carolina Press, 2006), 35–41, 67, 87; Sally Schwager, "Educating Women in America," *Signs*, 12.2 (1987): 333–372; Lynn D. Gordon, "Female Gothic: Writing the History of Women's Colleges," *American Quarterly*, 37.2 (1985): 299–304; Kathryn Kish Sklar, *Florence Kelley and the Nation's Work: The Rise of Women's Political Culture, 1830–1900* (New Haven, CT: Yale University Press, 1995), 51–52.

5. Catharine E. Beecher, *A Treatise on Domestic Economy, for the Use of Young Ladies at Home, and at School* (1841; New York: Harper & Brothers, 1846), 27, 33, 37.

6. Contributions to this voluminous debate include Barbara Welter, "The Cult of True Womanhood, 1820–1860," *American Quarterly*, 18.2, pt. 1 (1966): 151–174; Cathy N. Davidson and Jessamyn Hatcher, introduction to *No More Separate Spheres! A Next Wave American Studies Reader*, ed. Cathy N. Davidson and Jessamyn Hatcher (Durham, NC: Duke University Press, 2002), 7–26; Nancy F. Cott, *The Bonds of Womanhood: "Woman's Sphere" in New England, 1780–1835* (New Haven, CT: Yale University Press, 1997); Lora Romero, *Home*

Fronts: Domesticity and Its Critics in the Antebellum United States (Durham, NC: Duke University Press, 1977); Marc Egnal "Historicizing Domesticity: The Impact of the Woman's Rights Movement," *Canadian Review of American Studies*, 45.2 (2015): 238–258.

7. Anne M. Boylan, "Women in Groups: An Analysis of Women's Benevolent Organizations in New York and Boston, 1797–1840," *Journal of American History*, 71.3 (1984): 497–523; Anne M. Boylan, *The Origins of Women's Activism: New York and Boston, 1797–1840* (Chapel Hill: University of North Carolina Press, 1992).

8. Marc Egnal, *Clash of Extremes: The Economic Origins of the Civil War* (New York: Hill and Wang, 2009), 128–132; Dorothy Sterling, *Ahead of Her Time: Abby Kelley and the Politics of Antislavery* (New York: W. W. Norton, 1991), 60–68; Boylan, "Women in Groups," 504–514, 517–518. Ruth Bloch, in "American Feminine Ideals in Transition: The Rise of the Moral Mother, 1785–1815," *Feminist Studies*, 4.2 (1978): 100–126, provides the phrase "moral mother."

9. Lori D. Ginzberg, "'Moral Suasion Is Moral Balderdash': Women, Politics, and Social Activism in the 1850s," *Journal of American History*, 73.3 (1986): 601–622, quote on 612; Lori D. Ginzberg, *Women and the Work of Benevolence: Morality, Politics, and Class in the Nineteenth-Century United States* (New Haven, CT: Yale University Press, 1990), 98–213.

10. Ginzberg, "Moral Suasion," 606; Carolyn M. Moehling and Melissa A Thomasson, "Votes for Women: An Economic Perspective on Women's Enfranchisement," *Journal of Economic Perspectives*, 34.2 (2020): 3–23; Kathleen Feeney, "Amelia Jenks Bloomer," in American Council of Learned Societies, *American National Biography* (New York: Oxford University Press, 2000–), online edition; Andrew G. Wood, "Dorothea Lynde Dix," in *American National Biography*.

11. Joseph R. Gusfield, "Social Structure and Moral Reform: A Study of the Woman's Christian Temperance Union," *American Journal of Sociology*, 61.3 (1955): 221–232; Ruth Bordin, *Frances Willard: A Biography* (Chapel Hill: University of North Carolina Press, 1986), 69–79, 105–154, 175–180; Sklar, *Florence Kelley*, 73–75.

12. Bordin, *Frances Willard*, 97–103, quote on 98.

13. Glenda Elizabeth Gilmore, *Gender and Jim Crow: Women and the Politics of White Supremacy in North Carolina, 1896–1920*, 2nd ed. (Chapel Hill: University of North Carolina Press, 2019), 31–60, quote on 46.

14. Martha S. Jones, *Vanguard: How Black Women Broke Barriers, Won the Vote, and Insisted on Equality for All* (New York: Basic Books, 2020), 21–47, 149–158, quote on 153.

15. Mina Carson, *Settlement Folk: Social Thought and the American Settlement Movement, 1885–1930* (Chicago: University of Chicago Press, 1990); Rivka Shpak Lissak, *Pluralism and Progressives: Hull House and the New Immigrants, 1890–1919* (Chicago: University of Chicago Press, 1989).

16. Jane Addams, *Twenty Years at Hull-House* (1910; New York: Signet Classic, 1960), 76.

17. Elisabeth Lasch-Quinn, *Black Neighbors: Race and the Limits of Reform in the American Settlement House Movement, 1890–1945* (Chapel Hill: University of North Carolina Press, 1993).

18. J. Stanley Lemons, "The Sheppard-Towner Act: Progressivism in the 1920s," *Journal of American History*, 55.4 (1969): 776–786; Carolyn M. Moehling and Melissa A. Thomasson, "The Political Economy of Saving Mothers and Babies: The Politics of State Participation in the Sheppard-Towner Program," *Journal of Economic History*, 72.1 (2012): 75–103.

19. Alexis de Tocqueville, *Democracy in America*, ed. J. P. Mayer, trans. George Lawrence (1835, 1840; New York: Harper & Row, 1966), 590.

20. Marc Egnal, *A Mirror for History: How Novels and Art Reflect the Evolution of Middle-Class America* (Knoxville: University of Tennessee Press, 2024), 48–55.

21. Sarah M. Grimké, *Letters on the Equality of the Sexes and the Condition of Woman* in *Feminism: The Essential Historical Writings*, ed. Miriam Schneir (New York: Vintage Books, 1972), 35–48, quote on 45; Moehling and Thomasson, "Votes for Women," 4–6.

22. Kelley, *Learning to Stand*, 112–152, quotes on 149, 151.

23. Louisa May Alcott, *Little Men* (1871; Toronto: W. Briggs, 1996), 229–230; *Jo's Boys* (1886; New York: Grosset & Dunlap, 1949), 5–6; Egnal, *Mirror for History*, 98–101.

24. Sklar, *Florence Kelley*, 69–71, quote on 71.

25. Sklar, *Florence Kelley*, 75–186, quotes on 113, 132–133.

26. Clare Hemmings, "In the Mood for Revolution: Emma Goldman's Passion," *New Literary History*, 43.3 (2012): 527–545, quotes on 533, 538; Rachel Hui-Chi Hsu, "Propagating Sex Radicalism in the Progressive Era: Emma

Goldman's Anarchist Solution," *Journal of Women's History*, 30.3 (2018): 38–63; Rachel Hui-Chi Hsu, *Emma Goldman, Mother Earth, and the Anarchist Awakening* (Notre Dame: University of Notre Dame Press, 2021).

27. Charlotte Perkins Gilman, *Women and Economics*, ed. Carl Degler (1898; New York: Harper & Row, 1966), 340.

28. Alex Baskin, *Woman Rebel* (New York: Archives of Social History, 1976), quote on viii; Joanna Scutts, *Hotbed: Bohemian Greenwich Village and the Secret Club that Sparked Modern Feminism* (New York: Seal Press, 2022).

29. Egnal, *Mirror for History*, 118–123.

30. "Declaration of Sentiments and Resolutions," Seneca Falls Convention, July 1848, in *Feminism*, ed. Schneir, 78.

31. Lisa Tetrault, *The Myth of Seneca Falls: Memory and the Women's Suffrage Movement, 1848-1898* (Chapel Hill: University of North Carolina Press, 2014), 28.

32. Sally G. McMillen, *Seneca Falls and the Origins of the Women's Rights Movement* (New York: Oxford University Press, 2008), 149–228; Johanna Neuman, *And Yet They Persisted: How American Women Won the Right to Vote* (Hoboken, NJ: Wiley Blackwell, 2020); Brooke Kroeger, *The Suffragents: How Women Used Men to Get the Vote* (Albany: State University of New York Press, 2017).

33. Jones, *Vanguard*, 73–117, quote on 95; Tetrault, *Myth of Seneca Falls*, 21; Rosalyn Terborg-Penn, *African American Women in the Struggle for the Vote, 1850-1920* (Bloomington: Indiana University Press, 1998), 8–19.

34. Terborg-Penn, *African American Women*, 115–123; Elna C. Green, *Southern Strategies: Southern Women and the Woman Suffrage Question* (Chapel Hill: University of North Carolina Press, 1997), 9–12, 28–29, 89–90; Nancy F. Cott, "Feminist Politics in the 1920s: The National Woman's Party," *Journal of American History*, 71.1 (1984), 43–68.

35. Cott, "Feminist Politics."

36. J. Kevin Corder and Christina Wolbrecht, *Counting Women's Ballots: Female Voters from Suffrage Through the New Deal* (New York: Cambridge University Press, 2016), 254–273; Cott, "Feminist Politics"; Jo Freeman, "Social Revolution and the Equal Rights Amendment," *Sociological Forum*, 3.1 (1988): 145–146; Paula A. Monopoli, *Constitutional Orphan: Gender Equality and the Nineteenth Amendment* (New York: Oxford University Press, 2020); Eileen Boris and S. J. Kleinberg, "Mothers and Other Workers: (Re)Conceiving Labor,

Maternalism, and the State," *Journal of Women's History*, 15 (Autumn 2003): 90–117.

37. Louise Michele Newman, *White Women's Rights: The Racial Origins of Feminism in the United States* (New York: Oxford University Press, 1999); Jones, *Vanguard*, 175–202; Mary-Elizabeth B. Murphy, *Jim Crow Capital: Women and Black Freedom Struggles in Washington, D.C., 1920–1945* (Chapel Hill: University of North Carolina Press, 2018); Rosalyn Terborg-Penn, "The Nineteenth Amendment and Its Outcome for African American Women," *Journal of Women's History*, 32.1 (2020): 23–31; Liette Gidlow, "More Than Double: African American Women and the Rise of a 'Women's Vote,'" *Journal of Women's History*, 32.1 (2020): 52–61.

38. Blanche Wiesen Cook, *Eleanor Roosevelt*, vol. 1, *1884–1933* (New York: Viking, 1992), 258, 329, 384–386; Annelise Orleck, *Common Sense and a Little Fire: Women and Working-Class Politics in the United States, 1900–1965*, 2nd ed. (Chapel Hill: University of North Carolina Press, 2017), 122, 141–149.

39. Blanche Wiesen Cook, *Eleanor Roosevelt*, vol. 2, *1933–1938* (New York: Viking, 1999), 67–69, 77–79, 234–235, 248–249, 266, 457, quote on 78–79; Orleck, *Common Sense*, 141, 150–167; Freeman, "Social Revolution," 147; Kathleen Banks Nutter, "Rose Scheiderman," in *American National Biography*; Susan Ware, *Beyond Suffrage: Women in the New Deal* (Cambridge, MA: Harvard University Press, 1981).

40. Cook, *Eleanor Roosevelt*, 2: 159–161, 270, 278–280, 565–568; Darlene Clark Hine, "Mary Jane McLeod Bethune," in *American National Biography*; Rebecca Tuuri, *Strategic Sisterhood: The National Council of Negro Women in the Black Freedom Struggle* (Chapel Hill: University of North Carolina Press, 2018).

41. Rebecca DeWolf, "The Equal Rights Amendment and the Rise of Emancipationism, 1932–1946," *Frontiers: A Journal of Women Studies*, 38.2 (2017): quote on 64.

42. DeWolf, "Equal Rights Amendment," 62; Orleck, *Common Sense*, 126–127; Cynthia Harrison, *On Account of Sex: The Politics of Women's Issues, 1945–1968* (Berkeley: University of California Press, 1988), 7–12.

43. DeWolf, "Equal Rights Amendment," 47; Freeman, "Social Revolution," 145–152; Nancy F. Cott, *The Grounding of Modern Feminism* (New Haven, CT: Yale University Press, 1987), 180–185, 209–210; Michael E. Parrish, *Anxious Decades: America in Prosperity and Depression, 1920–1941* (New York: W. W. Norton, 1992), 400–402; Richard Sutch and Susan B. Carter, eds.,

Historical Statistics of the United States (New York: Cambridge University Press, 2006), millennial edition online, series Ba340–354.

44. DeWolf, "Equal Rights Amendment," 65; Karen Anderson, *Wartime Women: Sex Roles, Family Relations, and the Status of Women During World War II* (Westport, CT: Greenwood Press, 1981).

45. DeWolf, "Equal Rights Amendment," 65–67; Freeman, "Social Revolution," 147.

46. The essays in Joanne Meyerowitz, ed., *Not June Cleaver: Women and Gender in Postwar America, 1945–1960* (Philadelphia: Temple University Press, 1994), challenge the accepted depiction of these years. This scholarship, however, suggests at most modifying, not completely revising, the familiar story.

47. DeWolf, "Equal Rights Amendment," 69; Harrison, *On Account of Sex*, 3–49, 89–92, 170–172; *Historical Statistics*, series Ba340–348, Ba4228–4230. Figures for the immediate postwar years are lacking, but the decline in women's relative wages after 1950 is clear. See Claudia Goldin, *Understanding the Gender Gap: An Economic History of American Women* (New York: Oxford University Press, 1990), 62.

48. Susan A. Hartmann, *The Other Feminists: Activists in the Liberal Establishment* (New Haven, CT: Yale University Press, 1998), 4; Harrison, *On Account of Sex*, 109–163, 176–187; Betty Friedan, *The Feminine Mystique*, intro. by Gail Collins (1963; New York: W. W. Norton, 2013).

49. Hartmann, *Other Feminists*, 13, 53–90, 176–177, 207–208, 214; Harrison, *On Account of Sex*, 192–206; Friedan, *Feminine Mystique*, 461–468.

50. Freeman, "Social Revolution," 145–152; David E. Kyvig, "Historical Misunderstandings and the Defeat of the Equal Rights Amendment," *The Public Historian*, 18.1 (1996): 45–63; Friedan, *Feminine Mystique*, 473; Robin M. Morris, *Goldwater Girls to Reagan Women: Gender, Georgia, and the Growth of the New Right* (Athens: University of Georgia Press, 2022); Michelle M. Nickerson, *Mothers of Conservatism: Women and the Postwar Right* (Princeton, NJ: Princeton University Press, 2012); Stacie Taranto, *Kitchen Table Politics: Conservative Women and Family Values in New York* (Philadelphia: University of Pennsylvania Press, 2017).

51. Hartmann, *Other Feminists*.

52. Sara M. Evans, "Women's Liberation: Seeing the Revolution Clearly," *Feminist Studies*, 41.1 (2015): 138–149, quote on 139; Benita Roth, *Separate Roads to Feminism: Black, Chicana and White Feminist Movements in America's Second*

Wave (New York: Cambridge University Press, 2004), 64–75, 93–96; Egnal, *Mirror for History*, 195–198.

53. Cynthia Harrison, "Creating a National Feminist Agenda: Coalition Building in the 1970s," in *Feminist Coalitions: Historical Perspectives on Second-Wave Feminism in the United States*, ed. Stephanie Gilmore (Urbana: University of Illinois Press, 2008), 19–47. Marjorie J. Spruill, in *Divided We Stand: The Battle Over Women's Rights and Family Values That Polarized American Politics* (New York: Bloomsbury Publishing, 2017), provides the fullest account of the Houston conference.

54. Wini Breines, "What's Love Got to Do with It? White Women, Black Women, and Feminism in the Movement Years," *Signs*, 27.4 (2002): 1095–1133, quote on 1097; Ula Y. Taylor, "Making Waves: The Theory and Practice of Black Feminism," *The Black Scholar*, 28.2 (1998): 18–28; Roth, *Separate Roads*, 185–189.

55. Hartmann, *Other Feminists*, 190; Breines, "What's Love Got to Do with It?," 1126; Roth, *Separate Roads*, 76–98, 129–176; Taylor, "Making Waves," 20–21.

56. Leonie Huddy, Francis K. Neely, and Marilyn R. Lafay, "The Polls—Trends: Support for the Women's Movement," *Public Opinion Quarterly*, 64.3 (2000): 309–350; Weiyi Cai and Scott Clement, "What Americans Think about Feminism Today," *Washington Post*, Jan 27. 2016; Amanda Barroso, "61% of U.S. Women Say Feminist Describes Them Well," Pew Research Center, July 7, 2020, https://www.pewresearch.org/fact-tank/2020/07/07/61 -of-u-s-women-say-feminist-describes-them-well-many-see-feminism-as -empowering-polarizing/.

57. OECD, "Early Childhood Education and Care," https://www.oecd.org /education/school/earlychildhoodeducationandcare.htm; Marc Egnal, *Divergent Paths: How Culture and Institutions Have Shaped North American Growth* (New York: Oxford University Press, 1996), 178–192.

58. Barbara Burrell, "Political Parties and Women's Organizations: Bringing Women into the Electoral Arena," in *Gender and Elections: Shaping the Future of American Politics*, ed. Susan J. Carroll and Richard L. Fox (New York: Cambridge University Press, 2018), 220–249; Susan J. Carroll and Richard L. Fox, "Introduction: Gender and Electoral Politics in the Twenty-First Century," in *Gender and Elections*, 1–14; "Women Members by Congress," History, Art &

Archives, US House of Representatives, https://history.house.gov/Exhibitions
-and-Publications/WIC/Historical-Data/Women-Members-by-Congress/.
The Center for American Women and Politics, at Rutgers Eagleton Institute of
Politics, reflecting resignations and elections, gives slightly different figures at
https://cawp.rutgers.edu/women-us-congress-2021.

59. Ashwini Tambe, "The Women's March on Washington: Words from an
Organizer; An Interview with Mrinalini Chakraborty," *Feminist Studies*, 43.1
(2017): 223–229, quote on 224; Susan Chira, "Donald Trump's Gift to Feminism:
The Resistance," *Daedalus*, 149.1 (2020): 72–83.

60. Laura Montanaro, "Discursive Exit," *American Journal of Political Science*, 63.4 (2019): 875–887, quote on 877; Farah Stockman, "Women's March
on Washington Opens Contentious Dialogues about Race," *New York Times*,
Jan. 9, 2017, https://www.nytimes.com/2017/01/09/us/womens-march-on
-washington-opens-contentious-dialogues-about-race.html; Jenna Wortham,
"Who Didn't Go to the Women's March Matters More Than Who Did," *New
York Times Magazine*, Jan. 24, 2017, https://www.nytimes.com/2017/01/24
/magazine/who-didnt-go-to-the-womens-march-matters-more-than-who
-did.html; Farah Stockman, "Three Leaders of Women's March Group Step
Down After Controversies," *New York Times*, Sept. 16, 2019, https://www
.nytimes.com/2019/09/16/us/womens-march-anti-semitism.html. On the
attacks against march leader Linda Sarsour, see Stephen Emerson, "The New
York Times, Linda Sarsour and Misinformation," JNS, Sept. 20, 2022, https://
www.jns.org/the-new-york-times-linda-sarsour-and-misinformation/.

61. Ashwini Tambe, "Reckoning with the Silences of #MeToo," *Feminist
Studies*, 44.1 (2018): 197–203; Sarah K. Burgess, "Between the Desire for Law
and the Law of Desire: #MeToo and the Cost of Telling the Truth Today," *Philosophy & Rhetoric*, 51.4 (2018): 342–367.

62. Kimberlé Crenshaw, "Demarginalising the Intersection of Race and
Sex: A Black Feminist Critique of Antidiscrimination Doctrine, Feminist Theory and Antiracist Politics," *University of Chicago Legal Forum*, 140 (1989): 139–
167; Kimberlé Crenshaw, "Mapping the Margins: Intersectionality, Identity
Politics, and Violence Against Women of Color," *Stanford Law Review*, 43.6
(1991): 1241–1299; Valerie Bryson, *The Futures of Feminism* (Manchester, UK:
Manchester University Press, 2021), 64–91.

63. Barroso, "61% of U.S. Women."

64. "Women in the Labor Force: A Databook," *BLS Reports*, US Bureau of Labor Statistics, Mar. 2022, https://www.bls.gov/opub/reports/womens -databook/2021/home.htm; Janelle Jones, "5 Facts About the State of the Gender Pay Gap," *US Department of Labor Blog*, Mar. 19, 2021, https://blog.dol.gov /2021/03/19/5-facts-about-the-state-of-the-gender-pay-gap.

65. Jessica Bennett, "Looking Back at *Ms.*, Age 50," *New York Times*, June 19, 2022.

7. Why Do So Many Americans Passionately Support Donald Trump?

1. Tom Llamas and Lauren Effron, "The Moment Donald Trump and His Family Knew He Won the Election," ABC News, Nov. 11, 2016, https://abcnews .go.com/Politics/moment-donald-trump-family-knew-won-election/story?id =43466026.

2. Tina Nguyen, "You Could Fit All the Voters Who Cost Clinton the Election in a Mid-Size Football Stadium," *Vanity Fair*, Dec. 1, 2016, https://www .vanityfair.com/news/2016/12/hillary-clinton-margin-loss-votes; John Sides, Michael Tesler, and Lynn Vavreck, *Identity Crisis: The 2016 Presidential Campaign and the Battle for the Meaning of America*, with a new afterword by the authors (Princeton, NJ: Princeton University Press, 2018), 154–156; Jonathan Allen and Amie Parnes, *Shattered: Inside Hillary Clinton's Doomed Campaign* (New York: Crown, 2017), 394. Clinton lost in the electoral college, 304–227 despite receiving almost three million more votes than Trump.

3. Samuel Lubell, *The Future of American Politics*, 3rd ed. rev. (New York: Harper & Row, 1965), 45–55.

4. Ira Katznelson, *When Affirmative Action Was White: An Untold History of Racial Inequality in Twentieth-Century America* (New York: W. W. Norton, 2005), 20–23, 38–49, quotes on 21, 48; Keneshia N. Grant, *The Great Migration and the Democratic Party: Black Voters and the Realignment of American Politics in the 20th Century*. (Philadelphia: Temple University Press, 2020).

5. Katznelson, *Affirmative Action*, 25–43, quotes on 36.

6. Lubell, *Future of American Politics*, 69–71.

7. Ian Haney López, *Dog Whistle Politics: How Coded Racial Appeals Have Reinvented Racism and Wrecked the Middle Class* (New York: Oxford University Press, 2014), 17–18; Joseph G. Rayback, "Our 'Dixiecrat' Revolts—A Case Study," *Social Science*, 29.3 (1954): 143–146.

8. Harry S. Truman, Civil Rights Message, Feb. 2, 1948, in *History of U.S. Political Parties*, vol. 4, *1945-1972: The Politics of Change*, ed. Arthur M. Schlesinger Jr. (New York: Chelsea House Publishers, 1973), 3402-3408; Taylor Branch, *Parting the Waters: America in the King Years, 1954-63* (New York: Simon & Schuster, 1988).

9. US Census Bureau, Historical Poverty Tables, table 2, https://www.census.gov/data/tables/time-series/demo/income-poverty/historical-poverty-people.html; Michelle Alexander, *The New Jim Crow: Mass Incarceration in the Age of Colorblindness* (New York: The New Press, 2020), 47-48.

10. López, *Dog Whistle Politics*, 211; Steven Hahn, *Illiberal America: A History* (New York: W. W. Norton, 2024), provides a still broader perspective, tracing these resentments back to the 1830s.

11. Dan T. Carter, "Legacy of Rage: George Wallace and the Transformation of American Politics," *Journal of Southern History*, 62.1 (1996): 3-26, quote on 6-7.

12. Dan T. Carter, *The Politics of Rage: George Wallace, the Origins of the New Conservatism, and the Transformation of American Politics*, 2nd ed. (Baton Rouge: Louisiana State University Press, 2000), 365-367; George C. Wallace, "Speech at Madison Square Garden," Oct. 24, 1968, in *History of U.S. Political Parties*, 4: 3491-3497, quotes on 3492, 3494.

13. Carter, "Legacy of Rage," 10, 11.

14. López, *Dog Whistle Politics*, 22-25, quote on 24.

15. Dan T. Carter, *From George Wallace to Newt Gingrich: Race in the Conservative Counterrevolution, 1963-1994* (Baton Rouge: Louisiana State University Press, 1996), 30; Alexander, *New Jim Crow*, 56-58.

16. López, *Dog Whistle Politics*, 3, 56-70, quotes on 58, 59; Alexander, *New Jim Crow*, 61-62.

17. For example, Nelson Bunker Hunt, scion of the ultra-rich Texas oil family, provided George Wallace with a suitcase full of money and created a million-dollar trust fund for Wallace's running mate, Curtis LeMay. Carter, *From George Wallace*, 10; Carter, *Politics of Rage*, 357-359.

18. Andrew Kahn and Chris Kirk, "What It's Like to Be Black in the Criminal Justice System," *Slate*, Aug. 9, 2015, https://slate.com/news-and-politics/2015/08/racial-disparities-in-the-criminal-justice-system-eight-charts-illustrating-how-its-stacked-against-blacks.html; López, *Dog Whistle Politics*, 51-66; Alexander, *New Jim Crow*, 62-68.

19. Carter, *From George Wallace*, 68–72; Alexander, *New Jim Crow*, 69–71.

20. López, *Dog Whistle Politics*, 106–112, quote on 111; Alexander, *New Jim Crow*, 71–73, quote on 71; Carter, *From George Wallace*, 88–92, 99–102; Thomas Frank, *Listen Liberal, or What Ever Happened to the Party of the People?* (New York: Henry Holt, 2016), 78–102; Ibram X. Kendi, *How to Be an Antiracist* (New York: One World, 2019), 74–78, 93.

21. John Ganz, *When the Clock Broke: Con Men, Conspiracists, and How America Cracked Up in the Early 1990s* (New York: Farrar, Straus and Giroux, 2024), 4. Referring to Pat Buchanan and a few other politicians, Ganz observes that "while they lost in the short term, they brought to the surface an intense anguish in American life, a politics of national despair that has returned with greater force."

22. Quotes from Pat Buchanan, "Time for Economic Nationalism," June 12, 1995, http://www.buchanan.org/pa-95-0612.html; and "Announcement Speech," Mar. 20, 1995, http://www.4president.org/speeches/buchanan 1996announcement.htm.

23. Carter, *From George Wallace*, 52, 54, 93–94, 122; "2000 Presidential General Election Results," https://www.fec.gov/resources/cms-content /documents/FederalElections2000_PresidentialGeneralElectionResultsby State.pdf.

24. Judith A. Center, "1972 Democratic Convention Reforms and Party Democracy," *Political Science Quarterly*, 89.2 (1974): 325–350; Mary Linehan, "Women in the 1968 Eugene McCarthy Campaign and the Development of Feminist Politics," *Journal of Women's History*, 29.1 (2017): 111–137; Jean Kirkpatrick, "Representation in the American National Conventions: The Case of 1972," *British Journal of Political Science*, 5.3 (1975): 265–322, shows the gap in outlook between McGovern's views and those of most voters; Frank, *Listen Liberal*, 30–34; "The McGovern-Fraser Commission Report (1971)," in *The Evolving Presidency: Landmark Documents*, 6th ed., ed. Michael Nelson (Thousand Oaks, CA: CQ Press, 2019), 215–220.

25. Frank, *Listen Liberal*, 39–45.

26. Stanley A. Renshon, "Lost and Found? Clinton's Political Center," *Presidential Studies Quarterly*, 27.1 (1997): 111–117, quote on 112; Frank, *Listen Liberal*, 47–108; Lily Geismer, *Left Behind: The Democrats' Failed Attempt to Solve Inequality* (New York: Public Affairs, 2022), 4–11, 45–50, 104–140. Jesse

Jackson called the Democratic Leadership Council "Democrats for the Leisure Class." Quoted in Katrina vanden Heuvel, "Workers Are Organizing Independently: Why Don't Our Politicians Seem to Care?," *Washington Post*, Aug. 23, 2022, https://www.washingtonpost.com/opinions/2022/08/23/nlrb-unions -organizing-labor-laws/.

27. Ezra Klein, *Why We're Polarized* (New York: Simon & Schuster, 2020), 8–17, 33–40, 130, 205, 211; Alan I. Abramowitz, "It Wasn't the Economy, Stupid: Racial Polarization, White Racial Resentment, and the Rise of Trump," in *Trumped: The 2016 Election That Broke the Rules*, ed. Larry J. Sabato, Kyle Kondik, and Geoffrey Skelley (Lanham, MD: Rowman & Littlefield, 2017), 204–205; Sides et al., *Identity Crisis*, 26–28, 95, 168–169; Pew Research Center, "Political Polarization in the American Public," June 12, 2014, https://www.pewresearch .org/politics/2014/06/12/political-polarization-in-the-american-public/; Jason Zengerle, "The Vanishing Moderate Democrat," *New York Times Magazine*, July 3, 2022.

28. Abramowitz, "It Wasn't the Economy," 206–208; Pew Research Center, "Political Polarization." Gavin Wright, in "Voting Rights and Economics in the American South," in *Lincoln's Unfinished Work: The New Birth of Freedom from Generation to Generation*, ed. Orville Vernon Burton and Peter Eisenstadt (Baton Rouge: Louisiana State University Press, 2022), 340–388, shows the gradual rise of Republicans in the South, with 1995, 2008, and 2010 as dates when Republican control ratcheted up.

29. Heather McGhee, *The Sum of Us: What Racism Costs Everyone and How We Can Prosper Together* (New York: One World, 2021), 62–68; López, *Dog Whistle Politics*, 110, 123, 191–208; Alexander, *New Jim Crow*, xvii–xix; Frank, *Listen Liberal*, 6, 28, 116–232; Sides et al., *Identity Crisis*, 167–168; Theda Skocpol and Vanessa Williamson, *The Tea Party and the Remaking of Republican Conservatism* (New York: Oxford University Press, 2012), 26–28.

30. Ed Pilkington, "Obama Angers Midwest Voters with Guns and Religion Remark," *The Guardian*, Apr. 14, 2008, https://www.theguardian.com/world /2008/apr/14/barackobama.uselections2008.

31. Skocpol and Williamson, *Tea Party*, 7–9, quote on 7; López, *Dog Whistle Politics*, 148–149.

32. Skocpol and Williamson, *Tea Party*, 5, 21–28, 186; Arlie Russell Hochschild, *Strangers in Their Own Land: Anger and Mourning on the American Right; A*

Journey to the Heart of Our Political Divide (New York: The New Press, 2016), 7; US Bureau of the Census, Race and Ethnicity in the United States: 2010 Census and 2020 Census, https://www.census.gov/library/visualizations/interactive /race-and-ethnicity-in-the-united-state-2010-and-2020-census.html. Hochschild sounds the same themes in her most recent book, *Stolen Pride: Loss, Shame, and the Rise of the Right* (New York: The New Press, 2024). She focuses on a Kentucky community.

33. Hochschild, *Strangers*, 23; Skocpol and Williamson, *Tea Party*, 77-80, quote on 46.

34. Skocpol and Williamson, *Tea Party*, 20-21, 29-32, 46, 75-77; Hochschild, *Strangers*, 25-35, 51-54, 62-68, 73-81, 121-122, 129-132, 139-145.

35. López, *Dog Whistle Politics*, 152-166, quote on 164; Skocpol and Williamson, *Tea Party*, 9-10, 16, 58-66, 83-118, 121-157, 173-178, 202; Hochschild, *Strangers*, 57-59, 126-27; Sides et al., *Identity Crisis*, 78. Nancy McLean, in *Democracy in Chains: The Deep History of the Radical Right's Stealth Plans for America* (New York: Viking, 2017), explores the intellectual (and racist) origins of the Kochs' ideology; Nicholas Confessore, "American Nationalist: How Tucker Carlson Stoked White Fears to Conquer Cable News," *New York Times*, May 1, 2022.

36. Hochschild, *Strangers*, 92-93, quote on 92.

37. Skocpol and Williamson, *Tea Party*, 42, 56-57, 64-67, quote on 66; Hochschild, *Strangers*, 61-62, 113-116, 135-140, 148, 158-161, 216-118; Sides et al., *Identity Crisis*, 28, 29, 168.

38. Hochschild, *Strangers*, 13-15, 200-202, quote on 221; Skocpol and Williamson, *Tea Party*, 35-39, 49-52, 57-60, quote on 38.

39. Skocpol and Williamson, *Tea Party*, 11, 69-74; Hochschild, *Strangers*, 146-147; López, *Dog Whistle Politics*, 5-6; Pew Research Center, "The Partisan Divide on Political Values Grows Even Wider—Part 4, Race, Immigration and Discrimination," Oct. 5, 2017, https://www.pewresearch.org/politics/2017/10 /05/4-race-immigration-and-discrimination/.

40. Gary C. Jacobson, "The Republican Resurgence in 2010," *Political Science Quarterly*, 126.1 (2011): 27-52; Todd Makse, "The Redistricting Cycle, Partisan Tides, and Party Strategy in State Legislative Elections," *State Politics & Policy Quarterly*, 14.3 (2014): 342-363.

41. Hochschild, *Strangers*, 221-227; Sides et al., *Identity Crisis*, 94.

42. Michael D'Antonio, *Never Enough: Donald Trump and the Pursuit of Success* (New York: St. Martin's Press, 2015), 79–84, 192, 261–262, 284–290, quote on 328; Sides et al., *Identity Crisis*, 5.

43. Sides et al., *Identity Crisis*, 86–94. The 2020 election only confirmed the sharp divergence in racial attitudes between the parties. See John Sides, Chris Tausanovitch, and Lynn Vavreck, *The Bitter End: The 2020 Presidential Campaign and the Challenge to American Democracy* (Princeton, NJ: Princeton University Press, 2022), 175–178. Thomas B. Edsall, in "The Unsettling Truth About Trump's First Great Victory," *New York Times*, Mar. 22, 2023, reviews the scholarship on race and partisanship and notes Trump's ability to attract many Republicans whose views were more moderate.

44. Amber Phillips, "'They're Rapists': President Trump's Campaign Launch . . . ," *Washington Post*, June 16, 2017, https://www.washingtonpost.com /news/the-fix/wp/2017/06/16/theyre-rapists-presidents-trump-campaign -launch-speech-two-years-later-annotated/.

45. Nurith Aizenman, "Trump Wishes We Had More Immigrants from Norway: Turns Out We Once Did," NPR, Jan. 12, 2018, https://www.npr.org /sections/goatsandsoda/2018/01/12/577673191/trump-wishes-we-had-more -immigrants-from-norway-turns-out-we-once-did; "Muslim Travel Ban," *Immigration History*, https://immigrationhistory.org/item/muslim-travel-ban/.

46. Donald Trump, "Addressing Egregious Actions of the Government of South Africa," Executive Order, Feb. 7, 2025, https://www.whitehouse.gov /presidential-actions/2025/02/addressing-egregious-actions-of-the-republic -of-south-africa/.

47. Trip Gabriel, "Trump Escalates Anti-Immigrant Rhetoric . . . ," *New York Times*, Oct. 5, 2023, https://www.nytimes.com/2023/10/05/us/politics /trump-immigration-rhetoric.html.

48. Michael D. Shear, "Trump's Derision of Haitians Goes Back Years," *New York Times*, Sept. 18, 2024, https://www.nytimes.com/2024/09/18/us /politics/trump-haitians.html.

49. Jamelle Bouie, "Don't Fall for Trump's D.E.I. Dodge," *New York Times*, Feb. 1, 2025, https://www.nytimes.com/2025/02/01/opinion/trump-dei -diversity-meritocracy.html.

50. Sides et al., *Identity Crisis*, 84; Heather Timmons, "Trump Shifted from Pro-Choice to Pro-Life Only as He Planned a Presidential Run," *Quartz*,

May 20, 2019, https://qz.com/1623437/trump-shifted-from-pro-choice-to-pro -life-as-he-planned-a-presidential-run/; Robert Costa, "Donald Trump and a GOP Primary Race Like No Other," in Sabato, Kondik, and Skelley, *Trumped*, 97–111. In office, Trump often turned to Fox News hosts for guidance. Martin Pengelly, "Texts Show Fox News Host Hannity's Pleas to Trump Aide After Capitol Attack," *The Guardian*, Jan. 21, 2022, https://www.theguardian.com/us -news/2022/jan/21/fox-news-hannity-texts-trump-mcenany-capitol-attack-6 -january-committee; Emma Green, "How the Federalist Society Won," July 24, 2022, *The New Yorker*, https://www.newyorker.com/news/annals-of-education /how-the-federalist-society-won.

51. Matt Lavietes, "Trump Repeats False Claims That Children Are Under- going Transgender Surgery during the School Day," NBC News, Sept. 9, 2024, https://www.nbcnews.com/nbc-out/out-politics-and-policy/trump-false -claims-schools-transgender-surgeries-rcna170217.

52. David A. Fahrenthold, "Trump Recorded Having Extremely Lewd Conversation About Women in 2005," *Washington Post*, Oct. 8, 2016, https:// www.washingtonpost.com/politics/trump-recorded-having-extremely-lewd -conversation-about-women-in-2005/2016/10/07/3b9ce776-8cb4-11e6-bf8a- 3d26847eeed4_story.html.

53. Edward Helmore, "Donald Trump Vows to Be the Protector of Women 'Whether They Like It or Not,'" *The Guardian*, Oct. 31, 2024, https:// www.theguardian.com/us-news/2024/oct/31/donald-trump-women -protector-wisconsin-rally; Larry Neumeister, "Judge Denies Trump Relief from $83.3 Million Defamation Judgment," PBS News, Mar. 7, 2024, https:// www.pbs.org/newshour/politics/judge-denies-trump-relief-from-83-3 -million-defamation-judgment.

54. Karissa Waddick, "Trump's Victory Speech: 5 Takeaways," *USA Today*, Nov. 6, 2024, https://www.usatoday.com/story/news/politics/elections/2024 /11/06/trump-victory-speech-takeaways/76086175007/.

55. Jackie Calmes, "Trump Scores Points on Trade in Debate . . . ," *New York Times*, Sept. 27, 2016, https://www.nytimes.com/2020/02/10/opinion/trump -budget-2020.html.

56. Paul Krugman, "How Trump Got Trickled Down," *New York Times*, Feb. 10, 2020, https://www.nytimes.com/2020/02/10/opinion/trump-budget -2020.html; "Trump Instructed Big Pharma to Draft 2017 Drug Pricing Plan,

FOIA Request Reveals," Oct. 30, 2014, *Public Citizen*, https://www.citizen
.org/news/trump-instructed-big-pharma-to-draft-2017-drug-pricing
-plan-foia-request-reveals/.

57. Katie Lobosco and Tami Luhby, "Here's What Trump Is Proposing for
the Economy," CNN, Nov. 6, 2024, https://www.cnn.com/2024/11/06/politics
/heres-what-trump-is-proposing-for-the-economy/index.html.

58. Jim Tankersley and Andrew Duehren, "Vance and Trump Don't See
Eye to Eye on the Economy," *New York Times*, Aug. 4, 2024; Noam Scheiber,
"Can the G.O.P. Really Become the Party of Workers?," *New York Times*,
Aug. 24, 2024; Tom Krisher, "Trump Praised Elon Musk for Firing Striking
Workers, Sparking a Clash with the UAW," *Fortune*, Aug. 13, 2024, https://
fortune.com/2024/08/13/trump-praised-elon-musk-firing-works-labor-uaw
-kamala-harris/.

59. Maggie Haberman, *Confidence Man: The Making of Donald Trump and
the Breaking of America* (New York: Penguin Press, 2022), 307–322, quote on 311;
Robert C. O'Brien, "The Return of Peace Through Strength," *Foreign Affairs*
(July/Aug. 2024), https://www.foreignaffairs.com/united-states/return-peace
-strength-trump-obrien.

60. Haberman, *Confidence Man*, 217–218, 275, 283, 308, 352–54, 382, 385–
387, 399–400, 501.

61. Oliver Milman, "'It's Ironic': How Climate Crisis Is Driving Trump
Push on Greenland and Panama," *The Guardian*, Jan. 13, 2025, https://www
.theguardian.com/environment/2025/jan/13/trump-greenland-panama
-canal-climate-crisis; Rob Gillies, "Canadian Leaders Say Trump's Talk about
Canada Becoming the 51st State Isn't Funny Anymore," Jan. 8, 2025, AP,
https://apnews.com/article/canada-trump-us-state-131dcff58a8f56116765f16
0d9f35460.

62. Stephanie Muravchik and Jon A. Shields, *Trump's Democrats* (Washington, DC: Brookings Institution Press, 2020); Abbey Meller and Hauwa
Ahmed, "How Big Pharma Reaps Profits while Hurting Everyday Americans," *CAP*, Aug. 30, 2019, https://www.americanprogress.org/article/big
-pharma-reaps-profits-hurting-everyday-americans/; Karl Aiginger, "Pop-
ulism: Root Causes, Power Grabbing, and Counter Strategy," *Intereconom-
ics*, 1 (2020), https://www.intereconomics.eu/contents/year/2020/number/1
/article/populism-root-causes-power-grabbing-and-counter-strategy.html.

Other books elaborate this same argument. See particularly Jacob S. Hacker and Paul Pierson, *Let Them Eat Tweets: How the Right Rules in an Age of Extreme Inequality* (New York: Liveright, 2020); Jonathan M. Metzl, *Dying of Whiteness: How the Politics of Racial Resentment Is Killing America's Heartland* (New York: Basic Books, 2019).

63. Pew Research Center, "Beyond Red vs. Blue: The Political Typology," Nov. 9, 2021, https://www.pewresearch.org/politics/2021/11/09/beyond-red -vs-blue-the-political-typology-2/; Michael H. Keller and David D. Kirkpatrick, "Their America Is Vanishing: Like Trump, They Insist They Were Cheated," *New York Times*, Oct. 24, 2022, https://www.nytimes.com/2022/10/23/us /politics/republican-election-objectors-demographics.html. Nate Cohn, in "The 6 Kinds of Republican Voters," *New York Times*, Aug. 17, 2023, https:// www.nytimes.com/interactive/2023/08/17/upshot/six-kinds-of-republican -voters.html, presents a similar analysis of the constituent elements in the Republican Party.

64. Phillips, "'They're Rapists.'"

65. Sides et al., *Identity Crisis*, 30, 75, 91, 174, 208; Sides et al., *Bitter End*, 269, 274.

66. Michael Hiltzik, "Here Are the Billionaires in Thrall to Trump, and Why," Oct. 29, 2024, *Los Angeles Times*, https://www.latimes.com/business/story /2024-10-29/column-here-are-the-billionaires-in-thrall-to-trump-and-why.

67. Eva Xiao et al., "Poorer Voters Flocked to Trump—and Other Data Points from the Election," *Financial Times*, Nov. 9, 2024, https://www.ft.com /content/6de668c7-64e9-4196-b2c5-9ceca966fe3f.

68. Emily Bazelon, "How Gender Became the Election's Crucial Fault Line," Oct. 5, 2024, *New York Times Magazine*; Pew Research Center, "Changing Partisan Coalitions in a Politically Divided Nation," pt. 3, Apr. 9, 2024, https:// www.pewresearch.org/politics/2024/04/09/changing-partisan-coalitions-in -a-politically-divided-nation/.

69. Kiana Cox, "Black Voters Support Harris over Trump and Kennedy by a Wide Margin," Pew Research Center, Aug. 22, 2024, https://www .pewresearch.org/short-reads/2024/08/22/black-voters-support-harris-over -trump-and-kennedy-by-a-wide-margin/; Mark Hugo Lopez and Luis Noe-Bustamante, "In Tight U.S. Presidential Race, Latino Voters' Preferences Mirror 2020," Pew Research Center, Sept. 24, 2024, https://www.pewresearch .org/race-and-ethnicity/2024/09/24/in-tight-u-s-presidential-race-latino

-voters-preferences-mirror-2020/; Scott Clement et al., "What the 2024 Election Tells Us About Trump's Voters," MassLive, Nov. 9, 2024, https://www.masslive.com/politics/2024/11/what-the-2024-election-tells-us-about-trumps-voters.html.

70. Tufts CIRCLE, "The Youth Vote in the 2024 Election," Nov. 6, 2024, https://circle.tufts.edu/2024-election; Ruth Igelnik et al., "Behind Biden's 2020 Victory," Pew Research Center, June 30, 2021, https://www.pewresearch.org/politics/2021/06/30/behind-bidens-2020-victory/. Disaggregated numbers are also important. Overwhelmingly, young, White men backed Trump.

71. Tufts CIRCLE, "Youth Vote"; Keith Johnson, "How Economists See Trump's Victory," *Foreign Policy*, Nov. 6, 2024, https://foreignpolicy.com/2024/11/06/trump-election-economy-trade-markets/.

72. Anthony Robledo, "'The American People Are Angry and Want Change': Bernie Sanders Slams Democrats for Loss," *USA Today*, Nov. 6, 2024, https://www.usatoday.com/story/news/politics/elections/2024/11/06/bernie-sanders-election-statement/76101511007/; Daron Acemoglu, "Why the Democrats Lost Workers—and the Election," *Social Europe*, Nov. 15, 2024, https://www.socialeurope.eu/why-the-democrats-lost-workers-and-the-election; Perry Bacon Jr., "The Six Wings of the Democratic Party," FiveThirtyEight, Mar. 11, 2019, https://fivethirtyeight.com/features/the-six-wings-of-the-democratic-party/; John Nichols, "Joe Biden Is Embracing His Inner FDR," *The Nation*, Feb. 14, 2023, https://www.thenation.com/article/politics/joe-biden-capitalism-fdr/.

73. Almost two-thirds of the twenty-one million adults who felt violence was justified to restore Trump to power agreed that "African American people or Hispanic people in our country will eventually have more rights than whites." Barton Gellman, "Trump's Next Coup Has Already Begun," *The Atlantic*, Jan./Feb. 2022, 30–31.

Conclusion and Acknowledgments

1. Jeff Benvenuto et al., "Colonial Genocide in Indigenous North America," in *Colonial Genocide in Indigenous North America*, ed. Andrew Woolford et al. (Durham, NC: Duke University Press, 2014), 1–25; Patrick Wolf, "Settler Colonialism and the Elimination of the Native," *Journal of Genocide Research* (Dec. 2006): 387–409.

Selected Bibliography

Progress in History

Hannah-Jones, Nikole, et al. *The 1619 Project: A New Origin Story*. New York: Random House, 2021.

Nash, Gary, et al. *History on Trial: Cultural Wars and the Teaching of the Past*. New York: Alfred A. Knopf, 1997.

Novick, Peter. *That Noble Dream: The "Objectivity Question" and the American Historical Profession*. New York: Cambridge University Press, 1988.

Sleeper-Smith, Susan, et al., eds. *Why You Can't Teach United States History without American Indians*. Chapel Hill: University of North Carolina Press, 2015.

American Revolution

Egnal, Marc. *A Mighty Empire: The Origins of the American Revolution*. With a new preface. 1988; Ithaca, NY: Cornell University Press, 2010.

Hattem, Michael D. "Revolution Lost? Vast Early America, National History, and the American Revolution." *William and Mary Quarterly*, 78.2 (2021): 269–274.

Holton, Woody. *Forced Founders: Indians, Debtors, Slaves, and the Making of the American Revolution in Virginia*. Chapel Hill: University of North Carolina Press, 1999.

Young, Alfred F., ed. *Beyond the American Revolution: Explorations in the History of American Radicalism*. DeKalb: Northern Illinois University Press, 1993.

Civil War

Egnal, Marc. *Clash of Extremes: The Economic Origins of the Civil War.* New York: Hill and Wang, 2009.

Lowenstein, Roger. *Ways and Means: Lincoln and His Cabinet and the Financing of the Civil War.* New York: Penguin, 2022.

Oakes, James. *The Scorpion's Sting: Antislavery and the Coming of the Civil War.* New York: W. W. Norton, 2014.

Woods, Michael E. "What Twenty-First-Century Historians Have Said about the Causes of Disunion: A Civil War Sesquicentennial Review of the Recent Literature." *Journal of American History,* 99.2 (2012): 415–439.

Homicides

Blackhawk, Ned. *The Rediscovery of America: Native Peoples and the Unmaking of U.S. History.* New Haven, CT: Yale University Press, 2023.

Currie, Elliott. *A Peculiar Indifference: The Neglected Toll of Violence on Black America.* New York: Metropolitan Books, 2020.

Hinton, Elizabeth. *America on Fire: The Untold Story of Police Violence and Black Rebellion Since the 1960s.* New York: Liveright Publishing, 2021.

Roth, Randolph. *American Homicide.* Cambridge, MA: Harvard University Press, 2009.

Vietnam

Anderson, David L., and John Ernst, eds. *The War That Never Ends: New Perspectives on the Vietnam War.* Lexington: University Press of Kentucky, 2007.

Goodwin, Gerald F. *Race in the Crucible of War: African American Servicemen and the War in Vietnam.* Amherst: University of Massachusetts Press, 2023.

Isaacson, Walter, and Evan Thomas. *The Wise Men: Six Friends and the World They Made: Acheson, Bohlen, Harriman, Kennan, Lovett, McCloy.* New York: Simon & Shuster, 1986.

Young, Marilyn B. *The Vietnam Wars, 1945–1990.* New York: HarperCollins, 1991.

Women's Movement

Boylan, Anne M. *The Origins of Women's Activism: New York and Boston, 1797–1840*. Chapel Hill: University of North Carolina Press, 1992.

Jones, Martha S. *Vanguard: How Black Women Broke Barriers, Won the Vote, and Insisted on Equality for All*. New York: Basic Books, 2020 (preface 2021).

Roth, Benita. *Separate Roads to Feminism: Black, Chicana and White Feminist Movements in America's Second Wave*. New York: Cambridge University Press, 2004.

Sklar, Kathryn Kish. *Florence Kelley and the Nation's Work: The Rise of Women's Political Culture, 1830–1900*. New Haven, CT: Yale University Press, 1995.

Trump

Haberman, Maggie. *Confidence Man: The Making of Donald Trump and the Breaking of America*. New York: Penguin Press, 2022.

Hochschild, Arlie Russell. *Strangers in Their Own Land: Anger and Mourning on the American Right—A Journey to the Heart of Our Political Divide*. New York: The New Press, 2016.

Klein, Ezra. *Why We're Polarized*. New York: Simon & Schuster, 2020.

López, Ian Haney. *Dog Whistle Politics: How Coded Racial Appeals Have Reinvented Racism and Wrecked the Middle Class*. New York: Oxford University Press, 2014.

Index

abolition movements, xi, 26, 37, 44,
50–53, 161. *See also* slavery,
American system of
abortion, 123, 126, 147, 150–151, 156
Acheson, Dean, 84, 98–99, 100–103
Acts of Trade (Britain), 33–34
Adams, John, 22, 27, 32
Addams, Jane, 115; *Twenty Years at
Hull House,* 112
Affordable Care Act (Obamacare),
143, 157
African American history. *See* Black
history
Afrikaners, 149–150
Alabama: Black-on-Black homicides,
79; civil rights politics, 135;
"Dixiecrats," 133–134; on
secession pre-Civil War, 56, 57
Alcott, Louisa May: *Jo's Boys,* 114;
Little Women, 114–115
American Constitution: class
divisions and, 26; convention to
write, 37; Eighteenth Amend-
ment, 112–113; Fifteenth Amend-
ment, 117, 131; Nineteenth

Amendment, 8, 118, 131; Second
Amendment, 63; slavery protected
in, x, 26–27, 38, 159; Thirteenth
Amendment, 3, 4, 78–79
American Equal Rights Association,
117, 118
American Revolution, 19–38;
alternative explanations, 22,
37–38; expansionist motivations
for, x–xi, 28–36, 158–160;
republican ideology and consensus explanations, 20–22, 23,
171n10; social transformations
and, 22–28, 172n17; study of, 5
Anthony, Susan B., 107, 117
Arbenz, Jacobo, 90–91, 102

Beecher, Catherine, 114; *Treatise on
Domestic Economy,* 108–109
Bell, John, 53–54
benevolent societies, 109–110, 115
Bethune, Mary Jane McLeod, 120
Black history: American Revolution
and, 26–27; "Black Cabinet"
(FDR), 120; civil rights politics,

expansionism and expansionists (*continued*) history and, 17–18; nonexpansionists, 30, 31–33; northern business interests, 100–103, 105; overview, x–xi, 22, 28, 37, 158–161; pre-Revolution divisions, 28–33, 36; religion and, 31–32, 37, 87–88; shifting ideals justifying, 87–90; White settler violence and homicides, 67–71

Federal Housing Administration, 132; redlining, 14, 74, 169n32
feminism, 106–107, 115, 123, 125–128. *See also* women's history; women's movement
Fifteenth Amendment, 117, 131
First Gulf War (1990–1991), 92–93
foreign policy: anti-Communism, 82–83, 83–87, 90, 98–100; capitalism, 96–100; Cold War era, 90–92; defending freedom, 92–94; expansionism and, 83, 87; modernization, 82–83, 94–96; northern business interests, 100–103; racism, 82–83
Franklin, Benjamin: expansionist, 29–33, 37, 158–159; Paxton Boys and, 24; *Pennsylvania Gazette*, 32; *Poor Richard's Almanack,* 32–33; religion, 31–32, 37; writing the Constitution, 37
French and Indian War (1754–1763), 29–31, 35
Friedan, Betty, 123; *The Feminine Mystique,* 107, 124
Fulbright, William, 103–104

gays and lesbians, history of. *See* LGBTQ communities, histories of
Goldman, Emma: "The Woman Suffrage Chameleon," 115–116
Gore, Al, 103–104
Great Lakes economy, 48–49, 53, 159
Great Recession (2008–2009), 140, 142
Grimké, Sarah: *Letters on the Equality of the Sexes,* 113–114
Guatemala, 90–91, 98, 102
gun culture of America: gun lobby, 65; guns and homicides, 62–65; regulation and deregulation, 64–66; statistics, 63–64, 182n9; Donald Trump and, 151; western gunfights, 70–71

Haiti and Haitians, 89, 93, 97, 149–150
Hancock, Thomas, 29, 33
Hannah-Jones, Nikole, 15–16
Harriman, Averell, 100–103
Hispanics, 69, 73–74. *See also* race and racism
history, progress in study of, 1–18; digital humanities, 10; liberal consensus in, 11–18, 20–23; methodology of historians, 2–5, 18; new findings, 6–10
Ho Chi Minh, 84, 98–99
Hochschild, Arlie: *Strangers in Their Own Land,* 144–146.
homicide in America, 61–81; Black communities and rates of, 72–75; early settlements to "Wild West," 67–72; gun culture and ownership, 62–66; incarceration of Blacks,